The Precarious Generation

This book draws on a wealth of evidence, including young people's own stories, to document how they are now faring in increasingly unequal societies like America, Britain, Australia, France and Spain. It points to systematic generational inequality as those born since 1980 become the first generation to have a lower standard of living than previous generations. While governments and experts typically explain this by referring to globalization, new technologies, or young people's deficits, the authors of this book offer a new political economy of generations, which identifies the central role played by governments promoting neoliberal policies that exacerbate existing social inequalities based on age, ethnicity, gender and class. The book is a must read for social science students, human service workers and policy-makers and indeed for anyone interested in understanding the impact of government policy over the last 40 years on young people.

Judith Bessant is a Professor in the School of Global, Urban and Social Studies at RMIT University, Australia.

Rys Farthing is a consultant based in London, UK.

Rob Watts is a Professor in the School of Global, Urban and Social Studies at RMIT University, Australia.

Routledge Advances in Sociology

The Precarious Generation

A Political Economy of Young People

Judith Bessant, Rys Farthing and
Rob Watts

Routledge
Taylor & Francis Group

LONDON AND NEW YORK

First published 2017
by Routledge
2 Park Square, Milton Park, Abingdon, Oxon OX14 4RN

and by Routledge
711 Third Avenue, New York, NY 10017

Routledge is an imprint of the Taylor & Francis Group, an informa business

British Library Cataloguing in Publication Data
A catalogue record for this book is available from the British Library

Library of Congress Cataloging in Publication Data
Names: Bessant, Judith, author. | Farthing, Rys, 1981– author. |
Watts, Rob, author.
Title: The precarious generation : a political economy of young people /
by Judith Bessant, Rys Farthing and Rob Watts.
Description: Abingdon, Oxon ; New York, NY : Routledge, 2017.
Identifiers: LCCN 2016053809| ISBN 9781138185470 (hardback) |
ISBN 9781315644493 (ebook)
Subjects: LCSH: Youth–Social conditions. | Youth–Economic conditions. |
Youth–Employment. | Equality.
Classification: LCC HQ796 .B429 2017 | DDC 305.235–dc23
LC record available at https://lccn.loc.gov/2016053809

ISBN: 978-1-138-18547-0 (hbk)
ISBN: 978-1-315-64449-3 (ebk)

Typeset in Times New Roman
by Wearset Ltd, Boldon, Tyne and Wear

Contents

Figures

Tables

Acknowledgements

This book was conceived a couple of years ago. The three of us found ourselves in Paris talking about the ways many young people were not doing so well, a fact that we recognized as owing much to decisions made by neoliberal policy-makers and other power elites since the late 1970s. Each of us had also been thinking and writing about these issues for many years. We came to the conclusion that it was a good idea to write a book about it. We began scribbling away on various scraps of paper in cafés and gardens roughing out the draft for a book proposal.

To our delight, Gerhard Boomgaarden, commissioning editor for Routledge, liked the idea and gave us the go ahead in the form of a contract. We are most grateful.

Developing the proposal proved the easiest part of the project – in our naiveté and optimism, we thought it would be a straightforward project. As it turned out, writing this book has been one of the most intellectually challenging and difficult research projects we have done. Trying to document what governments have been doing since the late 1970s, over five countries, each with very different histories and cultures was – to say the least – a big job. This is to say nothing of the challenges involved in describing the various ways neoliberalism was expressed by governments and experienced by young people, before trying to make sense of it all in the context of ongoing debates in disciplines as various as sociology, youth studies, criminology and political science. Suffice it to say that it has been a project during which we have learnt much.

There are many people who have helped us along the way. First, our respective work places. Judith Bessant and Rob Watts thank the Royal Melbourne Institute of Technology University, which employs us, for support in researching and writing this book. We also thank our friends, colleagues and students at RMIT University.

Rys Farthing would like to thank Humaira, Harry and Anclaudys for their helpful insights.

It has been a demanding project carried out over three years without any research funding. We have also had help from many young people directly and indirectly; something we would like to acknowledge. Crucially, we thank our dear friend and colleague Alex Hudson, who kindly gave his precious time, energy and professional expertise when editing the book and letting us know ever so nicely when we were being excessive in the way only academics can be.

We also thank our families for their patience, love and support.

Finally, we thank the editorial staff at Routledge, especially Alyson Claffey, Alexis Taylor, Matt Deacon, and Amy Ekins-Coward, for their patience and expertise in seeing this book to publication.

Introduction

It has long been a universally acknowledged truth that young people are trouble. For much of the twentieth century, mountains of research by sociologists, psychologists, criminologists and educationists was devoted to describing and explaining why so many young people are rebellious, lazy, amoral, delinquent, even criminal.

This common-sense idea about adolescents and 'teenagers' can be traced to the founding father of American psychology, G. Stanley-Hall (1904). His enduring contribution was to argue that 'youth' or 'adolescence' was one of a number of inevitable stages of human development. Adolescence was the most perilous, indeed dangerous, stage because it involved the transition from 'childhood' to 'adulthood'. He was particularly concerned about the tension between certain 'biological impulses' (mainly sexual) and the civilizational need to 'socialize' young people so they became well-adjusted, functioning adult members of society.

The idea of human development became a seductive and popular project, especially the idea that young people had to make that perilous journey from childhood to adulthood. The concern that some might not make the transition fed a preoccupation with 'delinquents', 'hooligans' and 'young criminals' from the late-nineteenth century, moving through to the fascination with youth cultures from the 1950s to the 1980s, to the more contemporary and variously expressed worries about 'youth-at-risk' from the 1990s.

While the vocabulary shifted, the underlying assumption continued: that we humans pass though phases in 'the life-cycle'. Much of the research was intended to 'explain' and 'predict' who would successfully make the transition to adulthood and who would fail. Implicit in this was the concern that – through personal deficits, bad choices or structural factors – some young people would not make it. Inevitably much of this work was informed by an interest in 'deviant' cases and the problems represented by tobacco, sex, drugs, crime, alcohol, music and revolting styles of clothing or hair.

Although many different explanations might be offered for this fascination, it reflected the certainty that 'society' or the 'economy' would provide the resources and opportunities – like education, community services and above all jobs – that would enable normal young people to make the transition to adult life.

In the 1980s several things happened. First, the assumption that society would provide enough of the appropriate kinds of education and employment began crumbling in the face of increasing and persistent unemployment and under-employment. Governments of all persuasions across western societies professed alarm and deep concern, urging young people to remain in schools and enrol in universities and colleges. Since the 1980s, governments everywhere have pro-moted the positive role education can play in helping young people secure a job and get on with life.

Today it is clear that the implied promise that more education would deliver jobs and the good life is in tatters. In 2014, the European Commission warned that one in four young Europeans was at risk of 'social exclusion'. By July 2015, 4.634 million young persons (under 25) were unemployed in the eurozone. More than one in five young Europeans in the labour market could not find a job. In Greece 51.8 per cent of young people were unemployed in May 2015, while in Spain 48.6 per cent were unemployed (Eurostat 2015). Another 7.5 million young Europeans between 15–24 were not employed, in education or in training. Similar accounts are available for countries like America, the UK and Australia.

Belatedly governments in Europe realized more needed to be done. One result was the *Youth Guarantee*, a policy framework introduced across EU countries in April 2013 that was widely promoted as a 'new' approach to tackling youth unemployment (O'Reilly *et al.* 2015). It promised that all people under 25 would have access to a good-quality, 'concrete offer' within four months of leaving formal education or becoming unemployed. What is the offer? The offer should be either a job, an apprenticeship, a traineeship, or continued education 'adapted to the individual's need and situation'. In recognition of the global scale of the problem, a meeting of G20 labour ministers (from the 20 major countries responsible for 80 per cent of global trade) in Melbourne on 10–11 September 2014 decided more should be done to implement policies like the *Youth Guaran-tee*, by taking concrete actions to place young people in education, training and jobs. In 2016 the *Youth Guarantee* had its budget cut significantly.

Faced with evidence like this, politicians, policy-makers and opinion-makers began acknowledging that something unprecedented was happening. It was a recognition summarized by the English journalist Larry Elliott:

> Perpetual progress has been at the heart of western society for the past 150 years or more. The idea has been simple: each generation should be better off than their parents.... *The idea that each generation would be more fortu-nate than the last no longer applies.*
>
> (Elliott 2016) (Our emphasis)

To justify his claim, he pointed to the fact that young people as a generation are likely to be far worse off as a generation than their parents. The so-called 'millennials' (people born since 1980) are on average 26 percentage points less likely to own their own home than those from the baby boomer gen-eration i.e. people born after 1945. They are also struggling to make a decent wage in an increasingly insecure and casualized labour market in which low pay is endemic.

It is evidence like this that has begun to change the way social scientists and researchers think about young people. The traditional way was to focus on young people who were disadvantaged, poor, working class, delinquent or just different. The new approach, initiated by groups in the youth studies field, focuses on young people as a generation rather than youth as primarily a transitional stage or phase of life. As scholars in this field like Wyn and Woodman argue, considerable evidence now exists in Australia and other western countries 'of similarities in new life patterns that could be considered to constitute a generational shift in contrast to an extended transition to adulthood' (Wyn and Woodman 2006: 496). As these writers – and others like Furlong, Cartmel, Côté, Threadgold and Faruggia – argue, the social, political and economic spaces in which young people have come of age since the 1980s have completely subverted the older stories and expectations that young people can and should make a 'successful transition to adulthood'. A further shift was that we need to focus less on particular groups of disadvantaged and 'deviant' young people and instead on understanding how each generation is located within a particular social, political and economic milieu.

Without at this stage saying whether we agree with this, we do argue a good case exists for looking at what has happened to young people born since the early 1980s and for posing the following questions, which we address in this book.

Key questions

What is meant by 'generation'? Can we talk about a generation of young people, and if so, how are we to best to do this? What has changed in the socioeconomic and political circumstances of the past three or four decades in countries like America, Britain, Australia, France and Spain that affects the lives of young people? What is the evidence that many young people in France, Spain, UK, USA and Australia now face an increasing social and economic burden of relative deprivation and disadvantage? How can we describe and make sense of old and new forms of socioeconomic disadvantage experienced by young people in these countries? Are they a consequence of policies and politics, reflecting deliberate choices by governments and other power elites? Are there age-based patterns of social and economic disadvantage attributable to policies adopted by governments and policy-makers? How do young people in these countries experience and understand these socioeconomic processes taking place? While acknowledging the tendency on the part of many researchers to see young people as more 'acted on than acting', how do young people experience their own lives? Do they respond to 'generational disadvantage' in ways that are aligned to action? Are some young people engaging politically in response to the problems they experience?

Our approach: a 'political economy of generations'

In this book, we offer a political economy of generations to address these questions.

We note that a key focus of any political-economy approach is on how various political relations and processes affect the shape and distribution of valued social resources. However, as we argue, our political economy goes beyond narrowly defined economic resources like jobs, wages, income or wealth to include a near-total ensemble of cultural, intellectual, symbolic and political resources. Our focus on generations also enables us to keep our eye on an entire generation of people while allowing for differences and inequalities of all kinds within that generation.

We structure the book in the following way.

In Chapter 1 ('The State of Play: How Young People Are Faring') we demonstrate how young people in Europe, UK, USA and Australia now bear a disproportionate and increasing burden of poverty and disadvantage. As writers like Willetts (2010), Howker and Malik (2013) and Sukarieh and Tannock (2015) show, the weight of that burden was amplified by the global financial crisis of 2007–2008. Standing went further, seeing this process as integral to the rise of 'the precariat' (2011, 2014). Standing describes the 'precariat' as a new social class formed by people experiencing precarious employment that shapes lives without predictability or security and that affects people's welfare and their sense of wellbeing.

We ask what the youth unemployment figures are and what they mean for young people in France, Spain, UK, USA and Australia. We observe increases in economic stress and poverty affecting growing numbers of young people. Attention is given to the ways unemployment and underemployment affects young people's income levels and their access to decent quality and affordable housing. More young people are now staying on longer in the parental home. Many in the UK, the USA and Australia are also accumulating increasing levels of education-related debt as more are persuaded that further education, and university in particular, continues to offer a golden path to good jobs and economic security.

In Chapter 2 ('A Political Economy of Generations') we engage with a debate launched by James Côté in his account of a 'new political economy of youth' (2014: 528). According to Côté, we can and should talk about 'youth-as-a-class', arguing that 'Gen Y', or the 'millennials', are victims of downward social mobility.[1] Côté's work is valuable because it triggered an important debate. It's a debate that centres less on agreed facts about the contemporary disadvantage of young people, and more on the vocabulary and interpretative frames used to make sense of what is happening. We agree with Côté about the value of a political-economy approach. It helps explain young people's education, labour-force participation and earning power – and how they are talked about and become objects of certain kinds of policy-making in capitalist economies (Côté 2014: 538).

We note, however, that a key problem in this debate is the reliance by Côté and by many of his critics on a 'substantialist' framing of reality, which leaves us trapped in various versions of the structure vs agency debate. We argue for a relationalist account of the kind offered by Pierre Bourdieu (1977, 1987, 1990). This has major implications for how we describe and use categories like class, gender or generation in our political economy of generation.[2] We articulate a relationalist account of reality, like that offered by Bourdieu (1977, 1987), then outline the relational nature of our political economy of generation. This means that 'generation' itself is one of a number of analytic factors that can be used to explain what is happening.

In Chapter 3 ('Neoliberal Social Policy and Young People') we explain the situation now confronting many young people. One dimension of our political economy of generations focuses on the politics and decisions by policy-makers working and living under the sign of the market and relying on a political frame of neoliberalism. Our interest is to understand neoliberalism as a political project and the strange and even contradictory shapes it assumes. We also document how decisions made in this context have affected the lives of young people born in that time. Equally, we highlight the role of policy-makers working within a neoliberal frame that informed successive 'reforms' that have impacted so negatively and disproportionately on young people. We document how deliberate and choice-filled public policy explains what has happened to the lives of so many young people. We give particular attention to historical processes that saw young people pushed and pulled in and out of labour markets as part of a neoliberal policy dynamic intended to resolve crises endemic to the contemporary capitalist economies.

We observe how, from the 1980s, entities like the OECD, the World Trade Organization and the European Union promoted the first wave of neoliberal reforms. It involved the deregulation of the financial and labour markets, suspending the commitment to full employment policies and cutting many key welfare state policies and programs in the name of a new 'active society' model. Policy-makers also privatized, marketized and contracted out what were key public activities. We note how these policies, in combination with trade liberalization policies and technology, wiped out entire industries like manufacturing and low-skill service and clerical work. It destroyed what was once a relatively stable full-time youth labour market. Unemployment and underemployment became the new norm for young people, while increased retention in schooling and post-secondary education was promoted. We then follow a second wave of reform, beginning in the late 1990s at the behest of the EU, the IMF, and the World Bank, driven by a concern with 'intergenerational equity'.

This project was informed by neoliberal economists, think-tanks and policy advisors relying on 'intergenerational accounting' to sustain a narrative that too many OECD countries had overly generous welfare states and were running unsustainable levels of budget deficit that would impose crippling fiscal burdens on later generations. It was an argument that promoted rounds of austerity policies in the late 1990s and early 2000s. Finally, we turn to the effects of the global financial crisis of 2007–2009 and subsequent interventions by many governments to stave off the collapse of the global financial system. This involved injecting debt-funded capital into the financial system while maintaining deficit-funded government expenditures. While this was successful, it also triggered a third wave of austerity measures, especially in southern Europe after 2009–2010, which impacted heavily on young people.

In Chapter 4 ('Intergenerational Equity and Justice') we explore ethical and social justice issues bearing on the relations between generations. For the past few decades, conventional neoliberal policy-makers and governments have said they are interested in 'intergenerational equity'. This agenda-setting exercise points to a demographic trend towards an ageing society and the likelihood that a large population of older people will need the support of a dwindling population of younger people. Neoclassical economists add that contemporary government policy is enabling older people to enjoy the benefit of government welfare benefits, health, education programs and employment, enabled by deficit spending and debt accumulation – bequeathing an unsustainable level of debt to future generations.

This is said to be unfair and a major contemporary long-term policy problem. The proposed solutions are 'austerity' measures, designed to cut government expenditure on welfare state benefits, health care or education; or to reduce investment in public goods. In this chapter, we demonstrate how this problem-framing exercise lacks credible theoretical or empirical basis and is one part of the neoliberal imaginary. Moreover, it has no ethical substance, because it is designed to justify the brutal policies that expel people – including young people – from their economies and their life spaces.

In the second part of the chapter we argue there is a more serious problem of intergenerational equity evident since the 1980s. The more serious intergenerational equity problem is the way various generational transfers have occurred. In some cases, this has involved inequitable transfers to advantaged older citizens from disadvantaged younger people; while in other cases it involves the transmission of poverty and disadvantage across generations. This has been taking place over the past few decades.

In Chapter 5 ('Broken Promises: Human Capital Theory, Education and Work') we document education policy in the UK, France, Spain, the USA and Australia from 1980–2016. Much of that policy assumed the human capital theory associated with key members of the Chicago School of neoclassical economics, like Gary Becker. Central to that body of work was the idea that the more individuals invest in their own education, the better off they become (in terms of accessing good quality jobs, high incomes and an affluent lifestyle). Equally, the more we pursue private goods (e.g. education and income), the better off everyone becomes. As the founding figure of classical economics, Adam Smith explained in 1776:

> Every individual necessarily labours to render the annual revenue of the society as great as he can. He generally, indeed, neither intends to promote the public interest, nor knows how much he is promoting it … he intends only his own gain, and he is in this, as in many other cases, led by an invisible hand to promote an end which was no part of his intention.
>
> (Smith 1776: IV 2.9)

Becker's advocacy for human capital theory in the 1960s and 1970s prefigured and aided attempts by governments facing a slowdown in employment, which began in the early 1980s, to encourage more people to stay on for longer and longer in some form of education or training. In this chapter, we outline the connection between neoclassical economics and neoliberal education policy and say why it has become increasingly problematic for young people. We speak of the 'broken promises' entailed by the false belief that a 'knowledge-driven economy accelerates the demand for employees with a college education' (Brown, Lauder and Ashton 2011: 2).

We provide a detailed account of the reliance on human capital theory and use this to explain how this theory has been used to justify the prolongation of education; and why that is problematic. This enables us to ask one of the big questions of our time: should we continue relying on an economic theory that has been disconfirmed to inform education and labour market policies as we move toward a new work order?

In Chapter 6 ('Penalizing the young and the justice system') we examine the evolution of policies that portray some young people as symptoms and sources of disorder. They are policies reliant on quite mixed messages about young people. As governments spend much time bemoaning the tragic state of youth unemployment or child poverty, they also talk up how increasing numbers of young people are a threat as progenitors of social dysfunction, crime and disorder as a prelude to introducing tough law-and-order policies. Meanwhile, commitments to caring for the young constitute the press releases of government departments. Added to this are everyday celebrations of youth in all their beauty, in their athletic prowess and exuberant energy. Young people continue to be represented as the symbols of hope and heralds of a golden future.

Against this rhetoric we observe how populist left- and right-wing governments in the US, UK, Australia, France and Spain competed to see which government could be most tough on law-and-order issues. As we show, political parties and governments now rely on long-standing conservative and authoritarian discourses about unruly, high-risk youth, teen gangs and all the rest of it. If we believe this, we can never have enough regulation, surveillance and retribution when it comes to controlling 'at risk youth' deemed unlikely to transit successfully into economically self-sufficient adults. Since 2001, this frame has increasingly implicated young Muslims, too often represented as incipient terrorists on an inevitable slide into radicalization. We trace the use of curfews, antisocial behavioural orders, electronic surveillance techniques and mandatory sentencing all directed at young people.

Among the many consequences of these highly punitive policies used to regulate young people is the fact that the USA now leads the world in the number and proportion of its population incarcerated in prison. Most of those jailed are young, poor and come from one of the dominant Afro-American or Hispanic minorities. We also point to the important differences in the ways governments and communities in the US, UK, France, Spain and Australia deal with certain groups of young people, reflecting different historical economic and cultural trajectories operating in these societies.

In the final chapters of this book we draw on the political economy of generation model to explore how young people understand themselves and their political responses. This involves sampling the ways some young people understand themselves and how many are now challenging and extending conventional understandings of politics.

In Chapter 7 ('Young People Making Sense of It') we discuss findings from recent surveys that suggest in most western developed societies people under the age of 30 appear to be becoming increasingly pessimistic. How representative and accurate are survey findings like this? How do young people in the US, UK, France, Spain and Australia make sense of their current lives and circumstances and what do they think about their futures? Do they feel let down by their parents' generation? What role does family, community and the new social media play in their lives and in shaping their hopes and expectations? In this chapter, we draw on material from interviews with individual young people and focus groups to address the questions about how they now understand and live their lives. We do this with regard to the often quite different circumstances confronting young people in the USA, the United Kingdom, France, Spain, and Australia.

In Chapter 8 ('Taking Action: Young People and Politics') using a number of small case studies detailing how young people describe various political problems, what they think about them and what they say is needed to address them. The vignettes capture the various ways young people engage politically to shape the political agenda today. We ask: are we seeing new forms of politics – and what role is technology playing?

The examples used are not meant to be generalizable or representative, but evocative accounts that give a little insight into what is happening. We survey a number of left, far right, and new and old politics, including anti-Muslim and immigration campaigns, denial of service action and cultural politics involving user-generated satire.

The final chapter ('A new Intergenerational Contract') begins by observing how – in spite of all the heartfelt talk about 'youth participation' and 'intergenerational justice' – young people continue to be largely missing from formal contemporary policy and political debates about matters of public interest. In addition to this, we acknowledge the breakdown of an implied intergenerational contract. By this we refer to promises made by governments and others over many decades that young people would accrue significant benefits if they agreed to spend more time in secondary and higher education. That investment in human capital would be rewarded with secure jobs, higher incomes and 'a good life'. That promise or contract has not worked. What we have is a growing gap between what was promised and what is offered. We argue for a new intergenerational contract.

Our political economy of generations approach relies on a number of key principles that, we suggest, can inform the development of such an intergenerational contract. As we explain, it is a non-reductionist approach, in that we do not attempt to explain complex, large-scale phenomena by referring to more basic or smaller-scale components of the phenomena. It is non-determinist, because we do not assume that social life can be explained by reference to causal factors that possess predictive power. It is pluralist in our acknowledgment that no one single social resource-cum-capital necessarily plays a more powerful role in shaping the quality of social life than any other. For example, possessing financial capital will not necessarily guarantee a good life for a person with poor bodily health (they are dying) and minimal or no cultural capital (they are friendless).

It is relational, in the ways it understands generation as human relations among people within a generation and between diverse generations, and less a thing. It helps to articulate a defensible account of how we might develop a descriptive *and* normative assessment of the extent to which a society now or in the future can promote intergenerational fairness. It reflects a valuing of critique and reflexivity for the purpose of exposing suffering and oppression. In these ways, it is a practice requiring an ethical framework that allows us to recognize suffering and oppression and to know why it is bad. Implicitly such an ethical framework points to the conditions a just society will promote.

In this chapter, we consider the kinds of principles and considerations that might help to shape the substance of such a contract. We begin by outlining a defensible ethical account of the purpose of any intergenerational contract and the policies and social norms that could inform such a contract. A number of cognate political design principles are then identified.

We recognize that we cannot be too prescriptive or preemptive given that the development of such a contract necessarily will only work as a deliberative and inclusive cross-generational process. We therefore need to avoid the fall into the trap of subverting the very principles we think ought to inform such a contract. Such an intergenerational contract involves young people and their elders in conversation, listening to and observing what each other are saying and doing. For this reason, we restrict ourselves to identifying design principles that might inform such conversations, and some of the substantive issues that we believe ought to be canvassed.

A final point

Our focus is on five countries – Australia, the UK, the USA, France and Spain – which we use to consider how policy- and decision-making generally was variously understood, implemented and experienced since the early 1980s with the resurgence of neoliberalism.

It is not, however, a conventional comparative study. Most comparative studies seem to be done by people committed to testing hypotheses and measuring the strength of relationship between a number of dependent and independent variables to reveal causal connections or explain why certain things happen. For example, scholars have tested whether having a social democratic party in government means that a country is likely to develop a strong welfare state (e.g. Esping-Andersen 1990; Korpi and Palme 2003). We are not attempting this kind of research.

We see value in asking how people in countries with different sizes and populations, with different political and cultural histories and patterns of economic development have been 'dealing with' their young people. We expect the differences and the similarities to be telling.

We draw on a large body of social economic and political research undertaken by organizations like the OECD, the World Bank, IMF, the European Union national governments, youth observatories and academic researchers, as well as our own research projects. This gives us a flexible, credible evidentiary base for describing and interpreting the contemporary circumstances and status of young people.

Notes

1 Côté refers to this as this 'proletarianization', which works metaphorically to establish a Marxist provenance because it suggests a systematic process of exploitation.
2 As we later argue, all language and thinking is metaphoric. Metaphors function by transferring meanings associated with one 'thing' to something else. The idea of 'feral youth' works metaphorically by transferring the meaning of feral [or wild animal] to a young person. In these ways, metaphors both conceal and reveal what is happening. Being mindful of this can help reveal the interests or politics of those using the metaphor. Terms like 'class' or 'generation' are categories that are also metaphors. As such they can engender confusion because they encourage us to imagine and see in terms of category. Metaphorically, any category is a 'box' or 'container' into which we put 'things' deemed to share traits or substances that we say define that category.

   In this book, we argue that when using categories (class, generation ...) there is value in being mindful of how that encourages us to think in terms of *things* rather than the *social relations* or *processes* that characterize what we are trying to see or find out. In this case 'class' or 'generation' is less a category reliant on *things* defined by substances or traits and more a social relation or process understood as a process of competition for unequally available resources.

1   The state of play

How young people are faring

In May 2015, Martin Parkinson, one of the most powerful bureaucrats in Australia, gave a graduation speech to young graduates in which he said 'your generation is at risk of being the first in modern history whose living standards will be lower than those of their parents' (Parkinson 2015: 4). Parkinson almost seemed to be apologizing when he added 'my generation has failed you'. Given his own role in working for a succession of governments whose policies arguably gave rise to the problem he appeared to be acknowledging, we cannot be quite sure what if anything he was apologizing for – or how authentically. So, is there a problem? Is the current generation of young people doing it tough?

Like Martin Parkinson, many writers have concluded that the generation born since the early 1980s do not enjoy a better standard of living than their parents. David Willets (2010) made an early case for this, while Gardiner noted how – in contrast to the taken-for-granted promise that each generation will do better than the last – people born in the UK in 1988 'are earning the same amount that 27 year olds did a quarter of a century ago. Indeed, a typical young person (18–34) earned £8,000 less during their twenties than those in the preceding generation – generation X' (Gardiner 2016: 5). In the US, Morabito concluded that American young people have 'less opportunity than any previous generation currently alive today' with 'lower incomes, fewer job opportunities, and less likely to own homes and cars' (Morabito 2016). Likewise, Augustine and Nash-Stacey (2016) concluded that unemployment for 18–34 year olds is above average, their income below average, they own fewer cars, and are unlikely to own their own home. One recent Pew study suggested living with a parent is now the most common living arrangement among American young people (32.1 per cent), while a smaller group are living in their own household with a spouse (31.6 per cent) or alone (14 per cent) – down from 62 per cent and 5 per cent, respectively, in 1960 (Fry 2016).

In Australia writers like Rayner (2016), herself a 'millennial', argues her generation is the first in more than 80 years to go backwards in work, wealth and wellbeing. She says Australian young people are doing badly, with the number working without fixed contracts jumping from 32 per cent in 1992 to 50 per cent in 2013. At the same time, wage growth more than doubled for 50–54 year olds between 1990 and 2013, while the 20–24-year-old age group were only earning

25 per cent more than in 1990 (Rayner 2016: 15). Like their American peers, the unemployment rate among young people is above average, they have below average incomes and are unlikely to own their own home. As Chris Richardson, a leading Australian economist, explained: 'There is a stunning generational unfairness in our settings, and all those disengaged young Australians need to wake up to the fact they're being massively screwed' (Richardson cited in Cooke 2016).

In Europe too, writers and activists argue that young people are losing out. Research by the Pew Research Center argues that young Europeans have a negative outlook about prospects for the next generation. When asked whether they thought children in their country would be better off financially than their parents once they grow up, only 38 per cent of young British, 37 per cent of young Germans and 15 per cent of young French were optimistic (Stokes 2015). In Spain and France, the high levels of youth (15–24) unemployment may explain the pessimism. In France, the youth unemployment rate has been increasing, peaking at 24 per cent in 2015. This may explain the success of social movements like 'Nuit Debout' ('Rise up in the night') in attracting young people to protest against recent French labour laws and other issues. In Spain too, the only 'good news' was that the youth unemployment rate in Spain dropped to 45.8 per cent in June, down from its all-time peak of 56.2 per cent in February 2013 (Eurostat 2016).

Writing about 'grand claims' like these, Sonia Livingstone highlighted the value of asking three questions: 'what's really going on? How can this be explained? And how could things be otherwise?' (2012: 19). These are the protocol questions that animate this book. Here we address the first question: what's going on for young people[1]?

In this chapter, we argue that people under the age of 35 in the UK, US, Australia, France and Spain do indeed face an increasing economic burden of deprivation, inequality and disadvantage relative to older people. We do this by exploring income inequality, wage rates and employment; highlighting both how young people today are faring compared to older people today, and looking at how young people today are faring compared to other generations when they were young. After exploring incomes, we then briefly address what this means for one major type of wealth and asset: home ownership.

But to start, we begin with a broad-brush picture of the five countries we are interested in. First, we outline the age structure of each country, because the proportion of each 'generation' has the capacity to affect the socio-political dynamics. Second, we turn briefly to provide an overview of their economies, highlighting their relative affluence and levels of inequality. Finally, we close by exploring the levels of inequality prevalent in each country.

While we explore five different countries, this is not a comparative study. Instead, we acknowledge some important similarities and differences in the broader patterns of economic activity affecting young people in these countries. We do this because while these countries share certain important similarities there are also important differences. We cannot provide the coverage or the depth of analysis that we would if we were looking at only one country.

Age structure

All five of our countries have a roughly similar age structure, with young people (18–34) representing around a quarter of the population. The main difference is the total population of each, with America being substantially larger and Australia noticeably smaller.

These societies are also marked by a high degree of affluence when looked at globally. Economic estimates of the gross domestic product (GDP) suggest these are all wealthy countries, and indeed America is still the wealthiest country on the planet.

The difference in total population size means a slightly different picture emerges when the GDP is distributed *per capita*: on this basis, Australia becomes more wealthy than the UK, Spain and France; America is still the richest of the five.

The recent recession affected countries differently. Australia uniquely managed to maintain high and increasing economic growth, largely because China kept buying as much iron ore and coal as Australia could produce. It never technically entered recession during the global recession, with its GDP starting

Table 1.1 Age structure in France, Spain, UK, US and Australia, 2013

Age	15–35	35–54	55–74	Total population (including all age groups)
France	15.2m 24.2%	17.07m 26.8%	13.68m 21.5%	63.7m
Spain	10.9m 23.5%	14.9m 32.0%	9.4m 20.2%	46.6m
UK	16.7m 26.4%	17.4m 27.4%	13.2m 20.9%	63.2m
US	86.9m 27.5%	84.4m 26.7%	64.6m 20.4%	316.5m
Australia	6.5m 28.1%	6.3m 27.2%	4.5m 19.5%	23.1m

Source: OECD (2016a).

Table 1.2 Rank order in terms of nominal GDP

Country	Value (US$)
US	US$16.77 trillion
UK	US$2.8 trillion
Spain	US$2.7 trillion
France	US$2.4 trillion
Australia	US$1.59 trillion

Source: IMF (2016).

Table 1.3 Rank order country GDP per capita (2014) (US$)

Rank	Country	GDP per capita
10	US	$55,805
16	Australia	$47,359
24	United Kingdom	$41,181
25	France	$41,159
32	Spain	$34,810

Source: IMF (2016).

at $1.05 trillion in 2008, and climbing unsteadily to $1.34 trillion in 2015 (in 2016 dollar terms) (World Bank 2016). US GDP has also grown – from $14.7 trillion in 2008 to $17.9 trillion in 2015 – although it did suffer an initial recession. The UK too, appears to have recovered, with its initial GDP of $2.8 trillion dropping then recovering back to the same level in 2015 (ibid.).

Spain and France were hit hard by the recession. Spain was particularly damaged, with its GDP starting at $1.63 trillion in 2008 and sliding steadily to $1.20 trillion in 2015 (in 2016 dollar values). The French economy dipped slightly less, from $2.92 trillion in 2008 to $2.42 trillion in 2015. Like many other countries in Europe, they are still struggling to restore previous levels of economic growth.

The relative affluence of all five countries does not mean, however, that everyone is equally well off, nor that everyone suffered similarly from the 2008 recession.

Economic inequality

If we turn to the way the economic cake is distributed within these societies, we see different economic, political and social differences shaping the life chances and wellbeing of citizens. In particular, each of these societies is becoming increasingly unequal, which has implications for young people.

Although the trend towards increased inequality was well underway before the 2008 recession, the recession exacerbated this trend (EU EMPL Committee 2015). It triggered significant unemployment in most countries (except Australia) and waves of austerity drives that adversely affected low-income families who relied on government pensions, benefits and vital social, health and educational services.

On the plus side, however, the recession and its impacts raised the issue of inequality. As Fenna and Tapper note, if the inequality of wealth and income was once rather marginal it has now well and truly become mainstream, as 'attention is being lavished on the measurement, explanation and criticism of the distribution of income and wealth' (Fenna and Tapper 2015: 1). Along with economists like Leigh (2013), Piketty (2014), Atkinson (2014) and Atkinson and Morelli (2015), organisations like the OECD (2008, 2011, 2014, 2015) have begun talking up the problem of increasing social and economic inequality in many advanced western societies. While some – the OECD in particular – are interested because of the impacts inequality can have on economic growth, others seem more concerned about the ethical, social and political implications of mounting inequality. Piketty (2014), for example, mounted a strong evidence-based case that, since roughly 1980, economic inequality has been rising in both Europe and America and this represents an impending threat to the stability of liberal democracy.

There are formidable problems involved in getting good evidence that enables the description and measurement of income and wealth inequality, and even more difficulty in explaining it (Fenna and Tapper 2015: 3). There are several kinds of evidence, methods and approaches. One approach adopted by Piketty (2014) is to use tax data and focus on the very top of the income distribution (that is, the top 10 per cent, 1 per cent and 0.1 per cent of income earners). Using this approach, Piketty says there has been an 'explosion' of income inequality, especially in the US, since the 1980s. 'The bulk of the growth of inequality came from 'the 1 per cent', whose share of national income rose from 9 per cent in the 1970s to about 20 per cent in 2000–2010' (2014: 296). Piketty argues that this is explained by the rise of 'extravagantly overpaid senior executives', whose 'greed' has meant 'the share of the upper centile in national income has risen significantly in the United States, Great Britain, Canada, and Australia' (ibid.: 315). This is confirmed by Alvaredo *et al.* (2013: 5) who note that between 1980 to 2007, when the top 1 per cent share rose by some 135 per cent in the United States and the United Kingdom, it rose by some 105 per cent in Australia.

Another way to describe the total picture of income inequality is to measure the share of income owned by each decile of the population and then calculate the 'Gini index'. The index ranges from 0 when everybody has an equal share of total income (perfect equality) to 1 when all the available income in the country income goes to just one person (perfect inequality). Looking at 'market incomes' – incomes from wages and capital before taxes are taken out or pensions and benefits added in – highlights the generally high levels of inequality in the countries we are interested in.

These already high levels of inequality appear to be broadly on the rise in the OECD; the OECD average Gini was 0.29 in the mid 1980s, rising to 0.316 in the mid 2000s (World Bank 2014). In four of our countries the Gini is holding steady or increasing, in the UK however, it appears to be decreasing slightly.

Table 1.4 Income (market incomes) inequality by Gini score, 2011

Country	Gini score	Ratio of richest 10% to poorest 10%
Australia	0.303	12.5
France	0.301	9.1
Spain	0.359	10.3
UK	0.324	13.8
US	0.490	15.9

Source: *CIA World Fact Book* 2015.

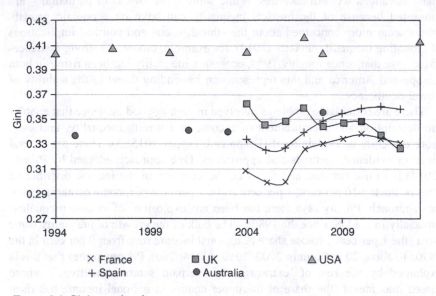

Figure 1.1 Gini over time by country.
Source: based on data from World Bank (2014).

High levels of inequality reflect serious problems with poverty. In the US, for example, there were 46.7 million Americans in poverty in 2014, almost the highest level for the 52 years poverty statistics have been published (DeNavas-Walt and Proctor 2015). In the UK, the poverty or social exclusion rate is on the increase, rising from 24.1 per cent in 2012 to 24.8 per cent in 2013; the same rate as the pre-recession 2005 figure. In Spain, an estimated 12.6 million people were at risk of poverty or social exclusion in 2013. In France, 20 per cent of the population is similarly at risk.

The differing levels of inequality and poverty, and its dynamics, can in large part be explained by the actions – or often inaction – of governments. Government affects the degree of inequality in a society via the kinds and scale of taxes it collects and how much money it gives back to mostly low-income people.[2] This is where the importance of long-term patterns of ideas and policy agendas becomes apparent. Drawing on Cavadino and Dignan (2006a), who amended a very influential model proposed by Gosta Esping-Andersen (1990), there are different ways governments deal with capitalist economies. These differences have certain effects like the degree of income inequality found in different societies. There are three kinds of regimes. Two we deal with here: neoliberal and conservative corporatist regimes.

The US, England and Wales and Australia are good examples of neoliberal political regimes. Neoliberal regimes are an expression of the late twentieth-century political project to cut back the scale of state intervention, and to promote wealth creation and free-market capitalism, which protects the interests of wealth owners, corporations and small-businesses, with the logic being that everyone does better when they do better. (We discuss the mess and contradictions real neoliberal governments create in Chapter 3). The general ethos is *individualist* and values individual wealth over egalitarianism. For neoliberals, the best kind of welfare state is minimalist, consisting mainly of means-tested welfare benefits, entitlement to which is often heavily stigmatised. We would expect them to have high levels of income inequality along with low total rates of taxation and restrictive, even punitive welfare policies. The evidence we draw on here (and in later chapters) supports this generalization.

The second kind of regime is the conservative version of *corporatism*. This kind of regime includes countries like France, Spain and Germany, where the overall socio-political ethos is *communitarian*. The state sets out to include and integrate all citizens within the nation, with individuals' membership of interest groups and other social groupings providing a vital link between the individual and the nation state. This explains why the Spanish and French states work to integrate national interest groups (like unions) into the national state and grant them a degree of control over those they represent on condition that this control is exercised in line with a consensual 'national interest'. In return, members of those national interest groups enjoy a range of benefits that are more generous than those associated with neoliberal states (Cavadino and Dignan 2006a: 444).[3] Conservative *corporatist regimes* should have a more equal distribution of disposable incomes, and less punitive welfare states.

When we look at the scale of their 'welfare states' (defined here simply in terms of the share of GDP allocated to various 'social expenditures') we begin to see some stark differences between them. In the countries with neoliberal regimes, governments provide, at best, very modest pensions and benefits that cater mainly to citizens on low incomes. France and Spain, on the other hand, as conservative/corporatist welfare states, rely on social insurance where most of the benefits for unemployment or sickness are entitlements based on an individual's previous insurance contribution. The contributions made and the benefits received vary according to the income of the individual. While we will need to explore what kinds of political frameworks have shaped the social policies of these countries, the table below shows a clear difference between the three 'neoliberal regimes' and the two 'conservative corporatist' regimes.

Table 1.5 Social expenditures as share (percentage) of GDP (1980–2014)

Country	1980	1990	2000	2005	2014
France	20.6	24.9	28.4	29.6	31.9
Spain	15.4	19.7	20.0	20.9	26.8
UK	16.3	16.3	18.4	20.2	21.7
US	12.8	13.1	14.2	15.5	19.2
Australia	10.2	13.1	17.2	16.4	19.0

Source: OECD (2016b).

Intergenerational income inequality

First, looking at a snapshot of young people's incomes in the here and now shows that young people have substantially lower incomes and earnings vis-à-vis older people's incomes. Across four of the countries we are interested in, young people's incomes are markedly lower than older people's.

In Australia, young people 17 and under currently earn on average AU$13.10, around one third of the hourly wages earned by 34–44 year olds at an average of AU$39.30 (ABS 2014). In the US, the median annual income in 2014 for households headed by 15–24 year olds was US$34,605, for those aged 25–34 it was $54,243 and for those aged 45–54, it was $70,832 (US Census Bureau 2015a). In Spain, France and the UK too, median annual income steadily increases with age (Eurostat 2016).

The recession affected young people's wages too, often driving decreases both in real terms and comparatively, driving up levels of intergenerational inequality. In Spain, for example, the annual incomes of 18–24 year olds decreased the most, to the extent that their average incomes are now the same as people under 18 (Eurostat 2016). And it's a similar situation in the UK. During the recession, all wage earners experienced a significant reduction in their hourly pay, but the biggest reduction was experienced by those aged 16–24 (ibid.).

Many of these countries legally mandate for lower 'minimum' wages for younger workers. Australia (Fairwork Ombudsman 2016) and the UK (Gov.uk 2016a) have a lower national minimum wage for younger workers, while the US (US Department of Labor 2016) and France (EurWORK 2016) have a lower rate linked to training or experience. Only Spain (ibid.) does not mandate for a lower

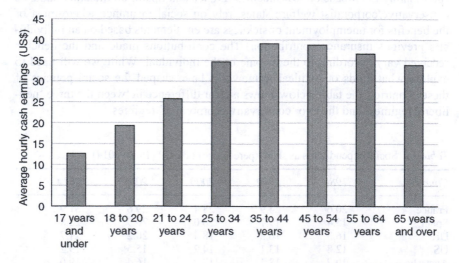

Figure 1.2 Average hourly earning of non-managers in Australia by age, 2014 AU$.

Source: based on data from ABS 2014.

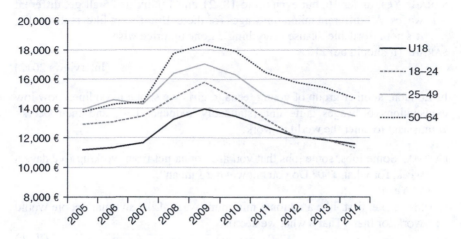

Figure 1.3 Spanish median income (equivalized), by age.

Source: based on data from Eurostat (2016).

minimum wage protection. While not all young workers earn the minimum wage, it does highlight the particular difficulties that low wage earning young people experience. The UK's minimum wage policy, for example, highlights growing issues for younger British workers.

From the introduction of the minimum wage in 1999, through the global recession of 2008–2015, the minimum wage for young British people slowly declined from 90 per cent to 79 per cent of adult wage for 18–20 year olds (Gov. uk 2016a). A new National Living Wage policy was introduced across the UK in April 2016, and is expected to increase by 13 per cent more by 2020 than it otherwise would have (Gov.uk 2016b). However, such a welcome boost to personal finances will not accrue to the young. Those under 25 are not covered by this new policy (ibid.), meaning their earnings will decline relatively and most probably in real terms compared to those over 25. For 21–24 year olds, in particular, who until April 2016 were classified as full adults earning the same as those 25 and over on National Minimum Wage, they will now be earning even less.

The reductions in the minimum wage, and its incapacity to provide adequate standards of living is not lost on young Britons. As young people from the North West of England who had spent time in state care explained, it was 'shocking' and only half of what they needed to lead a decent life – even before the National Living Wage was introduced:

SARAH: It's shocking.
JAMES: It's shocking! £6 something or £5 something for minimum wage.
SARAH: £6 I think it was …
ADAM: Under 16, isn't that £5?

SARAH: Yes, under 16, but even up to 18, 21 and I think its 25 all get different wages. All different minimum wages for there. But it's not like, realistically, it's not affordable, 'cause everything's gone up price wise.

SARAH: (It should be) £10.

(Interviews 2012)

In London, another group of young teenage girls we spoke to outlined how low expectations of wages quite understandably reduced their, and their peers', enthusiasm to enter the world of work:

FATIMA: Some jobs, some jobs that you are gonna get from working five days a week, for what, £50? Do you know what I mean?

SABA: Yeah.

FATIMA: Like, first, like a national minimum wage. Like summat people would work for that. (That's what we need).

(Ibid.)

America also adds a significant additional twist, reminding us in stark fashion that young people are not a homogeneous group. For example, households headed by black 15–24 year olds consistently have smaller incomes than Asian, white and Hispanic young people (US Census Bureau 2015b).

Second, while many of these differences can be partly explained by experience – older workers tend to have more experience and therefore command higher salaries – changes over time suggest that this does not explain it fully. Having a look at how the incomes of the young have fared over time, we see that today's young people are relatively poorer than previous generations

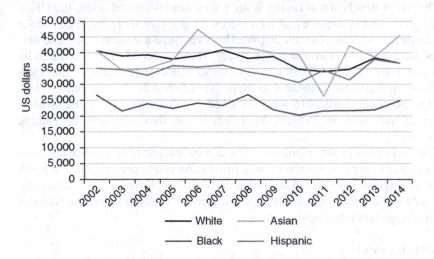

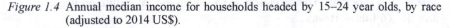

Figure 1.4 Annual median income for households headed by 15–24 year olds, by race (adjusted to 2014 US$).

Source: based on data from US Census Bureau 2015b.

In many of these countries, the income gap between the young and the old is growing. For example, while some people talk of the US economy having stalled since the recession (DeNavas-Walt and Proctor 2015), for households headed by 15–24 year olds, the stall began in 1967. Their median incomes have not improved in real terms since then, and neither has there been much growth for 25–34 year olds – 9 per cent in real terms over the last 50 years (US Census Bureau 2015a). Meanwhile, those over 65 have increased their incomes by 216 per cent. This means young people's incomes in the 'here and now' are not only less today than their elder peers in the US, but this gap is bigger for younger people than it was for other generations (US Census Bureau 2015a).

Charting the change in household disposable income (that is, incomes after tax) Barr and Malik (2016) found, while income growth for households headed by 65–69 year olds had increased in all of the countries we are interested in, it had decreased for the young in all bar Australia.

While the slight reduction in the UK – of 2 per cent – may not sound like such a huge reduction compared to the 8 per cent for France, 12 per cent for Spain or 9 per cent for the US, it potentially signals the first time since data has been recorded that we are witnessing one generation do worse than the last. In some countries, that generation is doing substantially worse, in others, less so. Even in the UK, Gardiner (2016: 25) suggests that the typical young person working throughout their twenties has earned £8,000 less than a typical person in generation X.

Uniquely in Australia, household disposable income (after tax) had grown 27 per cent above average for households aged 25–29 years old. So, while young

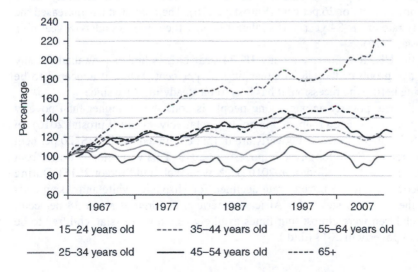
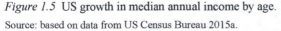

Figure 1.5 US growth in median annual income by age.

Source: based on data from US Census Bureau 2015a.

Table 1.6 Malik and Barr (2016)

Country	Age of head of household	Change (%)
UK 1979–2010	25–29	–2
	65–69	+62
France 1978–2010	25–29	–8
	65–69	+49
Spain 1980–2010	25–29	–12
	65–69	+33
US 1979–2010	25–29	–9
	65–69	+28
Australia 1985–2010	25–29	+27
	65–69	+14

Source: based on data from Malik and Barr 2016.

Australians confront a significant level of wage inequality in the 'here and now', it is clear that it is not getting worse. However, income inequality is not the whole story.

Intergenerational poverty

Young people's incomes are lower and, on the whole, getting worse and this is being reflecting in their poverty levels. In Spain, for example, the recession has dramatically increased youth poverty. Before the recession, there appeared to be a singular 'adult poverty' rate of around 17 per cent, below a relatively stable child poverty rate of 26 per cent (Eurostat 2016). The recession has increased the poverty rate of 18–24 year olds so that it is now the same as under-18 year olds (Eurostat 2016).

In the UK, too, poverty among 18–24 year olds is higher now than for any other age group in the UK, approaching 25 per cent. While it appeared to be reducing before the recession, it has been on a steady increase since.

In France, poverty among young people is consistently higher than poverty among any other age group, and is holding relatively steady (Eurostat 2016). In the US, inequality, race and poverty are intimately linked. In the US, 20 per cent of children (14.7 million) lived in poverty in 2013. This was actually down from 22 per cent (or 16.3 million), in 2010 (DeNavas-Walt and Proctor 2015). During this period, while the poverty rate declined for Hispanic, white and Asian children, the rate held steady for African-American children at about 38 per cent: these children were almost four times as likely as white or Asian children to be living in poverty in 2013 (ibid.).

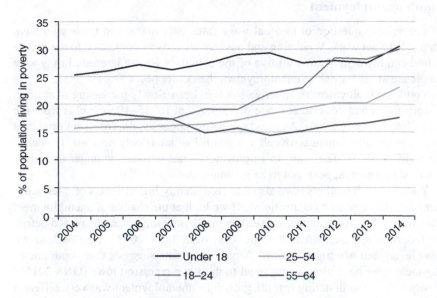

Figure 1.6 Percentage of population living in income poverty by age, Spain.

Source: based on data from Eurostat 2016.

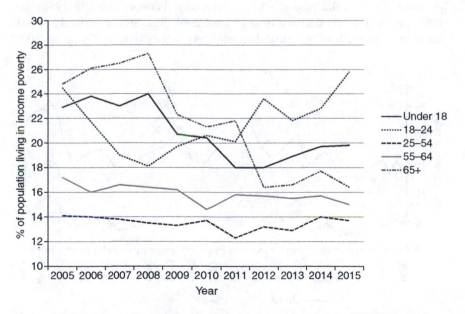

Figure 1.7 Percentage of population living in income poverty by age, UK 2005–2014.

Source: based on data from Eurostat 2016.

Youth unemployment

Of course, this question of unequal wage rates only matters to those who have been able to get work. Wellbeing and poverty are closely connected to the ability to find employment. Across all five of the countries we are interested in, young people are at higher risk of unemployment than older peers.

Youth unemployment in America has also been slowly increasing over time. Historically it had hovered at a rate of 15 per cent for 15–19 year olds from the 1960s into the early 2000s. As the graph below suggests, the recession produced a spike in unemployment across all age groups, which is only now slowly declining (OECD 2015). The 'gap' in employment rates between younger and older workers, however, appears not to be getting wider.

Young British workers have also had consistently higher levels of unemployment, but this appears to be declining. If we look at the change of unemployment rates since 1984, for example, we see that youth unemployment decreased before the recession – it decreased 38.17 per cent from 1984–2008 – rose back above 1984 levels, but has since declined. More recent data suggests that youth unemployment rates have almost recovered to their pre-recession lows (ONS 2016).[4] However, it is worth noting that the growth in unemployment was very different by age groups – everyone was affected by the recession, but the young more so.

In Australia too, the world of work does not appear to be particularly rosy for young people, despite the reduction in intergenerational inequality. Youth unemployment in Australia rose rapidly, if unevenly, between the late 1960s and 1993, before it slowly declined through until 2008. This almost certainly reflects the relative strength of the Australian economy through the 1990s up to 2013.[5]

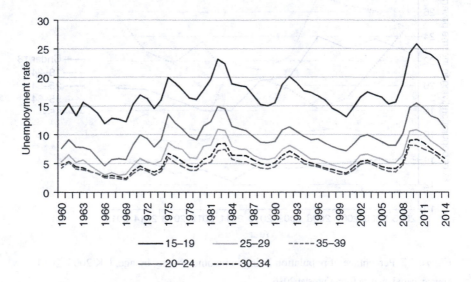

Figure 1.8 Unemployment rates by age, over time (US).

Source: based on data from OECD 2015b.

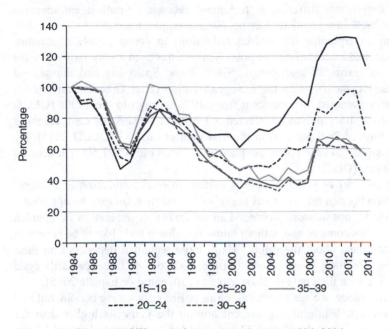

Figure 1.9 Changes to UK unemployment rate by ages, 1984–2014.

Source: based on data from OECD 2015b.

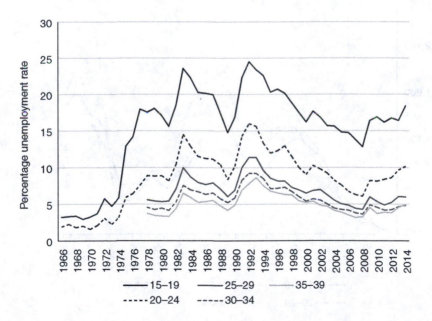

Figure 1.10 Unemployment rates by age, over time (Aus).

Source: based on data from OECD 2015b.

Curiously, despite not suffering a 'technical' recession, youth unemployment spiked after 2008, in a way that older people's unemployment did not.

In Spain, underpinning tremendous reductions in young people's incomes, and the associated increased risk of poverty, there has been a very large increase in joblessness across all age groups. Since 2008, Spain has had the second highest unemployment rate in the European Union (after Greece). Unemployment in Spain averaged 16.5 per cent from 1976 through to the 1990s (OECD 2015). By 2012, unemployment affected 5.3 million or 22.8 per cent, reaching an all-time high of 26.9 per cent in the first quarter of 2013 (OECD 2015). By 2013, joblessness rates for young people 20–24 years old was 1,500 per cent up on the 1970 rate (OECD 2015).

Because one in five young people is neither in work, education or training, this generation is often referred to as the 'ni-ni' generation (*ni estudia ni trabai* – or 'not in study, not in work') (Perez-Lanzac 2014). A generation of Spanish young people has come of age without knowing what it feels like to be secure in a job and confident about the future. Many have remained dependent on their parents long into their twenties and thirties: four out of five Spaniards aged 16–29 still live with their parents (Consejo de la Juventud de España 2015).

Finally, in France, we see something more positive for young people, but bad for older workers. While unemployment among the young is higher than for other age groups – in 2014, it was 32 per cent for 15–19 year olds and 21 per

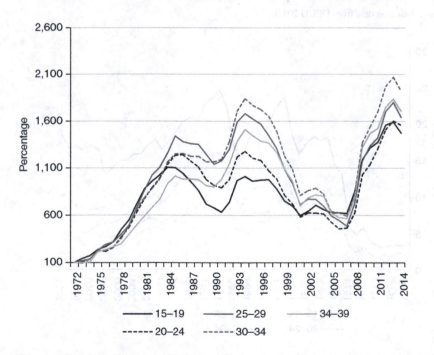

Figure 1.11 Unemployment rates by age, Spain.
Source: based on data from OECD 2015b.

cent for 20–24 year olds, compared to 8 per cent for 34–39 year olds – it appears to be improving over time (OECD 2015). Looking at changes to unemployment rates since 1983, unemployment among 15–19 year olds has held relatively steady. But the figure has increased to 30 per cent for 20–24 year olds, and increased by 90 per cent for 34–39 year olds (ibid.). 'Older' unemployment appears to be growing faster, shrinking the gap between unemployment rates.

Generation rent

What we see in these countries is evidence of economic inequality between younger people and older people in the 'here and now' *and* – Australia aside – persistent growth in this disparity. This has some profound consequences on the way young people live, particularly with regards to their housing. They are often 'locked out' of the housing market.

Home ownership rates among the countries we have looked at are relatively high – reflecting cultural norms that value home ownership. In Spain, 80 per cent of households own their own home, in the UK 74 per cent, in the US 72 per cent and in Australia 72 per cent; in France, fewer (68 per cent) do (IMF 2013: 11).

'Owning' a home however, can often fuel household debt via mortgages. As the IMF has made clear, the UK, US and Australia have excessively high levels of household debt. Using the ratio of household debt to disposable income as the key measure, the US ratio (in 2012) was 124 per cent, the UK's was 165 per cent

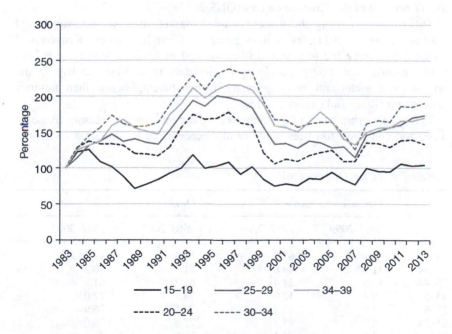

Figure 1.12 Changes to unemployment rate by age, France.

Source: based on data from OECD 2015b.

and Australia's was 153 per cent. France had a more manageable ratio of 99 per cent (IMF 2012: 18). By 2016, the Australian ratio was its highest ever at 177 per cent, largely driven by a speculative bubble in the housing market. If nothing else, this points to the value attached to home ownership in these societies and to the possibility that young people will feel strongly about being denied the chance to own their own home.

This debt however, is not always an economic drain. Rapid growth in the housing market – negative equity aside – means that households lucky enough to own their own homes have a significant financial asset that appreciates over time. Being locked out of the housing market therefore has three consequences. First, there are first the social consequences of being denied access to a social norm (think 'the great American dream'). Then there are long-term financial consequences because they cannot accrue housing assets. Finally, there are short-term financial consequences, because without access to the housing market, many are pushed to the more expensive private rental market.

In the UK, for example, while most Britons overwhelmingly still aspire to own their own home, nearly half of non-owners *never* expect to be able to buy a house (Bank of England 2015). Housing in the UK remains relatively expensive in comparison with other developed countries in terms both of house prices and private rentals (Clarke *et al.* 2016). Median house prices cost on average 8.8 years' worth of average wages, rising to up to 24 years in some areas of London (ONS 2015b). Rents aren't much cheaper, with the average English renter spending 47 per cent of their income on rent (ONS 2015a).

Difficulties accessing the owner/occupier market, and the state-subsidized market (Alakeson 2011), as well as potential lifestyle choices (Kenyon and Heath 2001), have led to a very distinctive sort of housing tenure for British young people, with young people proportionately more likely to live in the private rental sector and spending longer in their parental homes than previous generations (Rugg and Quilgars 2015).

Home ownership among the young in England has been decreasing for some time, and this trend has been significantly exacerbated by the 2008 recession.

Table 1.7 Rugg and Quilgars (2015)

Age	Private rental sector		Owner occupier	
	2008–2009	*2012–2013*	*2008–2009*	*2012–2013*
16–24	58.1	67.7	14.4	11.2
25–34	31.0	44.6	51.5	39.2
35–44	15.6	21.4	61.7	61.8
45–54	9.4	12.0	74.1	72.0
55–64	7.0	7.2	79.0	76.9
65–74	4.2	5.1	77.5	79.0
75+	5.2	5.1	71.9	75.5

Source: based on data from Rugg and Quilgars 2015: 7.

One result is that the share of under-35s in the homeowner population has almost halved in 15 years, and ownership rates among young people on low to middle incomes have fallen from above 50 per cent in the late 1990s to 25 per cent in 2013–2014 (Corlett *et al.* 2016). With access to social housing also restricted, this has meant more and more young people end up in the private rental sector.

The UK has a long tradition of valuing home ownership (Rowlands and Gurney 2000). The steady decline in ownership has, therefore, attracted policy attention. Recent government policies have reinforced the value of home ownership in the UK, highlighting the extent of the issue for British young people. Launching a 'Help to Buy' scheme in 2013, the Cameron government claimed that nothing less than young people's long-term economic security was at stake. Providing financial support to first-time homebuyers was designed to:

> … ensure that working people who were doing the right thing and saving for a deposit could achieve their aspiration of buying their own home through government support. Home ownership is a key part of the government's long-term plan to provide economic security for working people across the UK.
>
> (Gov.uk 2015)

It is too soon to say what the impact of 'Help to Buy' and similar schemes is or will be but, as long as young people's incomes remain comparatively subdued, it's likely that they will be locked out of the housing market.

In Australia, too, it is generally accepted there is an emerging housing crisis affecting young Australians. Homelessness is one consequence of this. Almost 44,000 children and young people in Australia were homeless, according to the 2011 Census (Mission Australia 2016). Further, over 112,000 young people sought assistance in 2014–2015 from specialist homelessness services (ibid.). Of these, about 42,000 were children under the age of 10 (ibid.).

House prices have far outstripped wage increases in Australia, pushing home ownership further away from young Australians, despite decreasing intergenerational inequality over time. Whereas, in 2001, an average home price in Australia was 4.7 times the average income, by 2011 this had increased to 7.3 times. While the cost of housing had, until 2001, risen in proportion to income growth, since 2001 the boom in housing prices has outpaced growth in household incomes. House prices increased by 147 per cent compared to income growth of just 57 per cent between 2001 and 2011. In dollar terms, the median price of a house more than doubled from AU$169,000 to AU$417,500 while after-tax income increased from just AU$36,000 to AU$57,000 (Senate Economic References Committee 2015: 20). For those on median incomes looking to purchase a first home (or at least a cheap one), the ratio has gone from 3.8 times median income to 6.2. Even cheap houses doubled in value between 2002 and 2014.

Not surprisingly, home ownership is becoming less and less common. The rates of home ownership overall have dropped from 64.4 per cent in 2002 to 59.7 per cent in 2014 (Senate Economic References Committee 2015: 20). One key effect is that many young people have been edged out of the housing market.

Home ownership is the major kind of wealth for most Australians and, while income inequality between the generations appears to be reducing, wealth inequality is *increasing*, most probably because of the astonishing growth in property values. While households headed by 55–64 year olds saw their wealth rise by AU$174,000, or 19 per cent, between 2003–2004 and 2011–2012, the households of 24–34 year olds lost AU$10,400 in wealth – a 4 per cent drop over the same time.

For those locked out of the housing market, even renting has become a problem, especially for young Australians on low incomes. A survey of 75,000 rental properties in Australia analysed their affordability for young people receiving Youthstart – the national income support scheme for unemployed or low income young Australians. Only 21 of the 75,000 rental properties were affordable for anyone on a Youthstart allowance – less than 0.1 per cent (Cooper 2016).

The situation facing young Europeans is more complex. As Bouyon (2015) explains, while Europe generally has quite high rates of owner occupation this is no uniform pattern. There are countries with rates significantly below the EU28 average (70 per cent) including Germany, Austria, and France; while other countries, like Spain and Italy, have rates between the EU28 average and 80 per cent (ibid.). At the same time, it seems clear that many young Europeans are facing more barriers than ever to affordable, high-quality housing. As Billari and Liefbroer (2010) argue, a new dominant pattern involving late, protracted and complex movement out of the family home is now taking place across Europe. Eurostat (2012) data shows that around 50 per cent of young people aged 18–29 who experience poverty (i.e. income less than 60 per cent of median) are paying more than 40 per cent of their income on housing: an increase of 10 per cent since 2008.

Spain certainly seems to value home ownership more highly even than Australia. In 2011 nearly 80 per cent of Spaniards owned their own home. At the same time, many European countries are experiencing an emergent generational phenomenon where the majority of people aged 18–34 are still living with their parents – 66 per cent of them in Italy, 58 per cent in Portugal and 74 per cent in Slovakia. Young Spanish people face a similar situation: 55 per cent of people aged 18–34 are still living with their parents. According to the EU's European Youth Portal (2013), most young people in Spain under the age of 30 live in the parental home, with only 7.2 per cent of those under 25 living independently. Spain is the country with the highest number of young people aged 25–34 living with their parents.

Paradoxically, Spain also has the highest percentage of young people (25–34) who own their own homes: 85.6 per cent versus 54.6 per cent in Germany. The paradox is explained by the fact that many of those who live in the family home do so to save the price of a housing deposit. However, recent trends are affecting their capacity to do this, including the effect of unemployment on young people's incomes. As Mínguez (2106) argues, while the price of buying a home and renting it has dropped significantly in Spain since the start of the crisis in 2007 (although costs began to rise again in 2012), this drop has been accompanied by a loss of financial independence among the young and job precariousness. 'The minimum income needed to buy a house exceeds [by] 80.8 per cent the average salary of a young person' (European Youth Portal 2013). The typical initial deposit is in the order of €45.000, while an employed young person from 16–29 would need to spend more than half of their net salary (54.2 per cent) on mortgage repayments. Equally the alternative of renting a house is also becoming more difficult. The average rent is €539.23, which represents 47.4 per cent of the average weekly wage of a young employee. (ibid; see also for disaggregated data Consejo de la Juventud de España 2013)

In France, we see a parallel situation, though one that needs to acknowledge that home ownership is not as strongly valued in France, where only 63 per cent of French adults own their own home (Trading Economics 2015). Perhaps it is not surprizing that young people aged 25–34 also have one of the lowest rates of home ownership in Europe next to Austria and Germany (Filandri and Bertolini 2016). Since the 2008 crisis, French young people, and particularly those with low incomes, found it difficult to leave the family home to rent and purchase their own homes as rents and housing prices have sky-rocketed (LiHumanite.fr 2015). This may reflect in part a persistent housing bubble in France. French house prices increased by 120 per cent between 2000–2008, briefly dipping

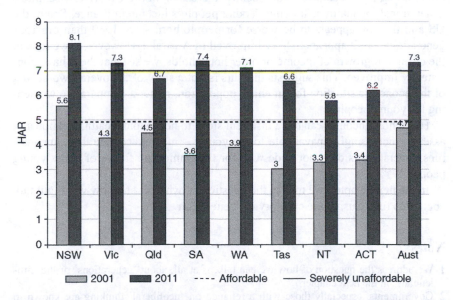

Figure 1.13 The 'Housing Affordability Ratio' is measured by dividing the median house price by the median income of the house purchaser. A ratio of five or less (that is, below the green line) is considered 'affordable'; a ratio of 7 or more (that is, above the purple line) is considered 'severely unaffordable'.

5.6 per cent in 2009, before increasing again from late 2009 to 2013. French policy-makers have expressed concern that property prices are highly overvalued, currently valued at 135 per cent of their historic price-to-income ratio and 150 per cent of their historic price-to-rent ratio. Young people are caught up in a wider housing crisis. Research by the Fondation Abbé Pierre (2015) showed that almost 10 million people were living in fragile housing, including 3.5 million in sub-standard accommodation, i.e. without a fixed home, living in hotel rooms, camp sites, squats; while 141,000 were living on the streets, in parks, under bridges and in makeshift camps. That number is made up of young and old people, the jobless, former prison inmates and asylum seekers. Around 38,000 people in France were currently housed in hotels waiting to find permanent accommodation. And 1.8 million households were on the waiting list for social housing, but only 450,000 are granted lodging each year.

Conclusion

The five countries we are interested in are all relatively wealthy countries marked to differing degrees by inequality. For the young, intergenerational inequality in the 'here and now' is present in all the countries we are interested in. Young people earn less on average and have higher levels of unemployment.

Over time, both overall inequality and intergenerational inequality change. The Gini index of most countries has changed rapidly over the last few decades – increasing in all countries, but recently decreasing in the UK. Likewise, intergenerational inequality is moving. Young people's income in France, Spain, the US and the UK appears to be worse for people born since 1980 than previous generations, but it appears to have improved in Australia. However, if we look at the change in growth of income of older households, we see that these have consistently improved. This suggests that this is not a story of the overall worsening of the economic situation for an entire population, rather a comparative worsening for young people.

Household incomes can tell a different story to household wealth, and housing assets – increasingly unavailable to the young – may exacerbate these inequalities. Overall, this does not bode well for the immediate future of many young people.

In the next chapter, we turn to the question of whether and how we might talk about this future using the category of 'generation'.

Notes

1 We address the question of how we can talk, if at all, about 'generations' or the 'millennials' in the next chapter.
2 Governments, especially those with a reliance on 'neoliberal' thinking are known to hand a considerable amount of money in the form of taxation expenditures back to high income earners and businesses. This is rarely measured and/or added into the redistributional effects. In Australia, for example, there were 290 kinds of tax expenditure in 2015, of which barely half were measured, but were still worth at least AU$130 billion

(ATO 2016). This compared with the $150 billion welfare expenditures (all recorded) targeting mostly low-income earners.

3 The third kind of regime is '*social democratic*' corporatism. This is both more egalitarian and secular than conservative '*corporatism*'. Typical examples include Sweden, Denmark and Norway. Social policy in these countries have been driven by a powerful trade union movement committed to the principle of 'universalism' and by a willingness on the part of employers to accept high levels of investment in return for wage restraint by the unions. The state undertakes a commitment to promote full employment, the pursuit of profit, the funding of generous welfare provision and an active labour market program that seeks to minimise the disruptive effects of deindustrialization and changes in economic conditions (Cavadino and Dignan 2006a: 445). This produces a corporatism with an egalitarian ethos and relatively generous universal welfare benefits.

4 www.ons.gov.uk/employmentandlabourmarket/peoplenotinwork/unemployment/ bulletins/youngpeoplenotineducationemploymentortrainingneet/may2016.

5 www.businessinsider.com.au/here-comes-australian-gdp-2015-12.

2 A political economy of generations

Talking about 'generations' is a ubiquitous feature of popular culture. As Woodman observes, journalists, market researchers and 'pop' academics find it convenient to generalize about certain social, cultural, emotional and political characteristics said to define people born in a given period (2013: 10). It is usually argued that a new generation appears every decade or so, and often that they have values diametrically opposed to earlier generations (Strauss and Howe 1997). For example, talk about 'Generation X' took off in 1964 when two journalists, Hamblett and Deverson (1964) released their book *Generation X*. Since then, and depending on the various generations being referred to, they have been described as materialistic, greedy, lazy, unmotivated, politically disengaged, media junkies and so on (Williams *et al.* 1997). Alternatively, 'Gen Y' or the 'millennials' – those born since 1980 or thereabouts, depending on the account – are confident, open-minded, disengaged, tech savvy, narcissistic and have an exaggerated sense of entitlement (Konrath *et al.* 2006; Twenge 2014; Stoerger 2009). As we already noted, a more serious tendency has been to talk up the idea that we are now in the middle of a 'generational war' as 'baby boomers' selfishly pursue their advantage to the detriment of the 'millennials' (Freedman 1999; Kamenatz 2007; Fishman 2010; Rayner 2016).

Yet if the generation category is so pervasive, and used to describe such an array of people and traits, is its use wise? Does such language confuse and obfuscate rather than help in figuring out what is going on? As we argue in this chapter, the concept of generation is useful.

The concept of generation is also controversial. Critics are concerned about the attribution of mostly negative traits to an entire age group and do not believe it has any value as an analytic or interpretive category. Others argue the category generation suffers from definitional confusion. Some point to the ways generation is used to refer variously to a 'principle of kinship descent', to an 'age cohort', to a 'life-stage' and to an 'historical period' (Troll 1970). Others say 'the term continues to be employed in a polysemous manner guaranteed to sow confusion' (Kertzer 1983: 126).

Others argue for a sociology of generations.[1] According to Woodman (2013: 1), some of this reflects an intention to redress the continual focus on excluded young people or spectacular examples of youth culture within sociology and youth studies. This focus, he suggests, means little research has addressed the experiences of 'ordinary' young people. This problem of the 'missing middle' reflects as much an absence of empirical research as it does 'conceptual problems', which he and his colleagues argue a sociology of generation can address (ibid.). We agree, though not for the same reasons.

We agree because many ordinary young people under 35 in America, Australia, France, Spain and Britain are systematically disadvantaged, socially and economically. Chapter 1 outlined a number of ways younger people are routinely 'losing ground'. For example, in the US, to reiterate, young men experienced real-term cuts in their weekly wages of 30 per cent between 1973 and 2010, while young women experienced a decline of approximately 10 per cent (Blanchflower 1999: 14). Given such evidence, how do we explain or understand what is happening and can the idea of generation help?

We argue that a political economy of generations is the best way to go. What this means, however, has yet to be established. A political economy acknowledges that important resources are distributed unequally and there is always a politics at play around this. A political economy acknowledges the many complex relations between advantage and disadvantage affecting young people, apart from the effects of age. The question is how can this be understood.

To answer this question, we begin with Côté's (2014: 528) advocacy for a 'new political economy of youth'. He argues we can and should talk about 'youth-as-a-class' because 'Gen Y' or the 'millennials' are victims of downward social mobility.[2] Côté triggered an important debate centring on the vocabulary and interpretative frameworks we should use to interpret what is happening. We agree with Côté about the value of a political economy approach and the need to explain how and why the education, labour-force participation and earning power of young people is changing (ibid.: 538). We do not agree that 'youth can be understood as a class' and, in this chapter, we identify a number of issues within Côté's account.

Côté and many of his critics rely on a 'substantialist' framing of reality, which leaves them caught in a version of the 'structure' versus 'agency' debate. Our preference is for a 'relationalist' account of the kind offered by Bourdieu (1977, 1987, 1990). This has implications for how we think about and use categories, like generation and class, in the political economy we offer here. In what follows, we draw on Bourdieu (1977, 1987) to develop a relational account of political economy of generations.

Given our focus is on young people born since 1980, we argue that a political economy of generation offers the best way to illuminate how young people are positioned, how they experience their world, and the nature of their relations with older people. Relations are particularly important, since older people often possess more economic, cultural and political power and will use these to further their own interests. We argue that generation itself is one of a number of important explanatory factors. In this political economy, categories like generation, class, gender, sexuality, ethnicity, geography and so forth, are presented in the way Bourdieu understands them. We agree with Antonucci's insight that it is misleading to position all young people's experiences as 'millennials', instead we need to acknowledge the 'reconfiguration of inequality occurring', which is 'profoundly influenced by intergenerational relations' among other factors (Antonucci 2016: 168).

Côté's political economy of youth

Côté (2014) argues youth studies tends to ignore issues raised by a 'political-economy-of-youth perspective'.[3] This matters, given the effects of several decades of neoliberalism, which saw governments systematically withdraw from correcting the serious consequences and contradictions of capitalist market economies. On top of this long-established trend, the 2008 recession exaggerated unemployment and underemployment, while increasing inequality in income and wealth. As he says, a political-economy-of-youth perspective:

> promises to be particularly useful in analyzing those societies in which government policies are unsupportive of youth interests, leaving youth cohorts open to exploitation by dominant economic interests ...
>
> (Côté 2014: 528)

His political-economy-of-youth perspective investigates:

> the root causes and consequences of the positioning over time of the youth segment in relation to those (adults) in a given society with political and economic power ... [while it also] ... provides a perspective with which to imagine radical solutions to youth exploitation.
>
> (Ibid.)

Central to this political-economy-of-youth perspective is the idea of youth-as-class. Côté draws on Marxist and Weberian approaches to class, arguing there are three 'common criteria' associated with definitions of class, which strengthen his case that we can think about 'youth-as-class' (Goldthorpe 1987; Wright 1978; Allahar and Côté 1998).

First, the idea of youth-as-class requires evidence of a demonstrable redistribution of resources as one group benefits from the other's exploitation and marginalization. In this case, given the claim that youth-as-class is an emergent phenomenon, it is necessary to show that younger adults of a certain age (e.g. 18–34) had a higher standard of living in the past in relation to older adults. Côté claims we have witnessed a significant redistribution of wealth in many societies influenced by neoliberal economics, within which age is an important axis. However, while we agree that the evidence points to significant generational inequality, it has yet to be established that inequality is to do with young people being a class.

Second, in making the case that this material disparity points to the role played by 'class', Côté argues there must also be evidence of a widely accepted 'ideological' justification for the differences between groups in access to wealth. Again, Côté is right to emphasise the evidence of a long-standing tendency to believe young people are naturally inferior or different from adults, which is often used to justify inequality of treatment. Claims about the 'inadequacy' of young people were originally made in arguments that adolescence was characterized by biologically generated periods of 'storm and stress' (Hall 1904). More recently, this idea resurfaced with experts pointing to deficiencies in the 'adolescent brain' (Côté and Allahar 1996: 2006). Côté also observes how education has long 'manufactured consent'. As he explains: 'the belief that education is a form of job preparation is usually sufficient for the public to accept these arrangements' (Côté 2014: 535).

Again, we grant Côté these points, although whether, or how, they sustain the idea of 'youth-as-a-class' is not clear, given that Côté allows that schooling itself is implicated in the 'reproduction of traditional social classes'. It is not made clear how traditional ideas of class relate to his idea of youth-as-a-class.

Finally, Côté argues there needs to be evidence of a 'consciousness' of difference between young people and adults. Côté refers to the use of binaries in public discourse like immature/mature, inferior/superior, dependent/independent, rebellious/responsible and so on (see also, Wyn and White 1997). He says the consciousness of adult–youth differences has increased significantly over the past few decades, evident in the growth of youth studies itself, in the bids by many governments to develop policies to placate youth activists, and to expand mass higher education to 'park' young people until their (cheap) labour is needed (Côté 2014: 530–531).

Côté's argument about youth-as-class seems to rely on an idea of 'false consciousness' found in parallel traditions of research and theory. He argues there are four examples of this false consciousness. First, he points to a more direct role for dominant interest groups in the 'manufacture of consent' through advertising and marketing, especially in the manufacture of *ersatz* youth cultures (Côté and Allahar 1996: 2006). Second, he points to psychological research for further evidence of the consciousness criteria, referring to representations of the actions of 'emerging adults' as expressions of 'free choice' interpreted as young people 'choosing' to delay the financial independence that comes from a full commitment to the workforce because they want to 'find themselves' (Côté 2014: 537). A third version of the consciousness criteria celebrates those born since 1980 for their coping capacity in the face of worsening economic prospects, which he attributes to Wyn and Woodman (2006) and Andres and Wyn (2010). The final consciousness criteria, he says, can be found in 'postmodernist' theories, such as 'post-subcultural' studies, that celebrate youth consumption cultures as 'resistance' (Bennett 2011).

We return to the implications of the emphasis on 'false consciousness' after briefly surveying some of the responses to Côté.

Critical responses to Côté

Most of his critics challenged Côté on theoretical issues, centring around the idea of class and class's relevance to youth studies (Farrugia 2013a, 2013b; Farrugia *et al.* 2015; France and Threadgold 2016).[4] This challenge was expressed in two ways.

First, in questioning whether youth is a class, critics have rightly suspected that Côté's claim is best understood as an attack on Beck (1992). Beck's work on 'risk society' and his individualization thesis had a major impact in youth studies. Beck argued that 'de-traditionalization' and 'structural fragmentation' are major defining characteristics of a change process underway in modern societies (ibid.). He is offered a microwaved version of Marx's account of the solvent effects of capitalism, Weber's account of the rationalization process, and Durkheim on anomie. 'De-traditionalization' refers to processes in which traditional 'taken-for-granted' beliefs and models for identity ceased to be generally accepted. In its place came an ethic of 'individual self-actualization'. Beck argues the change process is characterized by increasing structural fragmentation which leads to insecurity or 'risk' becoming a defining feature, hence his claim we now live in a 'risk society' (ibid.). For Beck, the primary driving force behind these structural changes is the capitalist labour market. The labour market treats workers as individual owners of their own labour, and the post-Fordist labour market removes them from collective forms of social life offered by union membership or through an identity as working class. The result is we all become 'reflexive', because we are compelled to see ourselves as an individual, and organise our lives actively to survive rapid social change. Individualized, reflexive subjectivities take the place of collectives, where collectives used to provide resources for identity and action, especially for the working class. Thus, instead of saying I am working class and belong to a union, the new tendency is to say I am just a person making choices.

This argument was taken up in youth studies with claims that young people were being 'disembedded' from traditional communal contexts and 're-embedded' in new contexts in which the ability to create life-paths and new identities was achieved through 'individual reflexivity'. McDonald argued that young people facing increased fragmentation of identity, needed to act as dissidents and 'resistance fighters' to assert their 'subjectivity' (1999: 7). Brannen and Nilsen used 'reflexivity' to describe the emergence of a 'new and powerful form of agency', in a context when 'social structures' like class were ceasing to shape young people's lives (2005).

However, Furlong and Cartmel rejected the idea that young people were being required to make more choices, be 'reflexive' or be actively involved in constructing their own 'biographies' (2006). Furlong and Cartmel argued that a political and social discourse that emphasized 'choice' had created a 'false reality' for the young. As a result, young people could no longer 'see' the 'wider forces' at play in shaping their lives. Furlong and Cartmel described this as an 'epistemological fallacy' because it sets young people up to believe they have control when they do not:

Blind to the existence of powerful chains of interdependency, young people frequently attempt to resolve collective problems through individual action and hold themselves responsible for their inevitable failure.

(Furlong and Cartmel 2006: 114)

Things heated up in 2009 when Woodman argued that Beck had been 'misunderstood' and misused. Beck, he argued, does not suggest 'class is dead' but that 'class theory' is the problem, because it is unable to explain the social changes taking place in 'late modern society' (Woodman, 2009). Roberts (2010) and Threadgold (2011) responded, suggesting such a position denies or fails to recognise that even when using 'objective' measures, class remains a significant influence in shaping what it means to be young. For example, educational outcomes are strongly 'correlated' to age, gender and 'class' (Threadgold and Nilan 2009). Others argue that social mobility is influenced by a person's class (Roberts 2010). For Platt (2011), factors like ethnicity or geography shape these outcomes; however, being working class or middle class is still a core feature of life. The question that matters, Threadgold adds, is not whether class is dead but whether class consciousness (or class identity) is dead (2011). Threadgold (2011: 388) also makes the point that 'people can be as reflexive as possible, but if they cannot put their choices into action, reflexivity becomes an intrinsic part of the reflexive experience of inequality'. For this reason, we need to understand better the disjunction between 'biographical choice' and continuing inequality (ibid.).

Critics also pointed to contradictions in Côté's work. While he rightly acknowledges that postgraduate degrees have becomes the 'new' undergraduate degrees in terms of 'advantage', he omits some significant social and economic inequalities that look to us like the effects of class (e.g. the reproduction of privilege through education).

This suggests a need for more clarity about what Côté means by class and how that intersects with his claim that 'youth-is-a-class'. A different kind of ambiguity also exists with categories like 'youth' and 'adult', which we see more as fuzzy or blurry classifications and not objective 'things' with clear boundaries. Moreover, as a large body of research on the notion of 'adult' shows, the markers of adulthood (e.g. full-time work, independent living and long-term relationships) are being deferred well beyond the age of 25, which is the age when most the 'legal' markers of adulthood are met, and are increasingly difficult to achieve at all (Crawford 2006; Blatterer 2007).

Second, what seems to have exercised most of his critics is his claim that young people suffer from 'false consciousness' (e.g. Côté 2014: 531, 535, 538). France and Threadgold say this is the weakest part of Côté's argument. Their critique is that the notion of 'false consciousness' represents 'millions of people as unthinking, mindless dupes' and it's an idea with little analytical or empirical value (France and Threadgold 2016: 618). Côté, they say, does not define what he means by the term and uses it as if it is a given, 'in spite a century's worth of critique of the notion that has largely rendered it inadequate'. They suggest that public perceptions of age distinctions are not evidence of 'consciousness', adding that depicting young people as empty, deluded and vapid is unhelpful, and contributes to age based stereotypes (ibid.). France and Threadgold (2016) add that when Côté argues 'the political-economy perspective draws attention to the problem of the manufacture of consent in the creation of false consciousness' (Côté 2014: 538), this reinforces the popular perception that young people are a 'problem' to be fixed (something Côté himself rightly says is a problem a few lines later).

His critics say 'false consciousness' cannot be 'evidenced' and that anyone doing research on young people will quickly discover they are reflexively aware of their own social position (France and Threadgold 2016; see also Threadgold and Nilan 2009; France and Haddon 2014). It is true there is much research telling us that young people talk about frustrations, setbacks and lack of status, a point recently attested to by Antonucci (2016: 84) in her study of university students. Yet it is also true that young people (like all people) do not always act in their own interests – whether those interests are economic, social, political or cultural (France and Threadgold 2016: 619). Arguing that this failure to act in a self-interested way demonstrates a 'false consciousness' is misguided.

Structure versus agency

Beyond criticisms of class, the other main category of critique of Côté's work has been a debate about 'structure' versus 'agency'. That is, behind the debates about the primacy of class structure versus the possibility of conscious thought, sits a longstanding and debate between advocates of structure and advocates of agency. Côté clearly accepts the relevance of a structure versus agency framework, as he does the older sociological tradition favouring causal structural explanations.[5] Côté defines this approach as a 'critical-realist macro theory' that examines the extent to which 'structural/materialist factors (or structures) that position people in society' can also be related to the ideologies they accept (Côté 2016: 854). He says he is not offering a theory of agency, but he does not deny our agentic capacity. According to Côté, political agency is highly relevant to his political economy perspective.

While not all of Côté's critics position themselves on one side or other of the structure versus agency debate, those who talk of 'individualization' imply the dominance of agency over structure while other writers re-assert the importance of structure for understanding young people's lives (Rudd and Evans 1998, Roberts 2001, 2007).

Evans (2002), for example, introduced the concept of 'bounded agency', proposing the need to recognise that individual choice was limited by structural location and position. More recently Roberts (2007), in responding to Wyn and Woodman's (2006) reassessment of generational theory, argued for an increased recognition of the importance of 'structured individualism' in shaping young people's lives and opportunities, presumably as part of a neoliberal discourse. Côté enlisted writers like Furlong and Cartmel (2006) and Sukarieh and Tannock (2015), who also use the structure versus agency frame. Furlong and Cartmel argue:

'Contrary to the ways in which some social scientists have (mis)interpreted our views ... we do not seek to deny the importance of subjectivity ... [or] agency ... [or] reflexivity.'

(2007: 138–139)

The structure versus agency frame has been central to recent discussion in youth studies (Farrugia 2013a; Roberts 2010; Threadgold 2011; Woodman 2009, 2010; Roberts 2012; Woodman and Threadgold 2014). Likewise, Sukarieh and Tannock (2015) use a structure versus agency frame, saying they are reacting to the over-emphasis on agency and the relative neglect of social and economic structures in much youth studies writing. Their focus, they say, is on broad discourses, the social and economic structures, and actions of elite actors in shaping the social category of youth and lives of young people in contemporary society, as these are too often overlooked and left in the background (Sukarieh and Tannock 2015: 138).

Woodman also accepts the structure versus agency frame and its underlying substantialism, while also wanting to assimilate Bourdieu into his 'middle ground' (2013). As he explains, this 'middle-ground' framework aims to fill a larger 'missing middle' in contemporary sociological theory, like that opened between recent approaches that 'over emphasise creativity and agency in the creation of the personal biography and incorrectly discount the impact of structural factors on life chances' (Woodman 2013).

Our view is that if we are interested in understanding young people's lives, we need an understanding of how the various ways what people *think and know* connects to what people *do* and *the circumstances* in which they act.

A political economy of generation, we argue, helps do this. This is possible, however, only if we sidestep the traps inherent in the structure versus agency frame. As we show, Bourdieu's account of practice provides a general political economy and, with help from Dilthey (2002) and Mannheim, suggests what a political economy of generation might look like.

Thinking about generation

Far from there being an objective basis for a category like generation, 'generation' is a concept that has always been shaped by its context. How the concept of generation worked throughout history is directly relevant to the contemporary conceptual character of generation. As Nash (1978) observed, the classical Greek root word *genos* had a verb form *genesthai* that meant 'to come into existence'. According to the classical Athenian understanding, the moment when a child is born simultaneously produces a new generation, separating parent and offspring, and reduces the idea of ever-shifting time. In this way, it can be seen how generation is time-bound *and* relative. It can be 'our generation', 'your generation' or it can mark 'allegiance, time of life, span of years, sameness with one group and otherness from the rest' (Nash 1978: 2).

With this in mind, we argue for clarity about generation. We can go some way towards achieving this by asking exactly what it is that we refer to when using terms like generation or youth. We say this while arguing that, when using words like generation, youth or even class, we engage in the practice of 'making people up'. That is, we attempt to make sense of the world by creating and using language categories. We note that most disputes about the definition of words and how we should use them rely on two assumptions:

The first assumption is that categories like class or generation refer to things and possess clear-cut traits that define them. This relies on an old assumption that in turn relies on the idea that the social world is made of things that have 'substances', promoted by philosophers belonging to the tradition of substantialism. It's also become a very popular idea that draws on the more modern 'classical theory of language'. This approach sees these words as amenable to a literal definition because they simply name things that exist in an objective sense. Philosophers like Wittgenstein (1953) and Rorty (1991), and cognitive psychologists like Lakoff (2004), demonstrated why this 'classical theory of language' is problematic, how people themselves constitute language and that metaphor plays a strong role in shaping how we think, see and use words.

In developing an argument for a political economy of generation we argue that we need to replace this preoccupation with *things* with a frame of inquiry that identifies *relations* and *processes* as the focus of inquiry. It's an approach that draws heavily on Bourdieu. We begin by identifying the problems associated with relying on a structure-versus-agency frame and its tacit reliance on a theory of things.

A relational political economy

The structure versus agency binary has dichotomized or polarized the social sciences for too long (Joas and Knobl 2009: 371). It has provoked sustained but fruitless debates between one absolutist position – that we are completely free to choose and act – pitched against the other absolutist position – that our actions are determined by various structures. It also supports the long-running methodological dispute between positivists and interpretivists.

While, ostensibly, these binaries are opposed, each part of the pair looks for causal connections and reduces the whole (of 'the social') to their preferred part, either society/structure or the individual/agency. While substantialists may be right on one level – the world does consist of 'things' like rocks and dogs – it also consists of social relations. The trouble begins when we see relations and processes as if they are things, or engage in what philosophers call reification. Reification means our thinking becomes trapped and we avoid recognizing important aspects of human life, like relations, intentionality and consciousness (Elias 1970: 112). As writers like Elias (ibid.) and Bourdieu and Wacquant (1992: 15) argue, we need to rid ourselves of such a 'commonsensical conception of social reality', which we perpetuate.

Bourdieu (1987) argues that this substantialist frame traps us by leading us to expect clear boundaries around the things we investigate. This is not possible in the social world: we have no clear-cut boundaries, no absolute breaks.

Drawing on metaphors, Bourdieu explains how the 'boundaries' between the theoretical classes we construct are like the boundaries of a cloud, in which the density of the water vapour is higher on one side than the other. They may be best thought of as lines or imaginary planes. Perhaps his most appropriate metaphor is that of a 'flame whose edges are in constant movement, oscillating around a line or surface' (Bourdieu 1987: 13). It's an idea that is anathema to many academics: 'Objects in the social world always involve a degree of indeterminacy and fuzziness, and thus present a definite degree of semantic elasticity' (ibid.).

Bourdieu argues that substantialism encourages us to:

> make quite senseless conceptual distinctions which makes it seem that 'the individual' and 'society' were two separate things, like tables and chairs, and pots and pans.
>
> (Bourdieu and Wacquant 1992: 15)

He argues that 'the real is relational' (1987: 3), and calls instead for a focus on relationality to better explain the nature of the relations, states and processes we are interested in (Bourdieu and Wacquant 1992: 15). Relationalism underscores the idea that human practices and actions are always transactional (Powell and Dépelteau 2013). Bourdieu was clear about what his focus on relations implied: 'what exist in the social world are relations, not interactions between agents or intersubjective ties between individuals, but objective relations' (Bourdieu and Wacquant 1992: 97).

Drawing on this we offer a political economy of generations. To do this we outline how Bourdieu thought about the use of classifications and categories such as 'working class', 'old', 'ethnicity'. He identified two conventional approaches: one realist, the other constructivist. Realists try to determine the properties or traits and the boundaries of the classification in question, sometimes even counting the numbers constituting that category. Constructivists, however, see a class like 'the young' as a construct of the researcher, with no grounding in reality.

According to Bourdieu, the realists who claim to discover ready-made classes of people and those constructivists who say a group (e.g. 'the unemployed') is a constructed artefact both share a common substantialist assumption. They both see the category in question as based on a substance.

Bourdieu argues that we will better understand what is happening if we begin with a relational frame, 'which identified the real not with substance but with relationships' (1987: 2). Being 'young' or 'upper class' is less about a certain substance than about the spaces in which the social relations and processes that these categories refer to take place. This emphasis on relations and processes involves a major revision in the way we interpret and write about the social world. It involves paying attention to the practices (and processes) that people in relations informed by ethnicity, economic power, age or gender engage in, as we struggle to add to the various resources we have.

His theory proposes that human *practice* is *habitus*, operating in a *field* of unequally distributed *capitals* (or powers characterized by inequality and continual conflict (Bourdieu 1984: 101). Practice here refers to all those activities and processes we engage in, like talking, thinking or going to school, and everything else we do. According to Bourdieu, most of our practice is habitual – hence his use of the term habitus.

Our habitus is what we use to perceive, understand, evaluate and act in the social world all the times. Bourdieu borrowed the idea of habitus from Mauss and expanded it. It refers to:

> a system of generated dispositions integrating past experiences, which functions at every moment in a matrix of perceptions, appreciations and actions and makes possible the achievement of infinitely diversified tasks.
>
> (Bourdieu 1977: 83)

Habitus is the person: it involves our emotions, ethical and cognitive life, tastes, and how we use our body. Practices and knowledge, he says, are bound together *in and by* the body. The social order inscribes itself in our bodies because we learn and express our knowledge bodily. This set of generative abilities is acquired through the interaction of the individual within the social world and in particular fields within it. Our habitus is the product of our particular history or trajectory through life.

Our reliance on habitus to engage in *practices* always occurs in what Bourdieu refers to as fields. By fields he means social spaces like family, education, work, the sports arena, the arts etc. All societies are compendiums of independent and differentiated fields. However, Bourdieu notes that any field involves social positions and relations based on power and endless struggles and conflicts over an array of *capitals* (Bourdieu and Wacquant, 1992: 97). In short, we compete in fields to multiply our economic, social, or cultural capital. Everyday life is thus nothing but continuous struggle in a conglomeration of organized fields.

Finally habitus and field refer to spaces comprising relationships dependent on capitals. Unlike Marx, who thought any society was defined by the dominant economic mode of production, Bourdieu thought in terms of many and different fields and kinds of capital. In Bourdieu's social theory, capital is different types of valued resources, distributed through the social body, which have an exchange value in the various fields that comprise the social world (Bourdieu 1977). For Bourdieu, each field involves a number of different capitals. In this way, each field tends to have one distinctive form of capital that agents seek to accumulate, bound by rules of competition that give the field a bounded integrity and relative autonomy. This is what makes Bourdieu's work a political economic account.

A capital is hierarchically arranged, according to 'the structure of the distribution' of the particular kind of power, social resource or 'species of capital' (Bourdieu 1990a: 119). The structure of the distribution refers to the many positions in those social relationships we occupy: e.g. as a parent *and* child; as a student *and* teacher; or worker *and* employer/manager. In those social relations we develop certain dispositions or habitus over time. Put differently, our habitus is the result of the inculcation of these social relations into the experiences we have of each other. At the same time, our habitus has historical dimensions because it encompasses all our past experiences. It is 'the product of history' as it signifies 'the active presence of the whole past of which it is a product' (Bourdieu 1977: 56).

Field and habitus involve a two-way relationship. Fields only exist if social agents possess the habitus necessary to maintain them and, reciprocally, by participating in the field, actors already incorporate into their habitus the specific rules that will allow them to constitute the field. Therefore, habitus enacts the field, and the field mediates between habitus and practice (Bourdieu 1977). This relational perspective has clear implications for how we think about and experience being young and old, which is what the idea of generations points to.

While Bourdieu is interested in capital, he does not claim there is one dominant form of capital. Indeed, anything can become capital when it presents itself as significant or desirable. Bourdieu offers a relational frame where no one element has causal privilege over any other (Emirbayer 1997). Our social world is best conceived as a multi-dimensional space comprising fields based on various capital, including:

- *economic capital* (e.g. wealth, commodities);
- *cultural capital* (e.g. education, experience and credentials);
- *social capital*, or resources based on connections and group membership – like the connections we do or don't have to high status or powerful people
- *symbolic capital* refers to prestige, reputation and honour. It depends on publicity, appreciation – and is associated with how much of the other kinds of capital we have or are presumed to have.

We all bring various forms and quantities of capital into fields. We draw on those capitals as we act in those fields. We also seek to add to those capitals in ways that are political and competitive. In this way, fields are hierarchically distributed, with those who populate them bringing different resources into those spaces.

All this has implications for how we can make sense of the world using categories like generation: we can construct categories because we can speak about people sharing certain kinds of conditions. The capacity to speak about groups is possible because the proximity found in a field like a family, a school or a workplace works to reinforce similarities. As Bourdieu observes, our 'occupation is generally a good and economical indicator of our position in society'. It provides valuable information like the effects of the work we do, such as the economic capital it generates and the access to social or cultural capital it can create. It can be as simple as the fact that space and the social relations in it are constructed in ways that mean the closer we are in a social space to others, the greater the probable number of common properties and, conversely, the further we are from each other, the fewer properties we will have in common. That is, when we occupy neighbouring positions in a field, we are placed in similar conditions and are subject to similar conditioning factors. Consequently, we have a chance of having similar dispositions and of producing practices and representations of similar kinds.

To be clear, Bourdieu does not suggest that people aggregated into a shared category by virtue of factors like generation, will have the same experiences, thought or behaviour. Nor does he imply that we can predict the behaviour of certain members of a class in a given situation. If this were the case, it would be a deterministic schema (Bourdieu 1977: 85). What he suggests is that, to a certain extent, members sharing the same features of a category will show homologous behaviour in a number of situations. This does not imply complete freedom of action because habitus shapes our practice. What Bourdieu suggests is that a degree of uncertainty remains in all social situations (ibid.: 9).

Having said that, Bourdieu is very clear that in this relational frame, the various factors that matter – like class or generation – are not real things in the way the substantialists believe.

A political economy of generations

Bourdieu argues we are distributed across three dimensions in society. One relates to the *quantity* of the capitals we possess. The second dimension relates to the *kinds* of capitals and their relative weight. The third relates to *the evolution of capital over time*, its volume and composition according to our historical trajectory in social space.

This third dimension points to the salience of time, the accretion of experience and the various forms of capitals that accrue across time and do so on a generational basis. Where we are positioned in historical time relates to the kinds and volumes of capitals we accumulate. Our trajectory over time and through a social space comprising many fields enables us to acknowledge the dimension of generation. For Bourdieu, generation is socially constructed through the conflict over various capitals within fields. These struggles can be intergenerational, as younger social actors struggle to impose new lifestyles and tastes within a field. They can also be intra-generational as some people use various kinds of social, cultural and economic capitals to advance their own position or reproduce a social position across generations. Some people are better equipped to take advantage of the possibilities afforded by changes to the rules configuring a field or to colonise emerging fields, where the rules of the game are less well defined (Bourdieu 1984: 357–358).

A political economy of generation, derived from Bourdieu, means we need to acknowledge that to make conceptual distinctions based on age is always a political exercise. This is also true of other classifications like gender, class, ethnicity, all of which impose limits so as to produce 'an order to which each person must keep' (Bourdieu 1993: 94).

The relationship between social age and biological age is also complex in that, while age is a biological fact, how we experience and 'know' age also depends on our social context. This is because each field and society has their own specific laws of ageing. Having this in mind is helpful in acknowledging all the ways a young person's life – as a worker, or student etc. – is shaped by time. It is time-defined and managed in ways that reflect the logics of specific labour markets, the reproduction of capital and how particular fields of work (bar work, lawyering) distribute material capital, both income and symbolic capital. Likewise, the student's life is variously shaped by school/academic time, regimes of study and so forth.[6] For the young student, these fields sustain what Bourdieu sees as a 'no-man's land of adolescence', in which students are 'adults for some things and children for other things'. The field of education is helping to influence habitus by shaping symbolic capital involving expectations: 'going to a *lycée* (public secondary school) means taking on the aspiration to become a *lycée* teacher or a doctor, a lawyer or a notary ...' (Bourdieu 1993: 98). At the same time, the *lycée* is implicated in the unequal distribution of cultural and symbolic capital. What all this means is that if we don't acknowledge 'the laws of ageing in each field', we risk abusing language when we start using a category like 'youth' to include within it 'social spaces that have practically nothing in common' (ibid.: 95).

Apart from paying attention to the ways each field has its own specific laws of ageing, Bourdieu also allows for a second and larger generational effect. This offers a different but complementary understanding, which, as we argue, Karl Mannheim anticipated in the late 1920s.

Bourdieu draws attention to this larger kind of generational effect when he acknowledges important policy-driven changes taking place in French education in the 1980s. The generation who entered a smaller, socially exclusive educational system in the early 1950s experienced quite different kinds of education to that experienced by those who enrolled into a 'massified' education system in the 1980s (Bourdieu 1993: 99). These changes affected the symbolic capital attributed to certain levels and kinds of cultural capital produced within the French schooling system. He argued that where access to a *lycée* represented a significant level of symbolic capital in the 1950s, it no longer did so in the 1980s, as more and more young French people stayed on in secondary school or university. When working-class children could not attend a *lycée*, the value of the symbolic capital accruing to those mostly middle- and upper-class children who did was greater. 'Consequently there's been devaluation as an effect of inflation ... a qualification that becomes more widespread is ipso facto devalued but it loses still more of its value because it becomes accessible to people "without social value"' (ibid.: 98). This, in turn, means that young generations 'will get less out of their qualification than the previous generation would have got' – or collective deskilling – which may, in turn, generate a level of disenchantment that spreads across that generation (ibid.: 101). In this way, there is a common generational effect, implying that apart from other differences grounded in gender or ethnicity, there is a collective experience because of generation.

Bourdieu points to other large historical changes. A generation, for example, forms certain expectations in relation to the availability and distribution of prestige and highly valued goods. For those born in the 1940s, buying a new car or having an overseas holiday in their twenties was a rare luxurious purchase. For many born in the 1960s, it had become a statistical banality.

Here we see a collective appreciation of how generation might be understood as part of a political economy. If a political economy of generation recognises the effects produced by the politics of unequal access to capitals in multiple fields arising from our trajectory through time, it also needs to acknowledge the effects of large-scale historical events. Amending Woodman (2013) slightly, a political economy of generations is a way of understanding social change and social reproduction simultaneously.

Mannheim and 'generation'

We agree that Mannheim's insight into generations needs to be resuscitated (Pilcher 1994; Wyn and Woodman 2006). His insight complements Bourdieu's political economy of practice, which acknowledges diversity within a generation while pointing to the effects of large-scale historical events on an entire generation.

As Woodman (2006) argues, this understanding of generation goes back to Mannheim's discussion of generational units, which traces 'both change and continuity but not as binary opposites' while allowing for the idea that a generation includes different kinds of people (Woodman 2013: 82). This concept of generation was first elucidated by Wilhelm Dilthey and later by Karl Mannheim (Bessant 2014b). While Mannheim's work has been acknowledged and discussed widely, Dilthey's contribution has been less well understood.

Dilthey was a nineteenth-century German philosopher of history who drew on the German phenomenological tradition that included thinkers like Heidegger and Hegel. Earlier phenomenologists, such as Hegel, were preoccupied with understanding the process of history itself and spoke of a *zeitgeist* or 'spirit of the time'. From this perspective, humans were seen not so much as rational, calculating machines but as culturally embedded actors attempting to 'understand' and 'interpret' (*verstehende*) the world. Linked to this older tradition, Dilthey was interested in the 'meta-historic rhythms' of western history. As part of his larger study of the human sciences (like art history, philosophy and history), Dilthey wanted to replicate for the 'human sciences' what Kant did for the natural sciences, namely to develop an objective theory of knowledge or epistemology while grounding this in lived experience (*Erlebnis*).

Dilthey, like later developmental theorists, saw early human life experiences as formative and as framing subsequent experiences and ways of seeing. As such, generations defined by certain shared assumptions created generally shared world-views, which worked to guide epochal change. Each period defines the life horizons that frame the outlook of those born into it, and to which, in turn, they orient themselves. Dilthey explained: 'such a horizon places life, life-concerns, life-experience, and thought-formation in a certain proportion' (2002: 198). Generations are recognisable by their 'permeating tendencies' or the ways they express the tendencies that dominate in particular times and create a historic consciousness:

> Those who receive the same impressions during their formative years form a generation. In this sense, a generation consists of a close circle of individuals who make up a holistic unit through their dependence upon the same events and changes which they experienced during their formative years in spite of other differences.
>
> (Dilthey 1875, cited in Jaeger 1985: 176)

For Dilthey, as older generations were succeeded by younger ones, each generation created change as tensions between 'opposing tendencies' embedded in particular historic time played out. Dilthey's work helped shape Mannheim's ideas on generation.

Karl Mannheim was one of the first modern theorists to develop a sociological account of generation and social change that departed from the then highly influential Marxist and Idealist traditions. While Marxism remained an influence on Mannheim, he also drew on phenomenology, appreciating how it helped make sense of what is happening and was interested in the historical context of what he studied.

That Mannheim drew on Marxism is evident in his sociology of knowledge, which he saw as an inquiry into the ways socio-historic conditions and 'world-views' shape knowledge. In this respect, Dilthey was Mannheim's forerunner in seeing that many factors shaped shared 'world views' of a given time and place, including our lived experience (Mannheim 1952: 291). Thus the worldview of a group, a class or generation was shaped by its historic location. As he explained:

> Were it not for the existence of social interaction between human beings – were there no definable social structure, no history based on a particular sort of continuity, the generation would not exist as a social phenomenon: there would be merely birth, ageing and death.
>
> (Ibid.)

Mannheim argued we can talk about generation as a unique social entity based on the dynamic interplay between being born in a particular period of time and the socio-political events that occur throughout the lives of those born in that period (McMullin *et al.* 2007: 299–300). For Mannheim, each generation has its own a distinctive historical consciousness that is shaped by the historical events of that time. Generation is a consciousness (*Zeitgeist* – spirit of the time) that guides one's view and approach to the world.

Those born into a particular time shared similar life experiences because they came of age in the same or similar milieu or 'fields of actions' as Bourdieu would later call them. As Mannheim explained:

individuals who hold membership in the same space and age group would share common space and time location in the socio-historical process, these commonalities would delimit their experiential situations and hence produce a common attitude, activities and behaviour.

(Mannheim 1952: 287)

Because our earlier years were seen as formative, that experience and time were considered particularly influential. Significant events during these years were said to predispose us toward certain ways of thinking and being, creating 'generation potentiality'. Thus a sense of generation is created by a generational consciousness and shared history.

For Mannheim, our experience of *historic events* (especially in periods of rapid change) produces a generation as *actuality*. He says that, like class, one's age position is a distinct fact that we may recognise or ignore even though we sense that we share a space in the socio-historical process. As mentioned, it does not follow, however, that exposure to the same events means we will all share the same characteristic attitudes and consciousness. How we each interpret and experience an event differs. Historic events affect us differently because human experience is mediated by our respective geographic position, ethnicity, gender, religion, and class. Such differences are part of belonging to a generation and what Mannheim called 'generational units'.

Like Bourdieu, Mannheim recognized time as a social phenomenon. Mannheim saw generation as a marker of time rather than (as positivists tend to) an objective thing or a dependent variable. Working within the phenomenological tradition, he saw time as an internal, subjective experience; this view encouraged him to acknowledge the diversity, differences and discord produced by the different social, cultural and geographic sites that make up a generation. Importantly, he recognized that 'within any generation there can exist a number of differentiated, antagonistic generation units' (Mannheim 1952: 306). This enabled Mannheim – and, later, Bourdieu – to see history as a process that encompasses change and persistence. Generation becomes useful for thinking about the complexity of understanding how change and persistence coexist in the biographical and historical dimensions of time.

Thus, while a generation consists of groups who are positioned unequally in terms of their access to different capitals, they still nonetheless belong to each other due to the ways certain large experiences and events encourage a binding connection that works to orient people of that generation toward each other. But politically and culturally, members of a given generation invariably disagree with each other on various issues or the value of certain practices or affiliations.

We argue that generation is a meaningful category that can help in understanding the specific circumstances many young people now experience. A generation is not a fixed homogenous 'thing', but a social entity bought together by dynamic socio-political events that happen in their lives, which provide a general 'worldview' or zeitgeist in the sense that a generation acknowledges certain events as highly significant.

The zeitgeist of today's generation

Specifically, we say three global events have defined a zeitgeist for people born after the early 1980s. The first, which is the primary focus of this book, is the rise and spread of a neoliberal worldview that powerfully shaped the policy-making processes of many governments and the popular culture of many societies. The second is the advent of digital technology, which had and continues to have global ramifications. Finally, there is a political-economic process of globalization, promoting processes of complex socioeconomic and cultural change across the globe.

Each of these events considered separately or together is comparable in scale and significance to earlier kinds of benchmark historic events, which, Mannheim argued, shape a generation. As we have mentioned, because a given generation is influenced by particular events or large-scale processes is not to claim that everyone is affected in the same way or has the same response. Mannheim, anticipating Bourdieu, went to great lengths to highlight diversity in how antagonistic generational units respond to the same events in different ways.

Within this diversity, however, these three events had important consequences in shaping the lives of young people born since 1980s in uneven ways. There were at least five notable effects.

First, we have witnessed the extension of the dependency traditionally associated with being a 'child' or 'adolescent'. Second, there is a growing gulf between the promises of education and the benefits said to flow from the human capital theory; and the reality of many unemployed graduates. Third, inequality and poverty among the young has increased, including an increasing number of well-educated young people and early school leavers who are socially and economically disadvantaged. Fourth, digital technology has reshaped the sensibilities, relationships, identities and experiences of being young. Finally, in political terms, complex and often contradictory shifts are taking place. Many who came of age in this period assume individualist neoliberal sensibilities and outlooks. At the same time, many young people have also developed oppositional stances to the political and economic status quo.

Generations include groups who differ from each other and who disagree but who, despite these differences, are oriented toward each other because of shared experiences. Our task is to make sense of the complex responses and sense-making on the part of those who came of age in a globalising world, dominated by neoliberal policies and with access to digital technology.

Conclusion

People born since the early 1980s belong to a distinct and important generation. They have been called many things, like 'Gen Y', 'millennials', and 'generation rent'. While many of these labels are used simplistically or to disparage, if used thoughtfully the category of generation can be helpful for making sense of what is happening in the world and, specifically, for young people.

We can and should talk about generation in this way because people born into the neoliberal zeitgeist have been shaped by a unique and unsettling combination of events, political ideas and policy practices set loose since the 1980s in most advanced societies. Our purpose here is to say how and why we can think about the lives of young people using the idea of a political economy of generation.

The political economy in which young people grew up from the early 1980s was profoundly shaped by policy and political decisions made by previous generations. We turn now to explore the transformation of socio-political and economic cultures that occurred in the early 1980s, promoted by the resurgence of a neoliberal worldview.

Notes

1 Pilcher (1994); Wyn and Woodman (2006); Andres and Wyn (2010); Woodman (2009, 2011, 2013); and Woodman and Wyn (2014).
2 Côté calls this 'proletarianization', which works as a metaphor to establish a Marxist provenance by suggesting systematic processes of exploitation.
3 The youth studies field has always exhibited some interest in class, e.g. the Birmingham School.
4 Côté seems to understate the continuing salience of class which has been, and remains, influential in discussions over the study of youth (Shildrick *et al.* 2009; Roberts 2010).
5 Structures are often referred to as rules that 'determine' or influence individuals' thoughts and behaviours. The structuralist perspective implies that people 'behave' or are programmed to act in accordance with the 'rules'. On the other hand, the voluntarism or agency perspective suggests that individuals are free in their choices and always have an array of alternatives (Hays 1994).
6 As Bourdieu explains, students in the French *écoles grandes* are denied adult status by being placed in 'semi-monastic enclosures' separated from the world to do gratuitous things: 'the things one does at school, exercises with blank ammunition' (Bourdieu 1993: 96).

3 Neoliberal social policy and young people

The story currently told about the generational conflict between baby boomers and millennials goes like this. After World War II, most western governments promised to secure the welfare of their citizens by promoting full employment. They did this by investing in public works and increasing spending on pensions, benefits, health, education and cultural activities. This Keynesian approach, which created the welfare state, became the dominant 'common sense'. Between 1945–1975 most western societies enjoyed economic growth, booming employment and a mass consumption lifestyle. Those born after 1945 ('baby boomers') enjoyed free education, secure full-time employment, cheap housing and the good life, and now enjoy high retirement incomes.

In the 1970s and 1980s, or so the story goes, this Keynesian political and policy common-sense was undone, courtesy of a mix of economic changes and neoliberal policies. The welfare state was dismantled or retrenched as governments cut social spending and restructured welfare programs. Wacquant, for example, argues the neoliberal 'centaur state' unleashed a triple transformation including the 'amputation of its economic arm, the retraction of its social bosom, and the massive expansion of its penal fist' (2009: 4) as the Keynesian welfare state was replaced by a 'workfare' state (Fisher and Reece 2011: 226). The story concludes that dismantling the welfare state means the millennials are now the first modern generation with living standards lower than their parents'.

As we have argued, we need to be cautious of accepting stories, even if they are popular or seem plausible. Instead, we ask 'what is actually happening?'

The story above is too simple. It misses many of the differences and complexities in the ways governments acted until the 1970s and 1980s, and how they changed their minds and have made policy since. There is a mass of literature that challenges the idea that a single coherent set of Keynesian ideas were rolled out across western societies after 1945.[1] Likewise, there is an equally large body of work challenging the idea that we can refer to neoliberalism to explain the specific and different changes that occurred in government policy-making between 1975–2016.[2] While some writers argue the welfare state has been destroyed or shrunk, others point to a more complex process of restructuring.

To establish what is going on, we link two ideas. One idea is that policy-makers rely on 'policy paradigms', which influence how they see and define policy problems and solutions. The other idea is that there are different kinds of 'welfare states' (Esping-Andersen 1990). When these ideas are combined, we have the idea of 'path dependence': the idea that it is hard to change policies and government institutions easily or totally.

Using a historical approach, we chart the rise and fall of the Keynesian policy paradigm between 1945 to the 1970s, and then document the rise of a neoliberal policy paradigm in the 1970s. We note that the neoliberal turn in policy-making did not mean every government did the same things, at the same time, or in the same ways. In some countries, neoliberal policy-makers shrank the welfare state, while in others they did not. We use a version of Esping-Andersen's typology of 'welfare states' to chart the impact of neoliberalism on different welfare states found in Britain, the US, Australia and France. This suggests that the liberal welfare states (Britain, US and Australia) embraced neoliberalism readily, although in some cases quite differently, while conservative welfare states like France proved less susceptible to neoliberal ideas.

On policy paradigms and welfare regimes

There is a common-sense tendency on the part of many who write about politics and policy-making to assume that the problems politicians or policy-makers deal with are obvious, and objectively real. One implication of this, if it were true, is that there would never be any case for disagreeing about the problems needing to be fixed. This, however, is not the case. We would rather insist that we need to pay a lot more attention to how policy-making communities understand or make sense of the world, i.e. what assumptions or beliefs they rely on to make sense of the world. Bacchi (2009) argues the value of working out how policy-making communities 'represent' the policy problems they think they are addressing, which involves working out which of several, even many, possible explanations for a given problem they have accepted as the one that will help them to develop a 'solution'.

It is becoming more widely accepted that policy-makers mostly rely on ready-made or common-sense frameworks of ideas and ways of thinking about problems and solutions. This reflects a general human disposition to rely on what cognitive psychologists call 'frames' or 'schemes' (Weick 1995; Weick *et al.* 2005). This does not mean that these frameworks, or what Hall (1990) calls 'policy paradigms', are all that realistic or rational. Policy-makers typically rely on a framework of ready-made ideas and standards that spells out not only the goals of policy and the kind of instruments that can be used to attain them, but also the very nature of the problems they are meant to be addressing. As Hall says:

> Like a *Gestalt* this framework is embedded in the terminology through which policy-makers communicate about their work, and it is influential precisely because so much of it is taken for granted and unamenable to scrutiny as a whole.
>
> (Hall 1993: 279)

The point then is to pay a lot more attention to what policy-makers think is happening and why they think certain solutions will work better than others. In this chapter, we will see how, for some decades, policy-makers relied on a Keynesian policy paradigm to identify the problems and solutions they thought would work and then how a new neoliberal policy paradigm emerged.

Yet we do need to acknowledge another problem. We agree with Hay when he points out that while Hall's account has some value, it involves too 'generic and abstracted a conception of the policy process' (Hay 2001: 198). Nor does Hall explain why an apparent receptivity to ideas like Keynes' full-employment theory gets translated into the specific policies that a government adopts or the institutional mechanisms it adopts to promote a policy. In other words, the link between a set of ideas like 'Keynesianism' or 'neoliberalism' and Keynesian or neoliberal policies is missing. Without this link, we are not able to explain how and why a particular kind of policy-making took place (Kus 2006: 499)

What is often missing is the specific historical and policy context, i.e. the ideas, the laws, the traditions and practices that specific governments have already adopted. This is the point of Gosta Esping-Andersen's (1990) study proposing a typology for classifying different historical styles of social policy. According to Esping-Andersen, there are three things that researchers need to do to make better sense of the 'welfare state'. The first is to establish the extent to which a government's routine daily activities are devoted to meeting the social needs of the households in that society. Esping-Andersen says that too many governments assume they are 'welfare states' without demonstrating that this is so. He notes, too, that not many governments actually passed this test until the 1970s. Second, Esping-Andersen says we need to draw on Titmuss' (1958) distinction between governments that adopt a 'residual mode' and those that adopt an 'institutional' form of intervention. The distinction is simple. The 'residual' approach means that governments only intervene when 'the market' or 'the family' has somehow failed and governments step in to meet the needs of disadvantaged people. This 'residual' approach is compared with those governments who try to address the needs of all of the population – what Titmuss referred to as 'institutional' forms of intervention (Titmuss 1958).

Esping-Andersen says this means we need to establish the extent to which a government sets out to 'de-commodify' relationships and promote human rights. Esping-Andersen says that, under the conditions of a capitalist labour market and economy, many things like housing, food, water or transport can only be purchased with money. This is because everything from eating to enjoying access to a museum has been turned into things or activities that have a price tag. (Even human labour has been commodified: having a job means selling your ability to labour to someone willing to buy that capacity for a wage). Esping-Andersen says that 'real' welfare states have moved to de-commodify many aspects of what have been made into commodities by market processes and to make sure that services like education, health and welfare are not commodities but are offered as a right to more and more people. This approach underpins Esping-Andersen's account of three different kinds of welfare state regimes.

Because we only deal with two of these types in this book we do not discuss his third or social-democratic regime.

'Liberal welfare states'

'Liberal welfare state' regimes refer to those governments that historically have made the smallest move towards a rights-based regime of welfare provision. The liberal welfare state is exemplified by the United States, United Kingdom and Australia, as well as New Zealand and Canada.

Conservative welfare states

The second kind of regime Esping-Andersen identifies is the 'conservative welfare state' regime. Typical examples of this type include Germany, France, Spain and Austria. Conservative welfare state regimes have moved towards a universal welfare system, typically through some kind of universal social insurance model. This is a 'welfare state' that relies on workers contributing via insurance to their own income support. The market is reinforced as the dominant institution since people need to be in the labour market to access the system. These societies typically give a much larger role and space to state sector economic activities than is usual in Anglo-Saxon societies; typically the public sector – as defined by scale of tax revenue, numbers of state employees or level of public expenditure – is much higher as a percentage of gross domestic product than in liberal states.

If Esping-Andersen is right, we should expect to see some interesting differences in the way different governments adopt both the Keynesian and the neoliberal policy paradigms. In what follows we highlight the key aspects of the Keynesian paradigm before showing how each government adapted aspects of this paradigm in ways that reflect the influence of history.

The Keynesian policy paradigm

After World War II, a new Keynesian policy paradigm emerged, shaping and structuring the thinking of many policy-makers across the west. Based on the thinking of John Maynard Keynes, governments began to 'frame' their management of economies in new ways. Keynes' ideas about how governments should use taxation and expenditure policies to run a total war economy (1940–1945) were drawn on after 1945 to shape full employment policies and encourage economic growth.

For Keynes, the 'curse of unemployment' was a consequence of unregulated markets. When left to themselves, the market alone could never achieve full-employment (Keynes 1971–1989: 16). Keynes challenged the core neoclassical economic assumption when he argued that markets do not naturally tend towards a state of equilibrium, and that governments needed to correct this chronic failure.

Keynes argued governments should promote full employment, protect the stability of their currency exchange rates and engage in a modest redistribution of national income. Keynes said three big policy changes would be needed to achieve these aims. The state would need to control the monetary system to provide adequate stimulus and investment. Governments would also need to directly regulate investment levels through public works. Finally, governments would need to impose progressive income taxation and use social services to reduce the incomes of the wealthy to improve the incomes of low income-earners.

In Britain, US and Australia after 1945, governments broadly committed themselves to a full-employment policy and this strategy 'worked' for three decades (Smyth 1994). But as we will see, even in these countries the Keynesian policy paradigm worked in different ways.

Britain's Keynesian welfare state

The onset of war in 1939 provided Keynesians with the opportunity to overturn decades of economic orthodoxy promoted by Britain's Treasury Department. The Treasury favoured low levels of public expenditure and balanced budgets and had argued against increasing government aid to the unemployed in the Depression, claiming the only way to relieve unemployment was to cut wages, because government spending would promote inflation and undermine the private sector's interest in creating jobs.

World War II shook Britain's government to the core, exposing it to new ideas and expertise. Keynes himself became a key advisor to the British government. The 1941 budget reflected a small triumph for Keynes as the government drew on some of his key ideas. Yet even after the end of war the triumph of Keynesian ideas was not absolute. The first post-war government (a Labour government) preferred nationalization and planning while the Chancellor of the Exchequer focused on manpower planning. Ironically, Keynes played hardly any role in shaping this emerging 'welfare state'. Keynes was not interested in social policy and had little involvement in developing Britain's policy commitment to full employment (Skidelsky 2000), nor did he develop a comprehensive plan for maintaining full employment after the war. His contribution as an adviser came more in the form of encouragement, commentary and criticism (ibid.: 270–271). The post-war Attlee government in 1945 implemented Beveridge's plan to provide comprehensive and universal welfare benefits for citizens. In 1942, William Beveridge, an orthodox liberal economist, had released his *Beveridge Report*. While he was antagonistic to Keynes' unorthodox economic doctrine, his report outlined a broad plan for what we might now recognise as the 'welfare state', involving family allowances, comprehensive healthcare and a full-employment policy (Beveridge 1942: 9–10).[3] Welfare benefits were to be centrally administered, financed by equal contributions from employers, employees and the state, with uniform benefits set at a subsistence level. However, Keynesian policy-makers helped draft the National Insurance Act, the National Health

Service Act, and the National Assistance Act that carried out Beveridge's ideals of a comprehensive welfare system (Hill 1993).

It can be said that it was only in the mid-1950s that the Labour Party and Conservatives embraced the Keynesian policy paradigm that lasted into the mid-1970s (Kus 2006: 503).

America's Keynesian welfare state

In America, the Keynesian policy paradigm only took root in the 1960s. This late development is peculiar given the earlier introduction of Roosevelt's 'New Deal' to respond to the Great Depression. Roosevelt responded quickly and vigorously to mass unemployment after his election in 1933 in ways that anticipated Keynes. New Deal initiatives included emergency jobs creation programs (Jansson 1997: 180) and social security legislation (Eitzen and Zinn 2000: 53). Alongside Social Security, a number of joint federal–state programs were established, including unemployment insurance, and the Aid to Families with Dependent Children (AFDC) scheme for white single mothers. Black mothers, who had always been expected to work, were not considered eligible to receive benefits (Berkowitz 1991: 15). The logic of America's welfare state was bifurcated and inconsistent from the outset: social insurance for the 'respectable' working majority and social assistance for 'the poor' (Quadagno 1987: 111). Health care notably remained off this early agenda.

After these early reforms, the US only adopted a Keynesian policy paradigm in the 1960s under the Kennedy, Johnson and Nixon administrations. The Kennedy and Johnson administrations responded to a growing awareness of US poverty (Harrington 1962) with new programs like Head Start, the Job Corps, and – responding to the Civil Rights movement – declared a 'War on Poverty' that expanded the scope of welfare entitlements under the AFDC program to include black women. Crucially too, health care reform was addressed. Medicare, which provided a federal hospital reimbursement program for older Americans, and Medicaid, the counterpart for low-income Americans, were established in 1965 (Jansson 1997: 216).

Even the Republican Nixon administration (1969–1974) expanded America's 'welfare state'. It presided over the creation of a food stamp programme and added Supplemental Security Income for the elderly, blind, and people with disabilities. It also implemented the Earned Income Credit scheme, providing the working poor with direct cash assistance through tax credits. By 1974, America had embraced a Keynesian approach.

The 1960s and early 1970s saw most of the current major welfare programs for low-income Americans established, formalized, or expanded. Between December 1960 and February 1969, for example, AFDC increased its registration numbers by 107 per cent and, between 1962 and 1968, federal spending on the poor rose from $12 billion to $27 billion.

Australia's Keynesian welfare state

Australia's approach to social policy was different from other developed countries. For example, their first Invalid and Old-Aged Pensions Act of 1908 provided a means-tested 'flat-rate' pension to both the elderly and people with disabilities that prevented them working. Unlike 'social insurance' models adopted in other countries – which link contributions paid into the scheme to the scale and duration of the benefits paid out – Australia's scheme pays a flat rate to all. It continues, and is still the largest part of Australia's income support.

As in Britain, Keynes influenced Australian policy-makers during the 1939–1945 war. When a Labor government gained power in 1941, income support schemes such as child endowment, unemployment and sickness benefits, maternity allowance, funeral benefits, and a pharmaceutical benefits scheme were introduced (Murphy 2016). These reforms were influenced by Keynesian thinking, as economists tried to create a 'total war economy', which used taxation to control inflation and welfare policies to legitimise this taxation (Watts 1987). Like the old-age pensions of 1908, later schemes like unemployment and sickness benefits (1944), maternity allowance (1943), funeral benefits (1943) and a pharmaceutical benefits scheme (1945) were flat rate, means-tested and financed from taxation.

Four years later, in 1945, the Full Employment in Australia white paper argued the need for full employment to secure social welfare, completing the Keynesian trinity of aims. In Australia, as in other liberal welfare states, linking welfare provision to labour market engagement positioned the nascent welfare state as a 'safety net' for those who 'fell out' of the labour market (Watts 1987; Kalecki 1943).

By the 1950s, Australia's policy community had fully embraced the Keynesian paradigm. As J.G. Crawford, Secretary of the Department of Trade, explained in 1959: 'We are all planners now' (Crawford 1959: 45–47). He meant that the government was focused on determining social objectives, like full employment, and devising comprehensive plans to achieve these objectives. This required the government to build an economic and political consensus and provide the welfare and economic infrastructure. As Smyth and Cass (1998: 92) note, this was the triumph of an Australian social liberalism shared on a bipartisan basis by all major parties between 1945 and 1975.

In the 1970s, the Whitlam Labor government won office committed to the Keynesian idea that

> A citizen's real standard of living, the health of himself and his family, his children's opportunity for education and self-improvement, his access to employment opportunities, his ability to enjoy the nation's resources for recreation and cultural activity … his scope to participate in the decisions and actions of the community, are determined not so much by his income but by the availability and accessibility of the services which the community alone can provide and ensure.
>
> (Whitlam 1985: 3)

In some ways, the Whitlam government kept faith with the Keynesian spirit. The income security system was revamped to be more accessible to previously excluded groups like single mothers. A universal healthcare system, Medicare, which still exists, was introduced in 1975. Yet as Battin observed, by 1975 the Whitlam government was making policies that resembled early anticipations of neoliberal policy (Battin 1997). In 1974, the Labor government cut tariffs by 25 per cent triggering significant unemployment. It abolished death duties thereby weakening of its capacity to tax wealth. Its 1975 budget 'was anti-Keynesian in sentiment' (ibid.:84). As we soon show, the 'crisis' that begins in the 1970s extends to a neoliberal makeover perpetrated by the Hawke–Keating government, another Labor government.

France's Keynesian welfare state

Between 1945–1975, successive French governments pursued a *dirigiste* policy framework where the state exercised strong influence over investment. *Dirigisme* involved a mixture of Keynesianism and a politically conservative program, especially under de Gaulle (1958–1969). The state guided the course of macro-economic development to promote growth across the economy rather than favouring particular interest groups, except to the extent that favouring such groups (in particular, big business) was seen as instrumental to collective prosperity (Vail 2014: 68–69). The central premise was that the French state would promote economic modernization more effectively without the participation of narrow interest associations. *Dirigisme* functioned effectively in the first 30 years (*les trente glorieuses*) following the Second World War until the mid-1970s, as France became one of the most prosperous countries in Europe.

At the heart of *dirigisme* lay the objective of speeding up the pace of economic modernization by channelling resources into key industrial sectors (Hall 1986; Levy 1999, 2010). This objective relied on a national planning system as well as state ownership of industrial sectors considered crucial for the country's development (such as nuclear power and high-speed trains). The French government also protected French industries from foreign competition, by aggressive devaluations in currency and providing cheap loans through a subsidized credit system.

Keynesian ideas, in particular, played a part in shaping *dirigisme*. Many prestigious technical schools like the ENSAE (*École nationale de la statistique et de l'administration économique*) and the ENA (*École Nationale d'Administration*), which trained the administrative technocracy or 'enlightened technocratic leaders', all taught Keynesian ideas (Boyer 1983: 7–10). Keynesian technocrats held key positions in government departments, and came to play prominent roles in the reorganization of the Treasury, in the introduction of National Accounts Statistics, and the development of new forecasting tools. They also successfully influenced the politicians' economic thinking and participated actively in economic policy decisions (ibid.: 17–23).

The post-war expansion of the welfare state in France was not closely linked with the country's post-war development paradigm. As Levy notes: 'for much of the post-war period the French welfare state operated in the shadow of the *dirigiste* model of economic development' (Levy 1999: 308). The size and structure of the welfare state changed in conjunction with the changes to the French political context. From the perspective of *dirigiste* policy-makers, whose primary concern was to make French industry competitive, the welfare state represented a waste of financial resources, which should have been allocated to productive investment (Levy 1999).

The high watermark of *dirigisme* came in the early 1970s when the Socialist administration of François Mitterrand undertook an ill-fated experiment with 'redistributive Keynesianism' designed to promote a 'rupture with capitalism' and promote workers' incomes and wages. This failure ushered in neoliberal approaches to labour market governance, which came to dominate French policy-making through the 1980s: centred on deregulation, limitations on benefits, and reductions in non-wage labour costs (Vail 2014: 70).

Most western societies experienced sustained economic growth between 1945 and the 1970s. An organic unity appeared to exist between successful, industrialized market economies shaped by Keynesian policy paradigms and the welfare state. Yet in the 1970s, this Keynesian model came under fierce attack by proponents of the neoliberal policy paradigm, and neoliberalism came to displace Keynesianism over the next few decades.[4] How and why did this happen? How do we explain the way policy paradigms change? One way is to use the idea of crisis.

The crisis of the Keynesian welfare state

Any crisis involves a combination of 'something' that is happening (or is believed to be happening) and the socially-constructed and shared 'frames' available to a community to make sense of what is happening. In this way, policy-making communities change their policy paradigms because they have made new sense of a 'problem' and the range of 'solutions', typically for various 'political' reasons. This is what happened in the 1970s.

Many policy-makers believed new economic conditions were emerging that required action. Governments began tinkering with the Keynesian paradigm. In Australia, the Whitlam government, which claimed a Keynesian provenance, began experimenting with neoliberal policies like the decision to cut tariffs by 25 per cent, which triggered significant unemployment in 1974 (Beilharz *et al.* 1992). In 1970, even as he was declaring himself a 'Keynesian', President Nixon ended the Bretton Woods agreement put together by Keynes in 1944 to stabilise global currencies. Nixon and his advisors announced the unilateral cancellation of the undertaking to convert US dollars into gold as well as freezing wages and prices for 90 days to combat potential inflationary effects (Bordo and Eichengreen 1993).

Then, in 1971, the US experienced a combination of an unemployment rate of 6.1 per cent and an inflation rate of 5.84 per cent. For the first time since the Depression, high unemployment and unprecedented inflation persisted, with government seemingly helpless to control either (Offe 1984). The combination of unemployment, inflation and Nixon's policy shift triggered one of the worst and longest stock market downturns in modern history, between January 1973 and December 1974 (Davis 2003). In parallel with the stock market crash, most western nations also experienced massive inflation triggered by the decision of the OPEC oil cartel to drastically raise oil prices in 1973–1974. Less noticed at the time were other large changes like increasing numbers of women in the workplace, and the onset of 'globalization' as employers began relocating manufacturing to cheaper developing economies like India, China and Indonesia (Mishra 1999: 20).

Suddenly, it seemed governments had lost control of their economies. Economists began to argue that Keynesianism was unable to deal with the new combination of unemployment and inflation (Battin 1997: 123). Other, sharper-eyed critics identified the real problem: the contradiction at the heart of the 'long boom' in the 1960s and 1970s was that electors wanted tax cuts *and* increased public services and goods (Myles 1984; Offe 1984). This contradictory impulse continues to influence policy-making into our own time

What few observers understood at the time was that the 'crisis' that the Keynesian policy paradigm was experiencing was also a consequence of a long-term political and intellectual campaign by those economists who had steadfastly opposed the Keynesian policy paradigm since the 1940s. The rise of neoliberalism owes most of its success to a global intellectual project-movement that became increasingly influential in the mid-to-late-1970s courtesy of a well-heeled and highly-organized network of neoliberal think-tanks dedicated to fighting Keynesianism. It was a campaign that began in 1947, when Friedrich von Hayek, accompanied by neoclassical economists like Frank Knight, Ludwig von Mises, George Stigler and Milton Friedman, and philosophers like Karl Popper, founded the Mont Pelerin Society. Their objective was to promote liberalism and defeat socialism and Keynesianism. It linked together liberal political philosophy and neoclassical economics. What began as an annual conference in the Swiss resort spawned a global network of think-tanks bankrolled by major businesses that would eventually come to make neoliberalism the next big policy paradigm (Cockett 1994; Mirowski and Plehwe 2009).

Neoliberalism

Like every important political concept there is plenty of disagreement about how to characterise neoliberalism. Brown (2015) usefully treats neoliberalism as a way of thinking in which everything is 'economized'. 'We are all converted into 'market actors', all fields of activity become 'markets', and every public or private entity, every person, commercial practice, or state is 'governed as a firm' (ibid.: 1). This is because neoliberals rely heavily on neoclassical economics. Neoliberals, like neoclassical economists, claim markets possess an inherent self-equilibrating or balancing capacity that is upset by 'outside interference', like government planning or union power, which prevents the market from functioning naturally and healthily. The economy, markets and 'individuals' all need to be left alone to self-regulate, or the exact opposite of what Keynes suggested. As Ronald Reagan explained in his inaugural address in 1981: 'The government is the problem.... It is time to check and reverse the growth of government which shows signs of having grown beyond the consent of the governed' (Reagan 1981).

Oddly, however, neoliberalism is a political project that relies on government setting up a complicated and contradictory relationship with 'the state'. Although neoliberalism claims to be antagonistic toward government, it relies on governments to promote its policies (Harvey 2005: 20). This was obviously the case when governments bailed out major banks in the wake of the financial crisis of 2008, as well as using Keynesian stimulus measures to deal with that recession. This was also the case when neoliberal governments imposed savage 'austerity' measures on their own citizens to pay for the bailouts (Crouch 2011). Neoliberalism is an anti-political project, yet one deeply reliant on the state (Harvey 2005: 3).

This inherent contradiction is the defining feature of neoliberalism. While neoliberalism claims to be an economic project separate from the state and the central principle of neoliberalism appears to restrict state interventions, it is actually a deeply political project that requires significant and persistent state intervention.

Australia's neoliberal welfare state

The Australian Labor Party and Liberal-National coalitions have been in office for half of the time between 1980 and 2016. Unlike Britain and America, where clearly 'conservative' governments took lead roles in starting a neoliberal turn around, in Australia, the Hawke–Keating Labor governments led a major neoliberal reform program which broke down the long-standing bipartisan Keynesian consensus. In 1983, using a framework negotiated between the government and the union movement, the Hawke–Keating government promoted an 'economic modernization' project that pushed a substantively neoliberal policy agenda legitimated by a peculiar appeal to 'fairness'. Subsequent governments, the conservative Howard Liberal-National government (1996–2007), the Rudd–Gillard Labor government (2007–2013) and the Liberal-National Abbot–Turnbull government (2013-present), either consolidated or enlarged these neoliberal foundations.

In talking about Australian policy, we make two points. First, neoliberal governments have not shrunk the value of income support or the number of people receiving support (Fenna and Tapper 2012). Australia's social expenditure as share of GDP was 10.2 per cent in 1980, 17.2 per cent in 2000 and had increased to 19 per cent in 2014. The Australian government spent AU$145.7 billion on income support (35.1 per cent of expenses) in 2014–2015, making it the largest single item of government expenditure, well above defence (5.8 per cent), education (7.1 per cent) and health spending (16.1 per cent) (Australian Government

2014).[5] The 'neoliberal attack' has not reduced the numbers of people receiving income support. The proportion of workforce-age people receiving social security payments grew from 4 per cent in 1966 to 27 per cent in 2014 (Henman and Perry 2002; Department of Social Services 2014b).

What neoliberal governments have done is introduce a new level of punitive, even stigmatising conditionality as a feature of its 'workfare' reforms. People in receipt of income support experience restricted agency and, some research suggests, harms that result directly from being a recipient of state income support (Carney 2006; Eardley *et al.* 2001). Income support is offered in stigmatising ways compared to paid employment, and involves a serious assault on freedom (Fryer and Fagan 1994). Centerlink – the state network designed to deliver income support – fails to give effect to a logic of citizenship as a right to full participation based on a premise of respect (Murphy *et al.* 2011: 168–72). For some 'client-customers' there is humiliation, while others experience painful intrusion into their privacy, and for many they face eligibility and activity tests (relating to activities, education, income, assets and looking for work), and long waiting periods before income security is available. The process of claiming benefits is stressful (Peel 2003). Recent government moves to introduce income management (quarantining part of income support payments for food and other essentials) will enhance the experience of stigma.

As ACOSS (Australian Council of Social Service) has pointed out, the unemployed in Australia experience an absence of rights, which results in penalties that affect large numbers of people with a severity greater than that of penalties for many other offences (ACOSS 2010) This is evidenced in a disturbing pattern of penalising low-income people for breaches of conditions attached to their benefits. In 2005 106,000 breaches were imposed in the 12 months to 2005, over half of them for failure to comply with activity tests involving suspension of payments for 26 weeks (Australian National Audit Office 2007). Since then, while some governments relaxed expectations, the system has become more punitive than ever before. The Department of Employment (2015) reported in 2014 that agencies managing work-for-the-dole schemes breached two-thirds of the 750,000 plus Newstart or Youth Allowance beneficiaries. In July–September 2015, of some 800,000 people receiving welfare in the form of the Newstart or Youth Allowance, 276,000 job seekers had their welfare payments suspended. It also reported that 6,000 indigenous people in remote and regional areas had their work-for-the-dole payments suspended for eight weeks between July and December 2015.

The conventional justification offered for this is that the system is designed to help unemployed people find jobs. This is nonsense. On a simple measure in August 2016 the ABS reported that there were 721,000 unemployed people and a total of 175,300 job vacancies: that is, there were approximately four times more unemployed people than jobs available. This kind of ratio has been the case since the 1990s, though it would be a courageous government that acknowledged this uncomfortable truth. The more brutal truth is that each Australian government has found it useful to convert the real problem of unemployment into the false problem of the unemployed and their 'deficits', before punishing them. As a result, 'citizens' become 'denizens'. Like asylum seekers, many income support recipients in Australia lack the capacity to claim or enforce rights for fear that asserting a claim right would have a high probability of retributive consequences or disastrous costs (Standing 2014: 7–9). As Standing argues, the status of 'denizen' depends on the larger structural shifts engineered by neoliberal policy-makers, a new social identity characterized by job insecurity, short-term contracts, lack of rights at work and low pay (ibid.).[6] The fact that young people constitute a significant part of this precariat is a direct effect of the neoliberal makeover of the 'welfare state'.

America's neoliberal welfare state

When the neoliberal turn came to America in the early 1980s, many thought the welfare state would shrink (Jencks 1992; Grogger and Karoly 2005). However, as in Australia, the system expanded. Spending has continued to increase in comparison with levels set in the 1960s and early 1970s. There was no general attack on welfare per se (Moffitt 2015: 735), with total spending on the 16 biggest welfare programs rising from 9 per cent of GDP in 1985 to 12 per cent in 2007 (ibid.). Between 1990–1995, social security income spending grew by 80 per cent because of changes in eligibility rules and the increase in the number of aged people. The Earned Income Tax Credit grew by 274 per cent between 1988–1998. This reflected the design of America's welfare state regime and the reliance on America's traditional insurance-based programs. America's social insurance programs have never based eligibility on whether a person is a low-income earner but on their work history and previous earnings. In 2015, Americans established entitlement to Social Security age-benefits on condition they had worked at least 10 years in 'covered jobs' and earned at least $1,200 per quarter. As the numbers of the disabled and aged increased, so the scheme kept on paying out more, and beneficiaries enjoyed modest increases in the benefits they got.

The neoliberal reform project had a clear racial and generational bias. The same design principle that assisted the elderly was always likely to hurt minority and poor Americans. Given that many Black, Hispanic and low-income earners have histories of unemployment and low earnings, they were unlikely to ever become eligible for these programs. At the same time as the total level of welfare expenditures kept increasing (Moffitt 2015) America's neoliberal turn went further than it did in Australia because it targeted young, often black, low-income Americans by cutting support to them.

One group picked out for exemplary treatment were single mothers and their children (Moffitt 2015: 730). The Aid to Families With Dependent Children (AFDC) program was the largest federal system providing income support to low-income families. During the 1970s and 1980s, AFDC transformed into a major source of financial support for single mothers. It also became a key target of neoliberal 'reform' efforts,[7] with leading critics like Charles Murray (1984) arguing that AFDC actually hurt the poor by discouraging them from working, and even arguing that it encouraged single-parenthood. In response to these neoliberal critics, during the 1980s 40 US states established 'welfare-to-work' programs. The Reagan administration weighed in with its Family Support Act 1988, directing all states to phase-in comprehensive welfare-to-work programs by 1990. Each state was required to implement education, job training, and job placement programs for welfare recipients.[8]

In 1992, President Bill Clinton vowed to 'end welfare as we know it'. Clinton's 1996 Personal Responsibility and Work Opportunity Reconciliation Act, was the culmination of a 30-year campaign by neoliberals against government welfare programs. AFDC was replaced with a new program: Temporary Assistance for Needy Families (TANF). TANF introduced a five-year time limit for support (Moffitt 2007) and required single parents to find jobs.[9] These were objectives grounded in the neoliberal idea of individual responsibility backed up by a punitive ethos. Welfare was transformed into a block-grant system, where each state received a lump sum to spend on their own customized welfare programs but was also required to provide their own matching funds. This placed a ceiling on the number of families who could enrol, as funding was strictly limited. When Congress, as a cost-saving measure, did not uprate their federal grants with inflation, the ceiling dropped and the number of families who could enrol shrunk.

These reforms had a striking effect. The TANF legislation reduced the number of families assisted by 63 per cent in 10 years, while the value of their benefit was also cut. The poorest single-parent families – 80 per cent of whom are headed by single mothers – received 35 per cent less in income support than they did three decades ago. By 2012, four million women and children were jobless and without cash aid (Moffitt 2015).

We see a clear racial and generational divide: on average, older adults received 20 per cent more from the government in 2004 than they did in 1983. The average younger single parent received 20 per cent less (Moffitt 2015). The neoliberal reform redistributed benefits *away* from the young and poorest single-parent minority families *to* those with higher incomes (ibid.: 743). The only caveat is that the 2008 recession sponsored temporary increases for some programs. Benefit levels for the Food Stamp program were raised, eligibility requirements relaxed, additional funds were provided for the TANF program, income and payroll tax rates were temporarily reduced, and one-time extra benefits were given to Social Security retirement and SSI recipients (ibid.: 745). However, by 2015 most of these temporary expansions were being phased out.

Britain's neoliberal welfare state

The election of the Thatcher government marked the paradigm shift from Keynesianism to a neoliberal framework (Hall 1993). Thatcher quickly adopted a monetarist economic policy, which meant that limiting inflation, rather than commitment to full employment, became the economic policy priority. But the

Thatcher government claimed that Britain's economic problems were sympto-
matic of a deeper, more fundamental crisis that could not be handled by small-
scale changes. The Keynesian paradigm itself was not only redundant but
responsible for turning a great global economic power into a struggling
economy. As the Conservative manifesto in 1979 explained:

> The state takes too much of the nation's income; its share must be steadily
> reduced. When it spends and borrows too much, taxes, interest rates, prices
> and unemployment rise so that in the long term there is less wealth with
> which to improve our standard of living and our social services.
>
> (Conservative Party 1979)

In policy terms, the neoliberal turn had four objectives, including cutting social
security spending, restoring work incentives and ensuring the social security
system provided support only to those who were in 'real' need (MacGregor
1985). The result was paradoxical.

Thatcher's policies contributed to increasing unemployment, poverty and
inequality through the 1980s (Kenworthy 1999). This meant more people needed
income support. Thatcher presided over a net increase in the number of welfare
recipients by around 60 per cent during her first term in office, while applicants
for unemployment benefits rose approximately 200 per cent between 1980–1987
(MacGregor 1985). Yet, despite this substantial rise in the number of 'dependents', social expenditure was cut between 1980–1990. The Thatcher government
targeted unemployment benefits, reducing unemployment benefits by more than
50 per cent over 10 years. Maternity and death grants were abolished. Child
benefits were cut to a 30-year low and old-age pensions were curtailed (Daguerre
and Taylor-Gooby 2002).

In 1998 Blair's New Labour government outlined its 'New Deal' – a policy
ostensibly designed to cut unemployment by providing training, subsidized
employment and voluntary work to the unemployed. Since the government had
no intention of compelling employers to hire people or create jobs, it was clear
that Blair was dealing with the problem of unemployment by treating it as a
problem of the unemployed. Blair affirmed his neoliberal affiliations when he
said he wanted more 'active participation' in job searching, education and training and declared that traditional welfare policies encouraged passivity and
dependency by paying benefits without insisting the unemployed look for work.

While British commentators made much about the novelty of New Labour's
Third Way, they failed to appreciate the degree to which British policy-makers
were borrowing from precedents set in the US and Australia. Blair's New Deal is
a clone of Keating's Australian Labor government's Working Nation program
and the Howard coalition government's Work for the Dole program, both of
which can be traced back to American Workfare policies of the 1980s and 1990s.

Five years into the New Labour experiment in 2002, social expenditures in
areas consistent with New Labour strategy – health and education – were substantial (Glyn and Wood 2001: 58). But spending on benefits and social security

showed little advance (ibid.; Chote *et al.* 2010). Overall, public social expenditures increased slightly from 18.3 per cent of GDP in 1997 to 22.8 per cent by 2010, but most of that increase was counter-cyclical, driven up by the crisis years of 2008–2010 (by 2.7 per cent) (Chote *et al.* 2010).

The conservative governments since 2010 (including a centre-right coalition and a Conservative majority government) renewed a neoliberal commitment to shrinking the state and rapid welfare reform, under the mantra of 'austerity'. The Conservative manifesto (Conservative Party 2015: 9) outlined that their approach was 'focused on reducing wasteful spending, making savings in welfare, and continuing to crack down on tax evasion and aggressive avoidance'. Analysis of the cumulative impact of the government's agenda on household wealth shows that lower-income households lost out, while higher-income households benefited from the net impact of tax and benefit reforms (Browne and Elming 2015).

France's 'neoliberal' welfare state

While the French political economy has changed significantly since the 1980s, it has not experienced the depth of neoliberal policy seen in Australia, the UK and the US (Fourcade-Gourinchas and Babb 2002). 'France has managed to become a symbol of resistance to Anglo-American-style neoliberalism in popular opinion' (Prasad 2005). French tax revenue remains at historically high levels, one of the highest in the world. The number of people employed by the state is also high.

By the mid-1970s, contextual factors that had been favourable to *dirigisme* began shifting. The oil shocks of 1973 and 1979 exposed western Europe to a prolonged recession, ending the rapid growth France enjoyed during the post-war period. Exercising aggressive devaluations, which made an inflationary growth strategy feasible during the post-war years, became risky in the post-Bretton Woods environment. Additionally, the Treaty of Rome became fully active, forcing France to reduce barriers to its trade partners and face intense competition. As Cole notes, these external constraints weighed 'on the French economy, and the limited room for manoeuvring of its governments in initiating policies' (Cole 1998: 212).

In 1976, faced with declining industrial production and increasing unemployment, President Giscard d'Estaing appointed as prime minister Raymond Barre, an economist known for his liberal views on the economy. Barre was given the job to fix industrial stagnation, the foreign trade deficit and inflation. He understood France's economic problems to be related to the extensive role of the state in the management of the economy, particularly in the industrial sector. To remedy this, his government started an array of market-friendly reforms that included lowering of subsidies, dismantling price controls, and reducing restraints on the business sector (Levy 1999).

These reforms did not include welfare retrenchment. Indeed, during Barre's term, social spending increased drastically because his government's interpretation of the crisis did not centre on the welfare state, but on industrial policy.

Barre's economic strategy, known as 'industrial redeployment', signified France's first move toward neoliberalism in economic policy-making. However, it floundered. This was partly due to the aggravating effects of the OPEC oil shocks and partly, as Cole (1998: 215) notes, due to the 'belief that there was an alternative economic strategy, a belief not confined to the ranks of the left-wing opposition'. Neither the public nor the French political system was ready for a paradigmatic shift.

The 1981 elections saw a Socialist victory. Giscard was replaced by François Mitterrand, who promised to 'bring the state back in', and Pierre Mauroy became prime minister. The new socialist government argued the problem was not that there was too much state but rather there was too little of it (Levy 1999). According to government officials, 'what France needed now was a 'real industrial policy', and for the state to move to centre stage in restructuring France's economy (ibid.: 43–44). The Mitterrand government nationalized 38 banks, increased aid to industrial firms, raised taxes, and expanded social benefits (Hall 1990; Levy 1999). Just as in his predecessor's term, the expansion of the welfare state continued under Mitterrand's presidency.

Mitterrand's expansionary policies led to a massive balance-of-payments crisis. The exchange rate, pegged to the Deutschmark since 1979, came under severe pressure, and France was forced to devalue the franc three times. These developments threatened France's position in the European Monetary System, which was a major concern for the Mitterrand government. The economic crisis reached its peak in 1983 when, in a bid to remain within the European Monetary System, the government changed policy direction and began implementing an austerity program. Its traditional inflationary growth strategy was abandoned in favour of a neoliberal view of the virtues of 'competitive disinflation' (Levy 1999: 52).

The neoliberal turn in France took a different path to those taken in liberal welfare states. Unlike Britain, Australia and the US, the definition of the crisis and its solutions did not focus on welfare policy and social expenditures, but on the state's interventionist industrial policies. The welfare state was not represented as a 'problem'. The neoliberal reform undertaken by the Mitterrand government involved dismantling many key instruments of *dirigisme* but they did not include the withering of the welfare state (Fourcade-Gourinchas and Babb 2002). With the *dirigiste* paradigm acting as a brake on social spending through the post-war years, public expenditures in many areas increased after 1983. Social spending rose from 23.5 per cent of GDP in 1980 to 26.7 per cent in 1990. By 1995, France became the heaviest social spender in Europe outside Scandinavia (Levy 2010). This period also saw a reduction in inequality and an increase in the level of compensation provided to the unemployed.

Conclusion

Providing a full and nuanced account of the policy-making process in countries like Britain, France, Australia and America is well beyond the remit of a small book. What we have done is give some sense of the scale and complexity of the changes that occurred in different countries that have profoundly affected the lives of young people born since the early 1980s. This potted history provides five useful insights.

First, particularly in liberal welfare states, we noted an emerging neoliberal tendency to privilege capitalist markets and associated reluctance to regulate employer–employee relations. This is completely the opposite of the Keynesian paradigm, which saw full employment as a policy priority. The political value of free markets became politically promoted and this, in turn, changed the way governments delivered public services.

Second, embracing neoliberal policy framings has produced quite different effects in different countries. In Britain, for example, Thatcher's government treated neoliberalism as a solution to the alleged failures of Keynesian policies. In France, the crisis was understood to reside in the declining competitiveness of French *dirigiste* and industrial policy. This meant that in the UK, the 'welfare state' was a focus for much reform (MacGregor 1985), while in France it was largely left alone (Kus 2006: 490).

Third, there is an inherent contradiction in the extent to which neoliberalism claims to be state free. It is deeply dependent on the state. Many governments have retained some important Keynesian macroeconomic controls, while simultaneously using the language of the neoliberal paradigm to smooth over this inherent contradiction. This 'slippage' expresses itself differently. In Australia, for example, all governments since 1983 have used budget deficits to try to maintain economic growth – a practice invariably accompanied by a 'moral panic' about how bad debt is. Others, such as the UK, embraced Keynesian-inspired approaches to 'quantitative easing' to mitigate the impact of the recent recession, while talking about a need for deep and enduring austerity.

Fourth, since the early 1980s we have not seen the kinds of dramatic changes to welfare states that the neoliberal policy paradigm might have implied, despite their calls for 'smaller government'. As Cerny (1990) and Weiss (1998) have argued, societies are now more state-centric than at any time before and, as we discussed above, spending on social security in many countries has actually increased. If the 'welfare states' in the US, Britain and Australia have not been dismantled or retrenched, they have certainly been redesigned. In each case, governments found it difficult to cut the total level of welfare expenditure. While certain groups – such as single mothers and the unemployed – may have been targeted for exclusion and discipline as full-time work dries up, the welfare state is still picking up a larger proportion of the working-age population. It proved much easier to cut benefits to certain groups rather than achieving blanket reductions.

Fifth, while Keynesianism largely established work as the dominant institution for securing human welfare, the neoliberal policy paradigm shifted this relationship into an inherently more punitive, 'activation' approach. This happened at a time when the supply of full-time jobs was becoming increasingly problematic.

Because people born since 1980 have known only this neoliberal paradigm, many may find it difficult to imagine how things might have been different, a theme that we consider in following chapters.

Notes

1 An extensive comparative literature exists focusing on patterns of the development of 'welfare state' policy in the west after 1945 (Rimlinger 1971; O'Connor 1973; Gough 1979; Flora and Heindeheimer 1981; Offe 1984; Castles 1983, 1985; Hall 1986; Esping-Andersen 1990; Hall and Soskice 2001; and Cavadino and Dignan 2006).
2 An equally extensive literature exists emphasising this (e.g. Hall 1986, 2001; Weiss 1998; Hay 2001; Fourcade-Gourinchas and Babb 2002; Ferguson 2009; Mueller 2011; Smith 2012; Wilson and Grant 2012; and Wincott 2013).
3 By 1944 Beveridge came to accept *some* of Keynes' ideas in his book on full employment (Beveridge 1944).
4 Some aspects of the Keynesian policy paradigm have not been displaced: like the role of central banks in setting interest rates; and use of fiscal policy in emergencies like the 2008 recession to stimulate the economy or to nationalize failing banks.
5 Although this growth was above the OECD average, it is not generous. Most OECD states still spend far more as share of GDP on income support. Australia spent 8.6 per cent in 2013 while the OECD average was 13 per cent (OECD 2014).
6 As Standing notes, people become 'denizens' in a number of ways (2014: 9). They can be blocked by laws and regulations from claiming rights. The cost of claiming rights can be prohibitive. Rights can be lost due to changes in status e.g. by becoming unemployed. They can be deprived of rights by legal process and in de facto ways. They can lose rights by not conforming to moral norms, by having a lifestyle that places them outside the protection of the law.
7 It also became a major target for racist reformers. Eugenic racists like William Shockley claimed the AFDC encouraged women to have more babies, especially among 'less productive members of society' like African-Americans, who he argued, were genetically inferior to 'whites' (Shockley and Pearson 1992).
8 The initiative proved unsuccessful because states lacked the money needed for matching federal funds.
9 In practice, there were exceptions that saw some families keep benefits longer than five years.

4   Intergenerational equity and justice

Over the past few decades, many western governments in the developed world have repeatedly expressed concern about 'intergenerational justice'. They argue that actions taken today could detrimentally affect the lives of future generations, including people not yet born. This includes, for example, discussions around global warming and the fairness of bequeathing major environmental problems to future generations. Another claim – more pertinent to our concerns – is a looming 'budget crisis' that means many governments may not have enough money in the future to pay for health and welfare services for the next generation. The claims around emergent budget crises rest on an economic approach called 'intergenerational accounting'.

Intergenerational accounting emerged from concerns around rapidly changing social demographics, specifically, the historically unprecedented increases in the numbers and proportions of older people in most developed nation-states. This demographic shift, when explored through the lens of a particular form of neoliberal economics, has led to suggestions of serious trouble for future government expenditures (Cardarelli et al. 2002; McCarthy et al. 2011).[1] Non-government organisations, like the Intergenerational Foundation, have amplified these concerns, arguing that 'Europe let down its young' and that 'that intergenerational fairness is getting steadily worse across Europe as a result of ageing populations and increasing borrowing [i.e. government debt]' (Leach et al. 2016: 5).

The idea that governments are worried that policies in place today will benefit older people over the coming decades at the expense of young people seems highly commendable. However, there is a potential hypocrisy in these claims that warrants attention. Governments that claim to be worried about fairness and justice for generations *in the future*, seem, as we documented in previous chapters, to have had no qualms about loading-up young people *today* with mountains of debt. Millions of young people in the Anglo-American world must now take out loans to purchase their post-secondary education, while governments in Europe seem to have little worry about throwing millions of children and young people into poverty and unemployment in pursuit of 'austerity'.

Intergenerational justice must engage questions about justice between the generations in the future *as well as* now. The aim of this chapter is to critically analyse and explore intergenerational accounting and, importantly, the ideas about justice that underpin it. We suggest that taking account of the young people of today is as important as taking account of those not yet born.

What is intergenerational accounting?

Many national governments and intra-national entities, like the OECD, IMF and the European Union, began exploring the policy implications of the demographic shift towards the elderly in the late 1980s (Heller *et al.* 1986; Bonin 2001). This interest was sparked by the increasing authority of the neoliberal paradigm. By the 1980s, most governments were trying to generate economic growth by redistributing national income away from labour and towards capital, cutting taxes and government spending and increasing deregulation and privatization (Williams *et al.* 1997). Intergenerational accounting[2] was framed by this interest in 'balanced budgets' and 'fiscal sustainability', informed by the potential horror of 'public debt' (Auerbach *et al.* 1999; Bonin 2001; Gokhale 2009).

Relying on forecasts of fertility trends, economic growth and various assumptions about the impact of deficit budgets and public debt, most developed nation-states concluded that they now face a looming crisis of fiscal sustainability. The European Union, for example, began warning member states to avoid 'profligacy', high budget deficits and 'mounting debt' (European Parliament 2006) as it built in non-discretionary rules and about budgets deficits in its Stability and Growth Pact and in Article 104 of the Maastricht Treaty. This anxiety about budget deficits and 'public debt' seems to be directly connected to the idea that governments in the future will face 'crippling' deficits because of the changing ratio between young and old people.

The work of three neoclassical economists – Auerbach, Gokhale and Kotlikoff (1991) – was especially influential in promoting intergenerational accounting.[3] They developed a logic that began with a truth they considered self-evident: that all government spending must be paid for by someone, be it past, current, or future generations. This means that, into the future, taxes must be sufficient to pay for all government purchases of goods and services, transfer payments and debt service. Kotlikoff describes this as the 'inter-temporal budget constraint' (Auerbach *et al.* 1991; Kotlikoff and Raffelhüschen 1999).

Given that the interest of intergenerational accounting is to establish whether the ratio of current and future taxes is adequate to finance current and future liabilities on social expenditures, those who developed this accounting framework argued that the critical question is whether the sum of all generational accounts is the same as the 'inter-temporal budget constraint'. That is, the 'residual' of the present value of government consumption expenditures minus the net government wealth assets minus liabilities, must be greater than zero to balance the government's 'inter-temporal budget constraint'. This involves adding-up current and future generations' net payments, which in most European states with substantial social security obligations are negative, and subtracting the explicit net debt (wealth). This enables a calculation of the fiscal gap, with respect to those demands on future budgets that would ensure sustainable fiscal policy. This provides an estimate of what is said to be the 'true' government debt or wealth for the base year.

Neoclassical economists engaging in generational accounting claim they can measure the amount of the inter-temporal government deficit (or surplus) that needs to be funded by future-born generations. With this, they claim to be able to say that 20 year olds in 2040 will have a 'generational account' of such and such, either surplus or debit. The alleged value of generational accounting rests on its apparent ability to 'measure' the size of the 'debt burden' passed from current to future generations. If this future generation is in debt this is said to be unfair.

Neoclassical economists say they have revealed a serious degree of unfairness in the present and point to patterns of unfairness in the future. The policy implications of this are that future generations will face a fiscal deficit that will be unfair and overwhelming. Unfair, as Raffelhüschen argued because '... there are no free lunches, ... expenditures in the future have to be paid for either by present or future generations' (2002: 76). And overwhelming, as Kotlikoff and Raffelhüschen suggested:

> ... [their findings] are shocking. An array of countries including the United States, Germany and Japan have severe generational imbalances.... The imbalances in these, and the majority of the other 19 countries considered here, place future generations at grave risk.
>
> (1999: 165)

According to Kotlikoff and Burns (2004), we are all marching down a debt-strewn road to ruin. Looking forward to 2030, these researchers see 77 million baby boomers hobbling into old age, twice as many retirees as there are today but only 18 per cent more workers. Kotlikoff and Burns argue if the American government continues on its current course, the result will be skyrocketing tax rates, drastically lower retirement and health benefits, high inflation, a rapidly depreciating dollar, unemployment, and political instability:

> History is replete with examples of what happens when countries can't pay their bills. They raise taxes to exorbitant levels, default on their explicit or implicit obligations, and begin printing money like mad. This triggers inflation, drives interest rates through the roof, and sends exchange rates down the tubes. Businesses go belly up, and banks shut their doors. The result is financial and economic meltdown.
>
> (Kotlikoff and Burns 2004: xvii)

In short, the 'problem' said to be revealed by generational accounting is that future generations face unacceptable levels of debt and deficit financing, and this is unfair.

It is not difficult to see how such analysis relies on the idea that 'balanced' or preferably 'surplus budgets', especially if they are put in place now, are 'good' and will prevent future 'generational imbalances'. According to Auerbach and Gale (1999) the looming fiscal crisis in the US, said to hit in the 2040s, can only be alleviated by acting now and requiring people who are alive now pay higher taxes and/or by cutting social transfer payments. The practical implications of this are illustrated when Auerbach and Gale (ibid.) point out that countries like Italy, Japan, Brazil and the US would need to cut current government expenditures by between one-half (Italy) and one-fifth (US) to restore the projected intergenerational balance for the 2040s.

We have two questions about this: How confident can we be in processes of generational accounting? When intergenerational accounting claims an interest in equity or fairness, is it underpinned by a defensible conception of justice?

The credibility of intergenerational accounting

We suggest there are good reasons for questioning the credibility of intergenerational accounting, particularly because it misrepresents and misunderstands the nature of public debt.

There are major problems with the unstated assumptions underpinning the neoclassical economic animus against government debt or budget deficits. It assumes that categories like 'income', 'revenue', 'spending' or 'debt' always mean the same – that they are universal – or that when governments act (for example, to incur debt, generate income ...) they refer to the same kind of economic phenomena as when households or businesses act. With this assumption in mind, it follows that these categories should be understood and evaluated in the same way. This, we argue, is a problem involving a category mistake because they are not the same.

Galbraith *et al.* (2009) explained why we should not make such a category mistake.[4] Put simply, private income, spending or debt are not the same thing as public income, spending or debt. This is because a sovereign government is 'the monopoly supplier of its currency' (Tymoigne and Wray 2013). This means it can issue currency in any form and has 'unlimited capacity' to pay for purchases and to fulfil promised payments. It also has an unlimited ability to fund other sectors. For this reason, insolvency and bankruptcy of the government is not possible (ibid.).

Unfortunately, neoclassical economists and neoliberal policy-makers have successfully persuaded many people that public and private debt are the same things. This relies on a failure to understand the difference between private 'debt' and government 'debt'. There are two key differences.

First, as Galbraith *et al.* (2009) explain, one difference is that the interest of a household or business is solely in the realm of the private welfare of specific people (a family or business). The government's interest is not; governments are involved in providing basic 'public goods' in the public interest (ibid.).

In 1954, economist Paul Samuelson explained the concept of 'public goods' by saying they are social goods that are 'non-rivalrous' and 'non-excludable'. A 'non-rivalrous' good can be consumed by any number of people without running out. Knowledge, like a mathematical theorem or a poem, is non-rivalrous. Any number of people can recite the poem or use the equation and it will never be depleted or run out. A 'non-excludable' good benefits many people, and cannot be confined to an individual. This is the case with goods such as roads, education, the law, or police and defence forces because they provide public goods like the ability to travel, knowledge, security and public order to large numbers of people.

In short, a government's interest is in providing for a collective welfare. There is a difference between the public interest, which involves supplying basic public goods, and the pursuit of private goods by households and businesses because they 'rivalrous' and 'excludable'. The food available to a family, for example, is rivalrous and excludable. Families prioritise themselves to ensure that primarily their members consume available food. Likewise, businesses consume rivalrous and excludable resources (for example, mineral ore or trade-marked products) as well as sources of energy and labour that it cannot afford to share with other competitors. This is why firms and households need to ensure that there is a positive correlation between their earnings and expenditure.

While governments record certain economic activities to say whether they are running a 'surplus' or 'deficit', unlike private business or a household, they do not need to be as concerned about debt, because private income and debt and public income and debt are not the same. This is because of the sovereign power of the state. In most nation-states, the government is sovereign, unlike households and business entities.[5] In most households and businesses, income arises from the sale of material produced, such as when parents sell their labour for wages or business sell commodities or services. While governments can sell things, most of their income comes from raising taxes or issuing currency. Governments have a power or ability that no household or firm will ever have: governments have the power to tax and to issue money.

> The power to tax means that government does not need to sell products, and the power to issue currency means that it can make purchases by dispensing IOUs. No private firm can require that markets buy its products or its debt. Indeed, taxation creates a demand for public spending in order to make available the currency required to pay the taxes. No private firm can generate demand for its output in this way.
>
> (Galbraith *et al.* 2009: 7)

One way of making this point about the relation between state sovereignty and debt and why it matters is illustrated by the history of sovereign default and debt forgiveness (Reinhart and Rogoff 2009; Das *et al.* 2012). Both are common practices.

Sovereign default happens when the government or a sovereign state refuses to pay back its public debt (Borensztein and Panizza 2010).[6] This reflects the fact that most governments, by definition, control their own affairs, and are not and cannot be obliged to pay back their debt.[7] Sovereign default is something few citizens in the many countries that have used this device remember or know about. However, it is a fact that some 83 states have used this device in the past few centuries, including the US as recently as 1972, and Russia in 1991 and again in 1998. Most of the major Latin American and Asian states have also done so over the past few decades (Das *et al.* 2012).

Debt forgiveness is what happens when one government that loaned another government money forgets what they are owed. One case of large-scale debt relief happened in 1934 when the US and Britain, the two main creditor governments of the time, simply 'wrote off' the debt owed them by France, Greece and Italy. The amounts were substantial. In France, Greece, and Italy the debt relief accounted for 36 per cent, 43 per cent, and 52 per cent respectively of each country's GDP. The debts were fully written off and largely forgotten (Reinhart and Trebesch 2014).

As Graeber points out in his history of debt, this record points to a 'deep moral confusion' about the topic of debt. On the one hand, there is a widespread understanding or moral belief that 'we should always pay our debts' (2014: 14). On the other hand, as the case of 'sovereign default' suggests, this moral belief seems not to be binding on states. We might also remember that many individuals and businesses have for a long time availed themselves of legal rules and practices enabling them to make a declaration of bankruptcy. A declaration of bankruptcy has the simple effect of denying creditors any entitlement to more than token repayment of what is owed; on some occasions creditors receive nothing at all.

In summary: we should *not* treat government spending, revenues or debt as if these are the same kind of thing as what households or companies do. The economic activities of governments need to be considered in the light, first, of their public status, that is their obligation to supply public goods, and, second, in terms of their sovereign power to raise revenues when and how they like, to spend as much as they can, and to default on their debt when they like.

This matters when we think about the nature of 'public debt' or the way governments generate income. While it is conventional to see government tax revenue as 'income', this income is not like the income earned by firms or households. This is because governments raise tax revenues or impose new tax rates (Galbraith *et al.* 2009). In short, a government's 'spending' is not constrained by its revenues or borrowing. By growing public goods, they can grow the private economy and generate more income. This fact is poorly understood (ibid.) and reflects the successful effort by neoclassical economists to persuade people, policy-makers and political elites that private 'incomes', 'spending' and 'debts' and public 'incomes', 'spending' and 'debts' are the same when they are not.

This category mistake owes much to the persistent use by neoclassical economists of what Michler calls the most 'misguided of metaphors currently in use in public discourse ... the comparison of public finance to household finance' (Michler 2013: 1). A 'nation' is not a 'household', whatever the metaphor implies. For one thing, a nation is many times larger than any household and, as we mentioned, it can print its own money (ibid.).

Seeing fiscal policy as if it is exactly the same as household economics explains the current anxiety about the levels of public debt. The preoccupation with the scale of public debt into the future, which intergenerational accounting promotes, relies on such a category mistake and widespread economic illiteracy. The idea that governments should never spend more than they earn or run a deficit account, just as no household should spend more than it earns, forgets the important differences identified above.

One conclusion follows from this, namely that we should not be swept up with moral panics about the scale of public debt or budget deficits now, or in the future. Government debt is not the problem it is usually made out to be.

Relying on economic forecasts

The second key problem is that the argument made for imposing cuts on contemporary social expenditures, ostensibly to prevent a future of mountainous public-sector debt, is reliant on economic projections. The credibility of these projections and forecasts is critical to the intergenerational accounting project. They are also often 'contentious' (Combs and Dollery 2004: 463). There are good reasons for caution and critical analysis of these forecasts, two of which we address here.

First, there is an important distinction between 'predictions' and 'projections'. Philosophers and social scientists have long understood that predictions about human states of affairs should not always be taken as a matter of fact. Take for example, the 'Hawthorne' or 'double-hermeneutic' effects, which argue that research itself can change people's behaviour and thereby shape the research findings (Mayo 1949). This point was made by Merton, who argued that once predictions about social issues are made, people tend to accommodate their actions towards those predictions (1948; see also Popper 1959; Giddens 1990). More recently, 'momentum' political theories suggest that once a candidate has gathered momentum in the polls, other voters swing towards that candidate (Forsyth 2010). Studying something, or declaring it so, can alter outcomes.

This also applies to economic predictions; Soros recently argued that predictions shape the behaviour being predicted and that no economic modelling technique can take account of the role of contingency – mess, error and bad judgement – in human affairs (Soros 2008: 13–24).

Stiglitz's (2001) account of 'information asymmetries' further emphasises the vulnerability of all economic predictions. All economic projections rely on assumptions being made, but once those assumptions are embedded in an economic model, that very same model is used to prove the validity of those assumptions (ibid.). In short, an inherent circularity operates in economic modelling and the predictions it generates. The reliance on economic models to make predictions, then, points to the possibility that the economic paradigm and the policy prescriptions thus generated are seen as credible because they 'have served certain interests' (ibid.: 524).

On top of this, despite claims of credibility, one of the consistently reliable things about economic predictions is that they have repeatedly failed to predict major structural disasters like the Great Depression or the recent 2008 financial crisis. Even short-range forecasting is surprisingly inaccurate. Hendry and Ericsson observe that forecasting models cannot represent the complex dynamics of real economies (2006). In one study, for example, short-range forecasts produced by 13 agencies (including the OECD and IMF) of growth and inflation in Europe, covering periods of 12–18 months, were found to have 'average errors in forecasts of both growth and inflation [that were] large, in terms of both their variance and the importance of these variables' (Oller and Barot 2000: 311–312). Another American study confirmed that even for periods of 12–18 months economic forecasts were often wrong (McCracken 2009). Given this, there seem to be good reasons for caution about long-range forecasts provided by intergenerational accounting.

We can be partly reassured when the intergenerational accountants suggest, as they did in an Australian exercise, that 'that the aim of ... long-term modelling is *not* to predict the future, rather it is to assess risks associated with current trends and policies' (Gallagher 2006: 3). But more caution is needed.

Second, while observations like these may seem technical, they are also highly political, raising other critical concerns. Generational accounting exercises are designed to persuade contemporary policy-makers to change current policies so as to avert the forecast 'fiscal crisis' that those doing the predicting foresee. This persuasion has informed decades of austerity policies enacted by governments of all political orientations, with measures that reduce government spending by cutting budgets, social welfare payments and public sector jobs. This is a challengeable political agenda, not a 'factual given'.

Intergenerational justice

The idea that debt is *unfair* to future generations highlights the need to clarify what ideas about justice are – or are not – informing the generational accounting exercises. We have explained why we believe our common-sense assumptions about state debt are problematic. Another problem remains: what do we mean by fairness? Irrespective of whether the 'debt problem' is what neoliberal merchants of moral panic claim it to be, the question remains: what makes the flow of resources between generations now or into the future just or fair? It is a question of justice between different generations.

Below, we develop a defensible conception of justice that could better underpin a process of intergenerational accounting. We make two points. First, the ethics and obligations behind intergenerational justice need to be more clearly articulated than has so far been done. Second, that the obligations those who live in the present have to people of other generations, and to people not yet born, need to be re-examined.

We begin with the idea that it is unjust to leave young people in future with an 'unfair' share of the burden of debt. This is expressed by Canada and colleagues as a common-sense wisdom: the 'growing debt burden threatens to crush the next generation of Americans' (Canada *et al.* 2013:1). They refer to 'generational theft', which they claim is producing a 'deeper failing ... of essential fairness' (ibid.). Proponents of such intergenerational accounts argue the essential problem is 'fiscal sustainability', yet subsequently refer to different types of 'unfairness', invoking questions around intergenerational justice. As Thompson (2003: 3–4) and other commentators (Sabbagh and Vanhuysse 2010) highlight however, such accounts beg a rarely, if ever, addressed question: what is unfair about intergenerational debt? This question is not fiscal, nor technically economic, it concerns justice.

If intergenerational debt and inequity is a problem, then surely we need to identify the principles of fairness or justice that can be used to avoid it. However, the principles of justice underpinning intergenerational accounting remain implicit and underdeveloped. While neoliberal analysts and commentators emphasize the importance of 'equity' across generations, it is not clear what they mean (Lamm 1989; Longman 1987). Critics on the left call for a conception of 'equity' that emphasises intragenerational fairness (Kingson 2007), but this also lacks clarity. Discussions in Canada, for example, foundered on the lack of agreement about what is meant by equity (Foot and Venne 2005). Coombs and Dollery (2002) made similar points about the intergenerational accounting performed in the UK, New Zealand, Canada, and the USA. Even in the US, where heated debates have been running since the 1980s between progressives and neoliberals about whether to cut spending on social security, Medicare, age-based subsidized housing and age-based tax benefits, the underlying question of justice has not been made clear.

Talking about intergenerational justice raises questions about the principles of justice that inform these claims (Solum 2001; Tremmel 2009; Thomson 2013).

Many philosophers have contributed to the discussion about intergenerational justice. According to Thompson (2009), we see at least three broadly defined approaches to understanding justice.

The first is a 'mutual advantage' conception of justice. Here, a 'just society' is where each person, assumed to be rational and self-interested, derives the maximum benefit they can (such as wealth or other valued goods and services) from voluntary cooperation, so that the result of this process is fair. This account of justice however does not rest on credible assumptions. There is considerable evidence that humans are not rational and not always self-interested: many people gamble heavily, some rely on astrology and many act altruistically (Oord 2007).

The second approach is the 'desert' or 'entitlement' approach to justice (Nozick 1974). This is a libertarian account of rights and justice that appeals to a specific set of principles to establish the rightness of owning property in ways that can be unequal but are nonetheless 'just'. For Nozick, whether a distribution of property or resources is just depends on how the distribution came to be. If it came about according to rules of acquisition, transfer and rectification, then it is just, no matter how unequal it may be. For philosophers like Nagel, Nozick's argument is not credible (1975) because Nozick did not acknowledge the problems created by the substantive inequalities that characterize most societies.

Finally, there is the idea that justice involves 'fairness'. A just society is one in which its members think the relevant institutions and relations are fair. This approach is exemplified by Rawls (1971). For Van Parijs, intergenerational justice requires each generation to make sure the situation of the next generation is no worse than its own; a requirement that follows from Rawls conception of social justice (Rawls 1971; see also Barry 1977; Van Parijs 1999). Others have drawn on Rawls.

According to Tremmel, we have 'generational justice when the accumulated capital which the next adjacent generation inherits is at least as high as what the present generation inherited' (2009: 34). Tremmel argues for drawing on Rawls' 'veil of ignorance' to determine the principles of justice that might obtain between the generations (2009). A similar approach to designing a principle of intergenerational justice has been offered by Sunstein who has extrapolated the 'Principle of Intergenerational Neutrality' from Rawls' theory of justice (2007: 269).

Does Rawls offer a useful way of thinking about intergenerational justice? We argue that his 'Principle of Intergenerational Neutrality' does *not* provide a strong base for thinking about intergenerational justice. Sen's (2009) idea of justice as freedom is more appropriate for clarifying intergenerational justice.

Rawls and intergenerational justice

Rawls' theory of justice as fairness purports to describe what a just arrangement of major political and social institutions like the political constitution, the legal system, and the economy in a liberal society would look like (1970). Unfortunately, it does not and cannot do this. What Rawls offers are some abstracted rules for thinking about what constitutes fairness, but he does so without offering any specific or helpful advice about what policy-makers might do to promote fairness.

His account of justice makes a negative and a positive claim.

Rawls' negative claim is that citizens do not deserve to be born into a rich or a poor family, to be born more or less gifted than others, to be born female or male, to be born a member of a racial group. His positive claim is that all social goods ought to be distributed equally, unless an unequal distribution is to everyone's advantage. Linking his negative and positive claims is that we should work out in a rational way what rules we might create that will ensure that any inequalities must benefit all citizens, and particularly must benefit those who will have the least (Wenar 2012). This does not, however, say how we will establish these rules to do this.

Rawls said we need to start with what he described as 'the original position', which would be agreed to by all reasonable members of a liberal society. The original position would enable those of us who reason well to work out what is fair. It involves making a fair choice, based on a commitment to just treatment, while assuming ignorance about those whose lives would be affected by the decision. Adopting this 'veil of ignorance', means that when someone makes a decision:

... no-one knows his place in society, his class position or social status, nor does anyone know his fortune in the distribution of natural assets and abilities, his intelligence, strength, and the like. I shall even assume that the parties do not know their conceptions of the good or their special psychological propensities. The principles of justice are chosen behind a veil of ignorance.

(1971: 11)

Rawls claimed that, in such a position, people would, on rational grounds, choose a model of justice that would include two key principles of justice. The first principle is that everyone has the same claim to an adequate scheme of equal basic liberties. The second principle is that any social and economic inequalities need to satisfy two conditions:

* They are attached to offices and positions open to everyone under conditions of *fair equality of opportunity*.
* They are to the greatest benefit of the least advantaged members of society (the *difference principle*) (Rawls 2001: 42–43).

Rawls sparked interest in intergenerational justice when he asked how an entire social system could be made to satisfy his two principles of justice. He implied concern for future generations in in his answer to this question:

The answer is bound to depend to some degree anyway, on the level at which the social minimum is to be set. But which in turn connects up with how far the present generation is bound to respect the claims of its successors.

(Rawls 1971: 284)

And, given his difference principle, it is not surprising that he stipulated the need for a 'just savings rate' whereby:

Each generation must not only preserve the gains of culture and civilization ... but it must also set aside in each period of time a suitable amount of real capital accumulation.

(Ibid.: 285)

By assuming a just 'savings principle', Rawls' social minimum is set, and the difference principle is satisfied. However, Rawls did not say how his theory of justice applied intergenerationally, nor how he resolved certain problems with intergenerational justice. Further he did not say how his two principles of justice might work as policy principles.

The problem with Rawls' approach to justice is that while it works as a philosophical exercise in reasoning it has no capacity to work as a policy framework or heuristic. By this we mean that it is one thing to assert, for example, that everyone should have the same claims to equal basic liberties and pointing to some arguments to support this, but it is never clear what it would mean to see this principle as a policy objective or as a criterion for evaluating a policy program. This point is validated when we turn to Sunstein's argument in favour of what he referred to as the principle of intergenerational neutrality.

The principle of intergenerational neutrality

Rawls' work inspired the development of the principle of intergenerational neutrality (e.g. Weiss 1991; Portney and Weyant 1999; Howarth 2005; Sunstein 2007). The principle of intergenerational neutrality argues that a problem exists if people born in say 1950 – who now make policy decisions designed to address issues (like global warming or future budget problems) – fail to consider those to be born in 2030 or 2050; seeing those people as worthy of less concern by virtue of their date of birth.

In environmental policy, the field where this idea has been discussed most widely, the principle of intergenerational neutrality translates into the protocol idea that present generations are 'obliged to take the interests of their environmentally threatened descendants as seriously as they take their own' (Sunstein 2007: 13).

According to Sunstein, the principle of intergenerational neutrality means that 'the decade of one's birth has no moral relevance any more than does one's skin color or sex' when addressing the question of justice or fairness (ibid.: 269).

It is a principle similarly applied to decisions not to use other identity markers like gender, sexuality or religion to discriminate against people. The use of markers like age to distribute valued resources unequally is destructive of many valued human goods.

On the face of it, methods appropriate to a philosophy seminar are used to arrive at an abstract principle that says we should pay attention to all kinds of important differences. It is *as if* we will reach the same end state of abstract justice by blanking out the real world in all its rich complexity. Sunstein never says why we would want to do this, nor what practical effect it would achieve.

Can we really achieve personal detachment or agent-neutral ethical deliberation as Sunstein and Rawls seem to require? Can a person be extracted from their own living place and time, and be void of values (Williams 2006)?

The Principle of Intergenerational Neutrality relies on the idea that a rule can be or should be followed without considering the actual people involved or what their circumstances are who try to apply that principle. Sunstein, like Rawls, operates *as if* using the rule of intergenerational neutrality can be applied by an abstracted human being who does not live as a real person of a particular age, class or educational background, who has lived a particular life with actual identities or a specific cultural setting. In effect, Sunstein makes all the rich details of real people's lives disappear while his principle promises an ideal solution with little if any practical application in our world. The problem Sunstein cannot make go away is that it is real people who would need to use his principle of intergenerational neutrality, and do so in the light of the particularities that shape of their lives, beliefs, passions and interests or by the differences which are being evaluated unfavourably.

This idealized approach does not provide a real basis for evaluating the merits of competing claims about the end purpose or the goods that inform a decision. It simply requires participants to consider who will be affected by decisions and to do so in ways that are not affected by their own interests.

Don't we need to acknowledge the differences people experience if we are to have any opportunity to enjoy certain rights (such as participating in decision-making etc.) and goods (such as respect). We cannot attain justice if we don a 'veil of ignorance' that encourages us to act as if these differences, like the different ways we are treated, do not exist. Justice, for example, may require reverse dis-crimination, which involves acknowledging how some inequalities are attached to or distributed according to identity markers (age, class etc.), requiring, for example, that the state uses a quota system to ensure that women or people with disability are employed in certain jobs, or that building codes ensure that people with a physical disability will be explicitly guaranteed access to a building.

In effect, the principle of intergenerational neutrality, like Rawls' conception of justice from which it derives, does not allow for determining the facts of the case that need evaluation, nor the basis for judging between competing claims about what goods should be pursued. For that we need two things: A defensible *account of justice* and a *capacity* on the part of policy-makers to establish the degree of current and intergenerational equity. Such an approach informs a project led by Sen and Nussbaum to develop the theory of justice as freedom.

Justice as freedom

An adequate theory of justice starts with acknowledging how our lives are marked by various significant differences – like income, gender, skin colour, religion, culture – which generate oppression, suffering and inequality. And, it begins by acknowledging how we live in a world where there are incommensur-able and multiple ways of evaluating what constitutes a good life and different ideas about justice or fairness (Berlin 2002; Gray 2007; Sen 1985, 2002, 2009).

Together Sen and Nussbaum crafted a framework for thinking about justice and how it might be promoted. Sen rejects utilitarianism, which shapes modern economics and much Anglo-American philosophy. In its place, Sen and Nuss-baum extend the classical liberal idea of freedom. They do this while outlining a framework for addressing the profound inequalities that exist, like unequal access to basic resources like food, water, health, and education – all necessary for a good life.

Sen does not believe we need one answer or one principle to work out what justice looks like. He accepts there are many ways of evaluating a good life and justice. For this reason, judgements about justice can accommodate different kinds of reasons and concerns (2009: 395). Sen argues for a conception of justice-as-freedom, which acknowledges a plurality of values, while being concerned with people's actual capacity to choose freely and being able to pursue the valued end that matter.

Freedom is valued because, if we have freedom, we have more opportunity to pursue those goods that we value. This is the 'opportunity' aspect of freedom. Freedom also requires that people have certain capabilities needed to make choices and to pursue their choices: a just society is one that supports freedom by enabling people to make and have the choices that define a free and a just society. Our quality of life can be judged by the extent to which we exercise freedom, choose between different ways of living and can then pursue what we have reason to value.

Whether a person is living a good life or whether a society or an institution is 'just' is determined by the extent to which people are free to choose between viable alternatives, and the degree to which they are, in fact, able to pursue the ends they value. This incorporates being free to value different ends (to choose between alternative conceptions of good, or what Sen describes as *functionings*) (Sen 2009: 233).

Sen and Nussbaum also focus on the opportunities a person has to live a certain kind of life or what they refer to as *capabilities*. As Sen said, he is not just interested in what a person ends up doing, but also in what they are in fact are able to do whether or not they choose to make use of that opportunity (Sen 2009: 235). The idea of 'capability' itself refers to our abilities to achieve various combinations of functionings that we can compare and judge against each other in working out what we value (ibid.: 214).

This account of justice as freedom is directly relevant to intergenerational justice.

Intergenerational justice

This approach is more attuned to political and policy processes because it stipulates a number of important practices. First, it directs policy-makers and communities to deliberate about the valued goods or functionings that community wishes to choose. Second, by highlighting the kinds of capabilities needed to achieve these functionings or goods the justice-as-freedom approach makes it possible to evaluate the extent to which a community is exercising its freedom and its use of various capabilities. That Sen was invited to join the French government's Commission on the Measurement of Economic Performance and Social Progress is illustrative of how this is so (Stiglitz, Sen and Fitoussi 2009). The work of Stiglitz, Sen and Fitoussi indicates there are good reasons for shifting the emphasis away from 'measuring economic production to measuring people's wellbeing' (ibid.: 12). They are also interested in 'assessing whether levels of human wellbeing can be sustained over time'. Recognizing this 'depends on whether stocks of capital (natural, physical, human, social) are passed on to future generations' (ibid.: 11).

They identify and assess levels of wellbeing within a given community and measure how this changes over time. The elements of wellbeing that are assessed include material living standards, health, education, personal activities including work, political voice and governance, social connections and friendship, the quality of the environment and the various kinds of insecurity. This approach to wellbeing seems compatible with a concern about intergenerational justice both *now* and in the *future*.

We see value in a conjoint approach to identifying social progress based on Sen's (2009) freedom-capabilities approach and the assessment of wellbeing within an intergenerational justice framework. Such an approach would help direct governments in assessing equity between existing age cohorts (e.g. by establishing whether younger age cohorts are enjoying the same kind of access to basic social resources, like housing or education as older cohorts, and whether they are also experiencing equity in terms of their taxation obligations). The question of cohort equity could also take into account status markers other than age, like gender, regional location, ethnicity or social and economic status.

The 'welfare state' has never attempted to address or measure intra-generational equity (Tapper 2002). Yet an implied contract exists between the generations, each sharing its burdens reciprocally in return for social benefits (ibid.). Coombs and Dollery concur in observing how the relevant literature focuses 'heavily on long-term fiscal sustainability' but overlooks intergenera-tional equity' (2004: 460).

We argue the situation is worse than Tapper (2002) or Coombs and Dollery (2004) suggest because the perspectives and interests of young people alive today have been omitted from much of the discussion about policy generally and generational accounting, in particular.

This is a major omission given the current size of the age cohort, for example those aged 12–25. That's to say nothing of the size of this same age cohort in say 2040 or 2050. Too little attention has been given to the current socio-economic circumstances that young people face now, which cause hardship and suffering. Descriptions of the looming 'demographic problem' have not addressed the 'youth factor', except to observe that 'they' are not going to be able to fund the costs of an ageing population.

In short, those who promote intergenerational accounting say a lot about fiscal sustainability. Yet they have said little or nothing about intergenerational justice. We also note that intergenerational accounting reports have not addressed the question of intergenerational equity. There is no discussion of the principles of acknowledging or addressing intergenerational equity in ways that address the interests of those yet to be born, but whose existence is implicitly factored in within the reports. Much of this work fails to ground concerns in a considered and conceptually coherent idea of intergenerational justice. We discuss later in this book ways of rectifying this situation.

Conclusion

We have made a number of points: First, that intergenerational accounting does not offer a credible way of thinking about intergenerational justice. Current versions of intergenerational accounting rely too much on the assumption that intergenerational equity is about one age cohort, namely the elderly.

Second, the ethical dimensions of intergenerational equity have generally not been considered, or dealt with poorly (Thompson 2003: 4). Economists, the group most involved in thinking about intergenerational equity, have generally avoided engaging in practical reasoning, preferring to develop technical fiscal accounting frameworks such as the 'generational accounting' framework (Auerbach *et al.* 1991, 2004; OECD 1997; Bonin 2001).

We also highlight the contradiction in the simultaneous expression by neoliberal policy-makers in governments of all political persuasions of concern about *intergenerational justice* in the future, while actively promoting *intergenerational injustice* in the present.

This apparent contradiction is resolved when we understand how the contemporary preoccupation with public debt in general is irrational, and when expressed by neoliberal governments, hypocritical.

If this is the case, it may be no surprise that the anxiety about future intergenerational justice is a technique designed to justify policies that cut present day spending on social security, education and health care. Taking intergenerational justice seriously requires consideration of *both* justice between neighbouring generations and justice between people alive now, *and* generations yet to be born. The neoliberal commitment to promoting austerity measures now, to promoting measures that disproportionately hit the young, and to promoting intergenerational accounting (to avert future fiscal crises), is antithetical to any defensible conception of intergenerational justice.

Notes

1 Governments in Argentina, Australia, Austria, Belgium, Brazil, Canada, Denmark, Finland, France, Germany, Ireland, Italy, Japan, the Netherlands, New Zealand, Norway, Portugal, Spain, Sweden, Thailand, the United Kingdom, and the United States all embarked on intergenerational accounting.
2 As a method, intergenerational accounting involves calculating the present value of total *net tax payments* over the remaining lifetime of a cohort born in a specific year. This present value of net tax payments is labelled the 'generational account'. The intergenerational distribution of the net tax burden is analyzed by comparing the generational accounts of different generational cohorts of the population. Typically, this is done by comparing the generational account of a 'newborn' in a base year. Beginning with the base year, the economists calculate the 'generational accounts' for that base year. The generational account is the present value for an age cohort of the net tax it pays over its whole life, i.e. its 'tax burden'. This is then done for the next age cohort. 'Generational accounts' can then be calculated for an unborn age cohort, say those who will be born in 2030, by making the relevant base year its year of birth. Generational accounting then involves calculating the present value of net tax payments and presenting this in a present value and a rest-of-life calculation for every cohort of people presently alive and/or born in the future.
3 Those governments now carrying out routine intergenerational reporting exercises, most using the method of generational accounting developed by Auerbach *et al.* (1999). These countries, most of them European, do so every 12–18 months.

4 This approach rests on detailed analysis of the fiscal and monetary operations of the institutions and practices found in Treasury departments and central banks of nations like the US, Brazil, Canada, Argentina, the eurozone, and Australia (Arestis and Sawyer 2007).

5 Most nation-states have sovereign power over their currency, but some do not. Modern monetary theorists note that some states surrender their monetary sovereignty either by pegging their currency to a metal like gold or to another currency, or by adopting a foreign currency altogether (for example the US dollar), and are constrained in their ability to finance their spending by issuing currency. Put simply this means public debt denominated in a foreign currency can create serious problems for that government.

6 Governments also have other options like promoting inflation, which is not 'sovereign default' in the conventional sense because the debt is honoured, albeit with currency that is worth less. Governments can also devalue their currency by printing more money to pay their own debt.

7 Historically, a major creditor nation could make threats of war or wage war against a debtor nation for failing to pay back debt. Today the UN Charter (Article 2 (4) prohibits use of force to recoup what it is owed. Today governments may face severe pressure from lending countries as happened in the case of Greece and the EU between 2012–2015. Usually today, a government which defaults may be denied access to further credit or face political pressure from its own domestic bondholders to pay back its debt. Finally, the IMF can extend loans to assist states to 'restructure' their sovereign debt. This topic has informed considerable discussion about trying to regulate sovereign default like regulating bankruptcies (e.g. Ryan 2014).

5 Broken promises

Human capital theory, education and work

For the second half of the twentieth century, many people and governments invested faith, hope and money in the idea that more education assured a prosperous future. Based on what became policy 'common sense', governments in western societies systematically expanded access to secondary schooling and then to their higher-education systems.[1] By 2000, 51 million 25–34 year olds in OECD countries had a university degree. Ten years later there were 66 million. In 2015, more than 42 per cent of 25–34 year olds in OECD countries had some form of tertiary education (OECD 2014: 31).

Yet now many people are not so sure about the promise implied in the expansion of higher education. Soon after the 2008 global financial crisis, writers like Brown and his colleagues (Brown *et al.* 2011: 1–5) argued that the implied intergenerational contractual promise that both society and the individual would be well rewarded if they invested in higher education had been broken. While many societies increased tertiary education enrolments and many young people – especially in Britain, America and Australia – took on increasing levels of debt to fund their higher education or technical training in colleges, they were rewarded with increasing unemployment and underemployment.

Expanding post-secondary education certainly increased the supply of educated workers, but reduced the bargaining position of university-qualified people to that experienced by low-paid factory workers in the 1880s (Brown *et al.* 2011: 1–5). The 'opportunity bargain' implied by mass university education was turning into an 'opportunity gap' as university-educated workers competed against each other for a diminishing pool of jobs courtesy of what Brown *et al.* (ibid.) called 'digital Taylorism,' as businesses outsourced work at a cheaper rate to every corner of the globe.

To appreciate the situation of young people today we need to understand why half a century ago people and governments invested enormous faith and money in expanding education and especially higher education. The answer is that people fell under the sway of the economic idea that individuals and societies should invest in 'human capital'. It was an idea advanced relentlessly, and continues unabated today. It assumes a clear connection between investment in education (human capital) and life-long economic rewards in the form of secure employment and high incomes. The more education a person has the better off they – and the society or economy they live in – will be. While the 'human capital' model may have now achieved 'common-sense' status, and may have even made some sense half a century ago, it no longer does. Berlant (2011) calls this an example of 'cruel optimism', which happens when we promote or desire something that, in fact, becomes an obstacle to our flourishing.

Here we explore what human capital theory is, as well as tracing its origins. We then outline some of the arguments that suggest it has passed its use-by date, and document some of the circumstances where large numbers of young people continue to experience this cruel optimism. There has always been a fatal flaw in the capacity of human capital theory to deliver on what it promised: its connection to the neoliberal political project.

As mentioned in Chapter 3, this policy frame drove changes like the collapse of the full-time youth labour market from the 1980s, the deregulation of global trade and financial and labour markets, cuts in income and company taxes, and cuts to public spending. By the 1990s, warning bells were sounding from the newly deregulated global financial system, which was committed to promoting massive private debt and speculative investment in markets, in everything from housing and currency to shares and derivatives.[2] By the 1980s and 1990s the preoccupation with speculative investment resulted in dramatic bubbles followed by crashes. Governments were urged to cut spending and fix their budget deficits by imposing what were forms of austerity policies. This began generating major increases in the inequality of income and wealth distribution across the OECD, especially in the Anglo-American world (Piketty 2014). In this context, governments in the Anglo-American world decided they did not have the resources to fund university expansion.

Instead, governments especially in Australia, Britain and America began insisting students should pay for their university education because it provided private benefits. They also insisted that universities be run as businesses, 'selling' education and competing with each other (Quiggin 1999). In short, while keeping faith with human capital theory, these governments decided to stop using tax revenue to invest in education and instead required students to pay for their own tertiary education, even if it meant going into debt.

Simultaneously a technological revolution was underway that also affected the labour market. As the World Economic Forum (2016) observed, new developments in genetics, artificial intelligence, robotics, nanotechnology and 3D printing, were laying the basis for a revolution far larger and more complex than Brown *et al.*'s (2011) 'digital Taylorization'. It is now evident this will be a more comprehensive and all-encompassing transformation in the relationship of technology and human labour than anything humans had ever seen (World Economic Forum 2016).

These developments raise one unprecedented question: how much longer will human labour define production and distribution of goods and services? This question needs to be asked given the origins of human capital theory in an industrial period that is passing away.

Human capital theory

Human capital theory sees people and their knowledge, abilities and skills, as 'natural' or 'real' resources (akin to land, mineral deposits, capital etc.), which education or learning enhances, thereby increasing our economic value. In this way, our abilities and knowledge are seen as assets in which we can 'invest' through education – in the same way we invest in housing or natural resources. This wasn't always the way people, and even economists, viewed education. For a long time, economists treated education as a consumption activity like going to the theatre or taking a holiday, which people spent money on for pleasure but no obvious economic gain.

Human capital theory has it origins in neoclassical economics. Key figures in the early development of neoclassical economics, like Marshall, argue humans were 'capital' (Marshall 1930: 787–788). The term 'human capital' appears to have been first used by Pigou (1928), a colleague of Marshall who claimed we could invest in human capital as well as material capital. It was not until the 1950s that human capital theory became the significant idea it continues to be.

Human capital theory was developed by economists associated with the University of Chicago School of Economics. Milton Friedman and Simon Kuznets (1945) made an early start at estimating the economic value of professional education. Lewis (1954) is credited with initiating 'development economics', which included reference to human capital. However, the first extended development of human capital in neoclassical economics is credited to Jacob Mincer (1958). Subsequently, it was popularized by Theodore Schultz (1961), chair of the Chicago School of Economics through the 1950s. The best-known advocate for human capital was Gary Becker (1964, 1975), another key member of the Chicago School.

Human capital theory was never the 'objective', 'scientific' or 'value free' theory that neoclassical economic advocates claimed it was. As we demonstrate, its underlying premise – that education increased people's employability – was not based on credible evidence. As Weick suggests, most people prefer plausibility to truth (1995: 61). The success of human capital theory owed much to the willingness of people and their governments to believe education was an 'obvious' source of economic growth and upward social mobility. This, in part, reflected the success with which members of the school of neoclassical economics (housed at the University of Chicago School) deployed their rhetorical skills.

The Chicago School is well known for developing and elaborating three key neoclassical economic claims. First, that the social world consists of individuals who are selfish, rational people ('rational economic man') calculating what will benefit them for the least effort ('efficiency'). Second, every aspect of human life is 'economic'. Finally, from the endless exercise of selfish individual happiness-maximising activity we create economic growth and affluence for all (Becker 1976).

The first claim implies that 'society' or the 'community' are not real because society really only contains individuals.[3] This was reiterated in 1987, by the then UK prime minister, Margaret Thatcher, when she said 'there's no such thing as society'. She was repeating the view of a long line of economists beginning in the eighteenth century with Jeremy Bentham, who argued:

> *The community is a fictitious body*, composed of individual persons ... The interest of the community [is] the sum of the interests of the several members who compose it. It is in vain to talk of the interest of the community, without understanding what the interest of the individual is.
>
> (Bentham 1789: 2 [our emphasis])

Since that time, neoclassical economists have argued that to understand a social or economic phenomenon, we need to assume the existence of individual choices and preference orderings as the basis of proper scientific inquiry. Moreover, social arrangements (such as family life or economic activity) are seen to be by-products of personal choices, as individuals act rationally to maximize their own interest (Green and Shapiro 1994).

The second claim is that individuals are rational creatures, who do their best to maximize their own happiness (also known as wellbeing or the 'utility function') (Green 2002). Neoclassical economists like to make their case using abstract rules and logical, even mathematical principles (Ayton 2012: 339. They say that because all rational individuals (*homo economicus*) are purposeful, work-shy, self-interested and utility-maximizing, they will – when making decisions – aim to get as much as they can for as little effort as possible. Writers like Friedman and Becker assume that rules like this make up a universally true theory that applies equally to everyone, and following a model of science, emulating physics, argue that 'rules and tastes are stable over time and similar among people' (Becker and Stigler 1977: 76). This assumed homogeneity is supposed to provide the basis for the mathematical treatment of our economic decisions relying on differential equations. Human activity is considered rational if it accords with the axioms that a rational person supposedly never violates.

The third claim by neoclassical economists is that every aspect of our human condition is economic, that everything is a rational, utility-maximising activity (Becker 1964). Getting married, committing a crime, and studying at a university are all economic activities as outlined above. We argue that converting education into an economic activity in this way is, however, a category mistake that has serious consequences.

According to Schultz, although it was obvious that people acquire useful skills and knowledge, it was not obvious that these skills and knowledge are a form of capital, or that this capital can be a product of deliberate investment (Schultz 1961: 1). He also argued that what was understood as 'consumption' is actually investment in human capital, citing examples like direct expenditures on education, health, and internal migration to take advantage of better job opportunities. In this way, education is not a form of consumption that represents a costly expenditure for government, but an investment that improves the economic worth of individuals (i.e. their human capital) and thereby raises a country's overall productivity and economic competitiveness.

For Schultz, human capital is akin to more physical forms like factories or machines that make production possible. This is because investment in human capital produces returns in the form of individual life-long income while creating economic growth for the community. It is a benefit or return that varies according to the amount and quality of the investment made in human capital formation. One implication of this was that governments ought to support education because additional investment would yield additional economic growth, more jobs and increased wealth. Equally, as Friedman began to argue in the 1960s, there was no reason why young people should not be required to invest in their own human capital by paying for their own education.

Key human capital theorists well understood that normal people might well reject a story that relied on treating people simply as 'assets'. Schultz, for example, understood that treating humans as assets that can be augmented by investment 'runs counter to deeply held values' (1961: 2). Schultz acknowledged that it might well be deeply offensive to treat humans as property to invest in, because this was the logic that underpinned slavery – something 'we abhor' (ibid.). Yet Schultz displayed a staggering disregard for elementary logic when he simply dismissed all such concerns and insisted that that 'by investing in themselves, people can enlarge the range of choice available to them. It is one way free men can enhance their welfare' (ibid.).

If nothing else, this is an example of the rhetorical skills of neoclassical economists seeking to appease readers who might be concerned about converting people into assets or property. While Schultz gives the impression that he rejects treating people as property, he is arguing that we can and should act that way. Like most neoclassical economists, Schultz is a methodological individualist who disregards our social relations or context and who insists that we can choose freely, because that is what free individuals do. Schultz, like Friedman and their mentor, von Hayek, argued that by investing in their human capital everyone could not only become free, but also a capitalist, by investing in themselves through 'the acquisition of knowledge and skills that have economic value' (Schultz 1961: 11).

Apart from the rhetorical skills of neoclassical economists another explanation for the success of human capital theory is that it was an idea with strong elective affinities to its historical and social context. Whether this is true now is an entirely different question.

Why human capital theory was so successful: the early years

Though it would eventually be used in the 1980s by neoliberal policy-makers as part of an increasingly inegalitarian policy agenda, the human capital model seemed initially to be a good idea because it aligned with meritocratic and egalitarian stories popular in America, Britain, and Australia that said people who worked hard could accumulate wealth and achieve social mobility.

At the start of the twentieth century, universities in western societies were small, elite institutions (Forsyth 2014). The higher education systems of

America, Britain, western Europe and Australia began to transform from 'elite' university systems into 'mass university' systems in the 1960s (Trow 1974). The advocacy for human capital theory was a core element in this transformation. It provided an attractive, common-sense story that seemed to explain why more education is good for individual people, the economy and society. A premise informing higher education policy in each of these societies was that governments were responsible for investment in higher education. As neoclassical economists made the case that investment in higher education would benefit individuals and society alike, so governments began to increase their investment in higher education from the 1950s onwards.

In America and well before the advent of human capital theory, Americans were attracted early to the idea that college education offered social mobility and economic success. In the second half of the nineteenth century, American governments, courtesy of the 'Land Grant' Morrill Acts of 1862 and 1890, established 70 universities all with a vocational orientation (Lambert 2014: 27–38). They offered 'utilitarian higher education' intended to further the development of agriculture and industry, and contribute to the general welfare (Nakosteen 1965: 494–495). In 1948, a renewed impetus for expanded higher education began when the Truman Commission on Higher Education argued America was not investing enough in post-secondary education, and recommended that higher education be expanded with no restriction of admissions based on race or religion. A second impetus for expansion of higher education came in the early 1960s on two fronts. First, the civil rights movement promoted the idea that African-Americans had equal rights to whites, including access to higher education. In 1964 the Johnson administration committed to invest in increased education as part of its 'war on poverty' (Lambert 2014). Increased investment in higher education was also seen as critical to promoting America's national security in the Cold War with Russia. America was keen to 'invest' in its capacity to win 'the space race', the 'arms race' and 'the scientific race' between the USA and Soviet Russia. Education seemed to offer the means for securing the expertise needed for the USA to secure its geopolitical global supremacy.

In Australia and Britain, universities were seen for a long time as best kept small and elite. At the same time Australia's university system was always shaped by a 'utilitarian ethos' in which most students and academics were 'primarily concerned with preparation for the professions' (Davis 2010: 27). In 1900 each major city had one university available mostly to young, middle-class men interested in professional careers. This pattern only began changing in the late 1950s when the Menzies coalition government began to increase the number of higher education institutions and student enrolments. To do this, the government created a dual post-secondary system with new Colleges of Advanced Education sitting alongside the universities. Universities would continue promoting the values of the old professions and high culture while the new, less expensive Colleges of Advanced Education trained 'new' professionals like nurses and social workers' (ibid.: 30).

For centuries, England had maintained a small and exclusive university system based on Oxford and Cambridge. It began enlarging its higher-education system back in the nineteenth century by establishing the 'redbrick' universities catering for professional education. As in Australia, a major expansion of student enrolment only began in the 1950s and 1960s. The Macmillan government developed a national system of mass higher education in the early 1960s based on the idea that universities were a public good because they encouraged a more just, meritocratic society and promoted individual economic growth and affluence (Shattock 2012).

Europe saw similar trends. From its inception in 1958 the European Economic Community promoted higher education.[4] Countries like France came under pressure in the 1960s to expand access to its elite university system (Musselin 2001). In the 1980s and 1990s, Spain likewise expanded the number of its universities and enrolments (Cruz-Castro and Sanz-Menéndez 2015).

In broad terms then we can say that between the 1950s and 1970s many governments increased their investment in higher education and did so because they were convinced that both individuals and the whole society would benefit. This investment was seen as part of a general policy commitment to promote full employment and sustained economic growth.

Then governments began to change their minds. Human capital theory would be retained but in a radically different political and policy setting, one shaped by the neoliberal political project.

Neoliberalism, the 'active society', higher education policy and human capital theory

When the OECD introduced its 'active society' model in 1988 this formally signalled the end of the post-1945 commitment by many western governments to a full-employment policy. Underpinning this was the then-new neoliberal position that governments were no longer responsible for ensuring full employment, with the OECD arguing that full-employment policies were too simple and inflexible (1988: 8). Creating jobs was now something best done by the market.

The 'active society' model also signalled an acknowledgement by governments that unemployment had now become a permanent feature of labour markets and that young people would be among those most affected. Part of this policy shift entailed representing those who got government income support as 'passive' and 'immoral' while government support itself was understood as bad policy and morally wrong. 'Giving' jobless people benefits and 'receiving nothing back' encouraged passivity and laziness. It exacerbated the problem by 'rewarding' citizens for being 'inactive'. If unemployed people wanted income support, then from now on they would have to demonstrate they were active, which involved proving they were 'genuinely' looking for work and/or participating in an approved education or training that improved their 'job readiness' (OECD 1988:10). Human capital theory was now to be reframed.

Human capital theory provided the dominant intellectual rationale for OECD policy in general, and European educational policy in particular, from the 1980s (Pascual 2007). The OECD enthusiastically promoted the idea that education developed human capital, which was vital for economic growth (Gillies 2011). From the 1980s the European Union committed itself to 'increasing investment in human capital through better education and skills' (Commission of the European Community 2009: 2). The general shift towards professional and vocational university degrees also dates from this time. Drawing on Bacchi's analytic for policy-making, the 'active society' policy was a consequence of representing the policy problem of unemployment as a problem of the unemployed who lacked the kind of job-ready skills they needed. This, in turn, reflected an underinvestment in education, a position sanctioned by the authority accorded 'human capital theory' (Bacchi 2009). In this way, the return of unemployment in the mid-1970s, which began to entrap increasing numbers of young people, enhanced the policy appeal of the human capital approach (Freeman 1976). Demand for higher education increased, and increasing it seemed a commonsense policy response to help 'activate' the young and prepare them for future employment. Yet the emergent neoliberal policy frame also meant that the old model in which governments simply spent more money on education was no longer seen as 'realistic'.

The bipartisan commitment to 'small state' neoliberal policies implied that governments should no longer foot the bill for education. Indeed, neoliberal governments began insisting that universities act as if they were businesses operating in competitive markets and earning their own income. This entailed that students would become 'customers' who purchased the education they wanted from the university. To promote this transformation from public education to private commodity, Anglo-American governments began imposing severe funding cuts, forcing universities to focus on revenue creation and become increasingly reliant on 'private' sources – like students (Slaughter and Rhoades 2004).

Here we see a new relationship between neoliberalism and human capital theory. In this case human capital theory, once used to justify the idea that governments should invest in higher education, was now used (in Anglo-American societies) to justify shifting the cost of that investment to students. In Europe, however, human capital theory was used to justify maintaining high levels of public investment in higher education.

Britain

In Britain, the neoliberal idea that 'the market' could provide the mechanism for university reform can be traced back to the 1976 Ruskin College speech by the Labour prime minister, James Callaghan. Callaghan argued for better education in a context of economic crisis brought on by the 1973–1974 OPEC oil embargo, which produced high inflation *and* unemployment ('stagflation'). Callaghan identified education as the cause of the crisis. In time-honoured fashion, he argued that the failure of education to produce graduates with the requisite skills and knowledge to compete in the modern market place caused the economic crisis. Britain's economy was in strife because its university system was out of date and needed radical reform. It wasn't until the election of the Conservative government headed by prime minister Margaret Thatcher in 1979 that we saw this argument extended and began to see major changes to higher education. It was also a policy trajectory supported and sustained by subsequent governments under the prime ministerships of Major (1990–1997), Blair (1997–2008), Brown (2008–2010) Cameron (2010–2016), and nascent under May (2016–).

Courtesy of Thatcher's policy initiatives, Britain's universities now operate under the 'sign of the market' (Shattock 2008). As Shattock (ibid.: 182) observes, increasingly Britain became subject not just to 'state steering', but to significant government 'interference' or 'micro-management' similar to European higher-education systems. Thus we see the contradiction between neoliberal arguments for 'a market' free of state 'interference' and the reality where proponents of neoliberalism produce policies that increase state regulation.

This came alongside an expansion of student enrolments starting in the 1980s, and a shift from the practice of government funding undergraduate education to a mixed system of student contributions, beginning with 25 per cent of the cost supported by low-interest government loans (Lunt 2008). This meant that while student enrolments doubled from 1990–1996, government funding per student fell by 30 per cent (Barr and Crawford 1998: 1). This funding shift continued. Both the Blair Labour government in 2004, and the Coalition in 2010 increased the amount students paid for their education substantively. Tuition fees, initially introduced in 1998 at £1,000 per year have increased steadily to £9,000 a year in 2010, generating widespread student protest (Coughlan 2010).

This continual expansion of higher education and parallel hikes in student fees was justified by reference to human capital theory. Under the aegis of neoliberalism one thing was clear: the growth of a mass system of higher education could not be publicly funded. The only way any expansion would happen was through significant private funding. As Barr and Crawford argue, education became 'a system which allows students to borrow against their future earnings' (1998: 2). The problem with this, however, is that for many graduates the prospect of future earnings has ceased to be a realistic prospect.

Australia

In Australia, the 1980s saw the emergence of a bipartisan commitment to a neoliberal reform agenda. As part of its radical restructure of public policy, the Hawke–Keating Labor government developed a new policy model for university expansion that included creating a higher education 'market'. One key plank of this initiative was the reintroduction of university fees in 1988. The old premise of education policy, that public higher-education policy should be broad and inclusive so everyone could enjoy the benefits of increased social mobility and economic growth – which justified state funding – was terminated in 1988.

Under the sway of neoclassical economic thought, and especially human capital theory, a succession of ministers for education beginning with John Dawkins claimed that public investment in universities was not affordable, desirable or defensible. The argument was that too many students, well able to afford to pay for their own education, were receiving tax subsidies in the form of 'free' education, paid for by taxpayers who were themselves unable to afford such an education. As part of the Dawkins reforms, students were required to take financial responsibility for their own education by taking on student debt (Bessant 2009: 64–74). The Australian government said it recognized the difficulties this created. To address these, it pioneered a deferred loan repayment scheme so students could borrow money to cover 'fees', and repay it when they graduated and got a job. As a result, many Australians now carry significant education debts. As we explained in Chapter 1, as student enrolments grew so too did their debt levels. In Australia, total student debt is forecast to reach AU\$70 billion by 2017 and \$185.2 billion by 2025–2026 (Bankwest Curtin Economics Center 2015).

The policy discussions that led to these reforms framed the problem in terms of the universities being out of touch with the needs of modern business in a globalized world that also called for a significant overhaul, including a systematic curriculum review (Dawkins 1988). Like the reforms elsewhere, Australia's Dawkin's reforms mandated the adoption of a 'market ethos' supported by changes in vocabulary. The language of markets turned students into clients and education into a business focused on 'economic outcomes'. By 2016, Australia had 43 universities and approximately 126 other higher-education providers, most of which are private.

America

We see a similar process in America. Cuts in government funding from the 1980s caused colleges and universities to concentrate on revenue creation, with many increasingly relying on student fees. The result was what critics have called the economization of learning, teaching and research, in which these practices come to be described instrumentally and valued in economic terms. This was accompanied by the adoption of market language and a focus on 'efficiencies'. It was a rationale that made having fewer tenured academic staff, and replacing them with cheaper, part-time, casual and adjunct faculty the 'obvious choice'. Paradoxically, at the same time as fewer faculty were employed to teach, student numbers increased and universities' administrative bureaucracies blew out (Slaughter 1998). While all this was taking place, university governance in the USA shifted from a collegiate approach to a top-down, managerialist practice (Ayers 2005).

The US has a large-scale and complex post-secondary technical education system incorporating six different types of 'providers', enrolling over six million students annually: public four-year institutions; private, non-profit four-year institutions; public two- to three-year institutions (community colleges); public vocational-technical institutes; private, non-profit less-than-four-year institutions; and private proprietary (for-profit) institutions (US Department of Education 2017). Within all this diversity, about one third of enrolments are governed by one piece of federal legislation, the Carl D. Perkins Career and Technical Education Act of 2006.

The complexity of the American higher education system owes much to its federal nature. Having said that, the federal government does not play a strong directive influence over investment in education. Rather a combination of federal and state government initiatives exists, designed to 'make economies' and marketize universities. It's system of private and public universities and colleges funded by various grants programs like the Pell Grant program, which in 2014 saw $33 billion worth of grants provided to nine million students to attend a post- secondary institution (Burke 2014). Various government and private credit options also exists which lend students and their parents billions of dollars (ibid.).

Europe

The European Union formally endorsed a single market and neoliberal policy frame in which education was central. Within this frame, member nation-states were independent and relatively free to pursue their own ways of achieving this new and common policy agenda.

In France, all universities are public, students pay no tuition fees, and academic staff are regarded as civil servants. In 2007, the French government brought in the Liberties and Responsibilities of Universities Act (Law Pécresse), intended to give universities greater financial and management 'autonomy' so the government could reduce their funding. It was a move that resulted in considerable protest from academics and students. Students clashed with police in opposing what they saw as the privatization of their universities and went on an extended strike. Blockades were established across the entrances of many universities, as protestors insisted that the government continue to provide funding.

While the full effects of the protests were not immediately clear, promises were made to increase university funding. Student fees remained negligible, and governing bodies of universities were reduced significantly in size. Greater autonomy was granted to university managers in budget expenditure, and they were authorized to raise private revenue; students' choice of the university in which they enrolled was no longer prescribed by the place in which they lived. The number of student enrolments increased, leading to concerns about overcrowding. By 2014, President Hollande began imposing considerable budget cuts on universities, and once more staff, students and others took to the streets in protest, leading to the president cancelling the proposed €70 million cuts. By 2016, Prime Minister Valls's socialist government announced that in the 2016 budget universities would receive an extra €100 million, taking the total university education budget to €200 million – double what it was in 2015.

By the 1980s, Spanish education policy was also reconfigured under the influence of policy advocates committed to a neoliberal agenda (Olmedo and Santa Cruz Grau 2013). While most of Spain's 83 universities are state funded, with only 33 of them privately funded, the effect has been felt most in the shift towards funding from students. University tuition fees have increased significantly since 2012–2013 as new policies 'adjusted' fee thresholds and linked them to the 'cost of provision' (ibid.: 7). The financial crisis of 2008 exacerbated this; the Spanish government implemented major budget cuts, reducing public spending on education and universities, in particular, as part of its 'austerity' policies. Moreover, the government required local governments to raise fee payments for students while also reducing the availability of scholarships. This came at a time when many young people were choosing to 'shelter out' the recession in higher education. The rate of university enrolment set a 'new high' in 2015 (Ministry of Education Culture and Sport 2015) and in 2014–2015, just under 30 per cent of 18–24 years olds were enrolled in university programmes at bachelor or master level (European Commission 2015a: 6–7).

Vocational education

Each country considered in this book has officially promoted the need to increase participation in vocational education and training.

In Europe, human capital theory has proved increasingly influential in shaping vocational education. The European Council (2000) declared that by 2010 Europe needed to be the 'most competitive and dynamic knowledge-based society in the world'. A key plank in that agenda was the 'promotion of employability and social inclusion through investment in education and training' (Harris *et al.* 2010b: 13). The Copenhagen Declaration of 2002 saw education ministers from 31 European countries and the European Commission agree to work to develop Europe's vocational education and training system (ibid.). Its latest 'skills' agenda remains welded to human capital theory, being designed to 'equip people in Europe with better skills' and 'make the most of Europe's human capital' (European Commission 2016).

While Britain and Australia historically had extensive systems of technical schools, they had greatly diminished by the advent of neoliberalism. By the 1990s, fewer than 0.5 per cent of British students were in technical schools (this compares with 60 per cent plus of German students). From the 1990s onward, however, under the aegis of a neoliberal concern with the 'need' to advance the 'knowledge society', British governments promoted vocational training within a 'National Vocational Qualifications framework'.

Similarly Australia allowed its network of publicly funded technical colleges to wither, while moving towards an increasingly privatized VET (Vocational Education and Training) model. The resulting system in Australia sees vocational training delivered by privatized registered training organisations under light regulation from state governments, against a national set of guidelines (the Australian Quality Training Framework). Approximately one million students are enrolled in state-run institutes of technology and with private, for-profit providers. The national government has applied the same technique it used with its university system: cutting public support to the state-run VET colleges, forcing them to increase fees, while establishing a VET student loan scheme to enable students to pay fees. Like the US, the Australian VET sphere is now largely privatized (National Center for Education Statistics 2016).

The growth of private VET providers in America and Australia has not always worked well. There have been widespread and well-founded allegations of corruption and predatory conduct on the part of many private providers accompanied by high student attrition rates (Commonwealth of Australia 2015). This was a problem to such an extent that it led to an American Senate inquiry into for-profit education in 2010 (US Senate Committee on Health Education Labor and Pensions 2010). Similarly, in Australia, legal proceedings were taken by statutory watchdogs like the Australian Competition and Consumer Commission (ACCC) against a number of VET 'private providers' that offer 'student loan'-funded courses. The case against the Australian Institute of Professional Education (AIPE) is illustrative of the general problem. In this instance, the ACCC claimed the AIPE's pattern of behaviour involved a long list of 'unconscionable' actions, including: 'failing to provide any, or adequate training or instruction to the agents and sub-agents to ensure that their conduct complied with the ACL'.

Using unfair tactics, including offering inducements to prospective Aboriginal students to enrol in a course (including Wi-Fi access and mobile phone credits); paying cash to assist in recruiting others, while failing to explain to students the nature of their VET FEE-HELP obligations if they enrolled in a course; not undertaking an adequate assessment of the literacy, numeracy or computer skills of the prospective students; and enrolling students into courses that were not suitable for them, having regard to their limited education, reading and writing skills; and the list goes on (ACCC 2016a: 18–19). Similar action was taken against other providers (ACCC 2016b).

Likewise, according to evidence presented to the USA's inquiry into the 'deceptive practices' of 'for profit' providers, companies made millions of dollars by preying on particularly vulnerable people (US Senate Committee on Health Education Labor and Pensions 2010). For-profit education companies encouraged students to accumulate huge debts for qualifications that had little or no substance and in a labour market where the chance of getting work commensurate with their qualification was minimal. As one hedge fund investor explained, after his company studied the for-profit education industry to understand how it operates and profits,

> Until recently, I thought that there would never again be an opportunity to be involved with an industry as socially destructive and morally bankrupt as the subprime mortgage industry. I was wrong. The for-profit education industry has proven equal to the task.
>
> (Eisman 2010)

He continued:

> The for-profit industry has grown at an extreme and unusual rate, driven by easy access to government sponsored debt in the form of ... student loans, where the credit is guaranteed by the government. Thus, the government, the students and the taxpayer bear all the risk and the for-profit industry reaps all the rewards. This is similar to the subprime mortgage sector in that the subprime originators bore far less risk than the investors in their mortgage paper.
>
> (Ibid.)

The industry, he argued, was unsound, and he predicted that millions of dollars will be 'lost' from students who default on their loans (ibid.; see also US Senate Committee on Health Education Labor and Pensions 2010).

The broken promise

In the twenty-first century, most governments remain committed to human capital theory. Increasing the numbers of young people in secondary and university education has been and remains a central policy objective. Yet the projected reductions of unemployment, which human capital theory says this increased investment in human capital should produce, have simply not happened.

Unemployment and underemployment remains a persistent problem. America had an official unemployment rate of 6.17 per cent in 2016 (World Bank nd). In mid-2016 Australia it was 6.0 per cent (ibid.), in the UK it was 5 per cent, in France it was 10.14 per cent, and in Spain a whopping 20.1 per cent (Eurostat 2016). As for youth unemployment, it is even higher now and has essentially not improved despite two decades of state and individual investment in young people's human capital. As the two tables below suggest, older teenagers face an especially difficult labour market in most cases while young adults confront a no-less challenging situation, especially in Europe.

A combination of persistent low economic growth and austerity-policy measures means that the youth jobless rate has stayed stubbornly high since 2008. Global economic growth has stalled since 2008 (OECD 2016). The number of unemployed people globally is predicted to hit 199.4 million in 2016, with

Table 5.1 Youth unemployment rates, 15–19 year olds

Unemployment rate %	1984	1994	2014
Australia	22.27	22.59	18.41
France	37.87	36.62	32.28
Spain	51.50	47.08	68.56
United Kingdom	22.25	18.45	25.29
United States	18.87	17.64	19.56

Source: OECD Stata 2015.

Table 5.2 Youth unemployment rates, 20–24 year olds

Unemployment rate, %	1984	1994	2014
Australia	12.87	13.31	10.15
France	20.31	27.58	21.03
Spain	36.71	41.27	50.32
United Kingdom	17.91	14.94	12.68
United States	11.46	9.72	11.17

Source: OECD Stata 2015.

an additional 1.1 million jobless predicted be added to the global tally in 2017 (ILO 2016).

Nothing now raises more questions about the credibility of human capital theory than the growing joblessness rates among highly educated young people Even the OECD now acknowledges that 'graduate unemployment' is a serious problem:

> Still, tertiary-educated people, especially young adults, are not immune to unemployment, and many governments are concerned about rising levels of unemployment among graduates.
>
> (OECD 2014: 13)

Or as the ILO explains:

> The increased access to education over the past decade has resulted in more young people aspiring to jobs in professional occupations. Unfortunately, there are currently not enough jobs available within this category to meet the supply of graduates.
>
> (ILO 2016: 30)

Overall, after two decades of sustained investment in their 'human capital', young people may be more educated, but remain equally unemployed and earn comparatively less than did earlier generations at a comparable point in history. While individual young people may become more competitive vis-à-vis other young people through costly investment of time, effort and money in their own education; collectively, young people are not benefitting. The problem of unemployment and stagnating wages is not due to a shortfall in particular skills and knowledge on the part of the workforce, something that 'better' and more education will fix. Nor is it that young people are work-shy. The problem is the absence of jobs, and it is not a short-term problem. It signals the emergence of a new kind of economy. The guarantees of investment in human capital appear not to have paid off for today's generation, even as they are now making the payments themselves.

There is now a clear mismatch between the educational qualifications and skills of young people and the actual number of jobs available to them – pointing to a 'demand-side problem' of the labour market, not a supply-side problem that represents the problem as young people's lack of human capital. MacDonald identifies four consequences of this (2011). First there will be more qualified workers than skilled jobs available. This will increase competition between qualified young people. This is because employers will continue to offer jobs to and hire the best, most-qualified person they can to fill vacancies. This will mean unskilled jobs will become de facto 'qualified' jobs, because those without qualifications are unlikely to get them. Finally, unskilled jobs will continue to pay less and this will decrease the return on the investment in education that individual young people have now paid.

It seems that governments still do not quite understand what is going on. It was only in early 2013 that the European Union accepted that Europe's very high rates of youth unemployment were a 'genuine social emergency'. In 2013 youth unemployment exceeded 25 per cent in 12 of the 27 member states. The EU accepted that youth unemployment also had a significant socioeconomic cost, which, taking unemployment benefits and foregone earnings and taxes into account, was worth around €153 billion (or 1.2 per cent of EU GDP) per year. In 2014, a total of 7.5 million young people were not in employment or education.

In response, the EU introduced its Youth Guarantee scheme in April 2013. The EU justified this decision with all the right words saying:

> High youth unemployment has dramatic consequences for our economies, our societies and above all for young people. This is why we have to invest in Europe's young people now.... This Package will help Member States to ensure young people's successful transition into work. The costs of not doing so would be catastrophic.

The Youth Guarantee scheme mandated a clear commitment to 'guarantee' that young people under the age of 25 would receive an offer of a 'good-quality' job suited to their education, skills and experience or acquire the education, skills and experience required to find a job in the future through an apprenticeship, a traineeship or continued education. (It should be noted this is not the same thing as a work guarantee). The EU budget initially allocated some €12.7 billion for 2014–2020 through the European Social Fund and a dedicated Youth Employment Initiative.

However, things have not gone well. In March 2015, the European Court of Auditors, which is the EU's independent external auditor, released a major report on the Youth Guarantee and it does not get a good report. Far from tackling youth unemployment the Youth Guarantee has presided over significant increases in youth unemployment. The average increase in youth unemployment rates between 2007–2014 was 11.9 percentage points. For non-euro nations, which Eurostat provides data for by way of comparison (i.e. Bulgaria, Czech Republic, Denmark, Croatia, Hungary, Poland, Romania, Sweden, UK, Iceland, Norway, US and Japan), the average change in youth unemployment rates between 2007–2014 was 4.6 percentage points. The reason for that difference appears to reflect fiscal policy in non-euro nations, where governments used deficits to stimulate employment. In mid-2016, some three years after the launch of the Youth Guarantee, in the worst cases the youth unemployment rate is still over 40 per cent: Spain (43.2 per cent), Greece (47.7 per cent) and Italy (39.2 per cent). The European Court of Auditors argues that the Youth Guarantee scheme has been underfunded, and that the quality of the activities (jobs, traineeships and apprenticeships) is questionable. Others would say it fails to encourage job creation and is overwhelmed by an austerity policy frame. Given the likelihood that things will not improve and unimpressed by the initial results, EU member states did not allocate the necessary credits for 2016. It seems that budget support for the Youth Guarantee will be cut from €6 billion over 2014–2016 to €2 billion for the next four years.

The future of work

The continuous and dramatic expansion of higher education and the steady increase in youth unemployment and precarious employment has been taking place in a context where technology is developing dramatically and radically transforming the labour market and the way work is done. Seven key technological transformations are underway:

1   *Information technologies* can now interpret information like – if not better than – humans, and use information to create specific content for individual users. Other digital technologies also have considerable disruptive capacity: from social media, to the 'internet of things' and artificial intelligence.
2   *Biotechnologies,* such as genetic therapies, stem cell research, surgical robotics and big data all allow for faster, more effective diagnosis and treatment. For example, a patient in New York may have her MRI sent digitally to Bangalore, where a highly skilled radiologist reads the scan at a quarter of the cost of a New York radiologist.
3   *New manufacturing technologies,* including robotics, automation, 3D printing and personalized manufacturing.
4   *Energy technologies:* including new forms of fossil fuels, like shale gas and new renewables; new storage technologies like long-life batteries; clean tech; and smart electricity grids.
6   *Financial technologies* affect payment systems, and entail the use of algorithms to handle high-volume financial transactions and credit checking.
7   *Defence technologies* include the use of robotics, drones and advanced weapons systems.

As Roubini (2016) argues, technological advances like these tend to favour those who already own or control capital because they are capital intensive, and those who already have a high level of technical skill because they are skill intensive. At the same time, the new technologies also offer labour savings.

There is considerable debate about the likely impact of the new technologies on the total number of jobs and the extent to which new technologies will create new types of structural unemployment (Roubini 2016). In Australia it is estimated that half the existing workforce will be replaced by automation in the next 10–20 years (CEDA 2015: 6). In a very careful study the Productivity Commission estimates that 40 per cent of jobs are at risk of automation, a finding relating to gross, not net employment (Productivity Commission 2016: 73). The most likely effects will be felt in a mix of routine tasks and some non-routine tasks that are amenable to automation (Frey and Osborne 2013). Autonomous or driverless cars and trucks are a good example of the increasing scope of automation (Durrant-Whyte *et al.* 2015). The kinds of occupations likely to be disrupted by technical change are labourers, machinery operators and drivers, and clerical workers. Equally, while most professionals and personal service workers have a lower probability of computerization, there are some jobs in these occupational groupings that are at higher risk of automation (Productivity Commission 2016: 74). The World Economic Forum has also pointed to 'the upcoming employment impact of artificial intelligence, although not on a scale that would lead to widespread societal upheaval – at least up until the year 2020' (World Economic Forum 2016: 11).

Many education systems do not seem well placed to think about or tackle this technologically induced transformation. The European Union (2014) admitted that modernizing higher education to face this technological challenge 'involves significant changes in how higher education institutions operate, as well as a change in culture and mindset' from where we currently are. Requiring young people to invest in their human capital via increasingly expensive, yet currently outmoded ways, has the capacity to further undermine the link between investment in human capital and social and personal rewards. Or, as Dewey explained a century ago, 'if we teach today as we taught yesterday, we rob our children of tomorrow' ... although this time we charge them for the privilege (1916).

Conclusion

The expansion of higher education since the 1980s was the result of policies that encouraged large numbers of young people to enrol in higher education for extended periods of time. It was a policy based on the rationale that extending education was an investment in 'human capital' that conferred lifelong socio-economic opportunities and benefits to the individual, to business and society.

It was the basis of an agreement or a compact between young people, their families, the state and others. As a metaphor, human capital provided an effective way of persuading people to see students and education in terms of an investment in economistic terms. It played a central role in the policy reforms of most western nations from the 1980s, and especially in Anglo-American nations, as they moved towards using student fees to replace public funding. It was a mechanism that increased rates of private contribution to a point where fees were substituting revenue from government expenditure.

While the neoclassical economic model remained the dominant way of framing policy directed towards increased education 'participation', it was a policy that also drew for its support on moral language, on ideas of fairness and inclusion. The moral argument said that access to higher education by groups that were historically excluded would encourage greater social mobility, enhance social inclusion, and create a more equitable society. From the 1980s, increasing education enrolments was officially identified as a way of enhancing 'access and equity' and thereby creating a more inclusive, fairer and just society (Anderson and Vervoorn 1983).

However, the promise inherent in human capital theory is now broken. Individual investment in human capital does not ensure that young people, as a collective, will be better off. Given this, what can and should we do?

As writers like Harvey (2005) and Berlant (2011) argue, the conventional social consensus we have long sustained about the 'good life', is coming to an end. The 'good life', for Berlant (2011: 2) is an idea of 'enduring reciprocity that binds couples together, particular family formations, particular institutional arrangements and political systems, markets and at work'. The social contracts embedded in these ideas 'have long since worn out' in the face of neoliberal reforms, the recurring economic crises, which have revealed the vulnerabilities of economics informed by neoclassical economic theory, and the influence of new technology on human work and the economy (ibid.).

How then can that idea of human capital investment endure, given the changed context? Do we still need this model? Is it not time for something different?

Notes

1 Higher education refers to post-secondary education, including universities, colleges, polytechnics or technical training institutions.
2 A derivative is a contract the value of which is based on an agreed financial asset or a debt security. It is an 'insurance' against possible loss, or a gamble about the prospect that an asset's value might increase or decrease. They are variously called 'futures contracts', 'forward contracts', or 'swaps' and are liked by financial speculators. The big sellers of derivatives include banks and financial houses and most are sold 'over the counter', without regulation. The current (2016) global market in derivatives is over US$750 trillion which is more than 20 times the total assets of the world's economy. The liquidation of US$4 trillion in 2008 triggered the Great Recession of 2008.
3 It is referred to as the 'rule' of methodological individualism.
4 Any discussion of EU higher education policy needs to acknowledge the diversity of Europe.

6 Penalizing the young and the justice system

Crime is one of the hottest topics of our time. If nothing else, this reflects the popular belief that we face ever-increasing levels of crime and violence, which means, unsurprisingly, that 'law and order' has become a major political topic. Politicians of all persuasions constantly try to outbid each other in being 'tough on crime'. What this can lead to for young people has been captured recently in two chilling videos.

The first video captured the arrest of an eight-year-old African-American boy in the third grade in Kentucky. The video shows the boy screaming in pain as he is handcuffed with his arms wrenched behind his back. The police officer, Deputy Sheriff Sumner was apparently responding to the school's call to deal with the 'threat' posed by this small eight-year-old boy (Pilkington 2015). The child, it was later revealed, suffers from both post-traumatic stress disorder and a learning disability. The video captures the chilling message of the police officer: 'You either behave the way you are supposed to, or you suffer the consequences'. When the American Civil Liberties Union subsequently took legal action, the Sheriff claimed that his deputy 'had done absolutely nothing wrong', that he had done 'what he is sworn to do and in conformity with all constitutional and law enforcement standards' (ACLU 2015).

The second video, released in mid-2016 in Australia, showed six boys in solitary confinement being tear-gassed. They were in a secure facility for juvenile offenders, mostly indigenous, in the Northern Territory. Conditions in solitary confinement were described by the children and staff as appalling and inhumane. They were locked in cells for nearly 24 hours a day with no running water, little natural light, and were denied access to school and educational material. A 14-year-old boy became upset about his time in isolation, so left his (accidentally unlocked) cell and refused to go back into it until he saw a senior officer. CCTV footage shows that instead of negotiating with the boy, prison staff laughed and mocked, calling the boy 'an idiot' and a 'little fucker'. The five other boys were still in their cells when 10 bursts of tear gas were sprayed into the solitary confinement area within one-and-a-half minutes, gassing all the children (Children's Commissioner 2015). Two boys can be seen on CCTV calmly playing cards before the CS gas is sprayed over them. The tear-gassing incident was initially described as a 'riot' by prison officials, who told the media the boys had escaped from their cells and threatened staff with weapons.

Are these two incidents evidence of some larger and more general trend affecting a whole generation of young people? The good news for most young people is probably not. The bad news, however, is that governments in Australia, America and Britain have been taking a tougher approach to crime, targeting some young people who are black or indigenous in disproportionate ways. Garland (2001) talks about contemporary juvenile justice policies in countries like the UK and Australia, referring to what he called their 'punitive turn'.

The punitive turn refers to a style of policy-making that re-emerged in the 1980s (Muncie 2008). Narrowly defined, it refers to a hardening in the way the criminal justice system works; governments criminalize more activities with new laws; courts hand out harsher sentences; police use 'stop and search' powers more; and so on. More broadly defined, the punitive turn describes new practices and approaches in the education and welfare systems as well. In American schools, this has meant a growing reliance on police, surveillance and security guards (Hing 2012) to regulate what young people do and say. Likewise, the welfare systems operating in Australia, America and Britain have also been subjected to several decades of increasingly paternalistic and punitive welfare reforms, which have increased the obligations of a range of welfare recipients while reducing the responsibilities of government, a process we discussed in Chapter 3 (Mestan 2014).

To understand the punitive turn in criminal justice we need to ask what is actually happening?; how do we explain or understand it?; and how might we do better? (Livingstone 2012). First, we map the extent of 'criminalization', noting an increase in the number of laws and harsh punishments being handed out in the UK, Australia and the US, but to a lesser extent in France and Spain. Second, we count the number of people, including young people, being put in prison, noting similar increases.

Exploring why this may be highlights the importance of challenging taken-for-granted political narratives, to say nothing of the assumptions people make about crime. While many politicians and citizens believe we are witnessing a tidal wave of criminality driving this punitive turn; this belief is not well grounded. It also highlights the need to critically interrogate academic theory. As Cavadino and Dignan observe, there has never been any shortage of theories offered explaining criminal justice policies and practices, but most tend to run aground on the hard rocks of messy reality (Cavadino and Dignan 2006a: 346). Certainly, some differences in the scale and evolution of the punitive turn raise questions. For example, if neoliberalism is the pervasive policy frame we have said it is, why are things like the rates of imprisonment so different between the different countries? Second, if neoliberalism claims an interest in promoting freedom, why is it so intent on denying some people their freedom by putting them in prison?

We begin with the punitive turn itself.

The growth of criminalization

There has been a dramatic increase in criminalization by governments of all kinds of political orientations in America, England and Australia (Lacey 2009, 2012; Husak 2008; Zedner 2007, 2009).

Arguably, the US played a lead role in the development of a tough-on-crime movement, involving the transformation of the American criminal law code, law enforcement, and sentencing policies. Congress, for example, created around 500 new crimes a decade between 1980–2007 (Baker 2008). Britain embraced an even more exuberant approach to criminalization. From 1988–1997, the Thatcher and Major governments legislated to create around 500 new crimes. And from 1997 on, Blair's government created an astonishing 3,023 new criminal offences before 2006 (Morris 2006). Australia too took a punitive turn in the 1980s. While there is no current estimate available for the creation of new laws across all of Australia's jurisdictions, we can explore the growth of remand in custody, which accounts for 23 per cent of all Australian prisoners (ABS 2012: 14), as a proxy. Here, in one Australian state alone, New South Wales introduced 89 amendments to the Bail Act between 1979–2011 (Brown 2013: 618), whittling away the presumption in favour of bail.

In France, there does not seem to have been anything like this frenzy of legislation, but there was a focus on increasing the maximum penalties for crime by Mitterand's socialist government in the 1980s. The most symbolically significant legislation was the Security and Liberty Act 1980 (Kensey 2005: 27–28), which increased maximum sentences for violent crimes to 20 years. Maximum sentences were increased again in 1986 for terrorism (to 30 years), in 1987 for drug crimes and again in 1992, when misdemeanours were raised from five to 10 years, and serious crimes raised from 20 to 30 years, the same as terrorism.

Spain appears to have bucked this trend towards more crimes and harsher penalties. In fact, there have been sporadic moves to make Spanish juvenile justice more coherent and strike a better balance between education and punishment (Alberola and Molina 2007: 324). The Juvenile Court Reform Act 1992, for example, promoted a 'dual framework of education and punishment'. However, this was not a universally popular push. The later compilation of all juvenile justice regulations into a single and complete system (the Juvenile Criminal Act 2000) was subjected to a significant public campaign that demanded tougher 'law and order' policies and tougher action against offenders. Despite this, the act ensures that young people in Spain are subject to a different criminal system with its own juvenile court.[1] The court is limited to criminal acts only, and the system requires children who are in poverty, neglected or abused, or are at risk of becoming offenders, to be dealt with the civil jurisdiction instead (Ley Orgánica 5/2000).

Prison and punishment

Another way of mapping the 'punitive turn' involves counting the number of people given prison sentences. What we see in the US, England and Wales and Australia is not only very high rates of imprisonment but a disturbing pattern of ethnic or 'racial' discrimination and excessive incarceration of young people.

America

Uniquely, capital punishment continues to be a legal penalty in the US. Capital punishment has been progressively abolished in most developed countries – 25 countries abolished it by 1960 and 96 by 2004 (Zimring 2005: 1406) – however, in the US, the trend is reversed. In 1972, the Supreme Court struck down capital punishment statutes in all states on the grounds it was a cruel and inhumane punishment, and there were no executions in the entire country between 1967–1977. In 1976, the Supreme Court reversed its decision and most states passed new death penalty statutes. Between 1977–2015 more than 1,400 people have been executed. Notoriously, the US has executed 21 young men who were aged 17 when they committed a capital crime and one who was aged 16 at the time of his offence.

Aside from capital punishment, the US imprisons more of its own people than any other society on earth, incarcerating around 22 per cent of the world's prisoners. In 2013, 716 people per 100,000 of the population were incarcerated, slightly down from the 2009 peak of 754. On top of imprisonment, which 2.3 million Americans experienced in 2016, another 820,000 Americans were on parole and a staggering 3.8 million people were on probation (Wagner and Rabuy 2016:1). In total, around seven million people were under some form of penal control – almost 3 per cent of the American population in 2016 (ibid.).

The rate of imprisonment increased by 500 per cent over the last three decades to become the world's highest (De Giorgi 2016). American governments at all levels drove this project. The US Congress created new crimes, while state governments used 'three strikes and you're out' legislation, which created mandatory minimum sentences for offenders convicted of a third offence. Created in 1994 in California, by 2004 some 26 states had passed 'three-strikes' statutes – invoking minimum sentences of 20 years to life. On top of this, major increases in pre-trial detention and the criminalization of illicit drug use and distribution have played a part (Brown 2012).[2]

There is a persistent racist bias operating in the American justice system (Alexander 2010; Tonry 2011). For decades, police forces across the US have targeted African-American males as part of routine policing. One result of this is that while approximately 13 per cent of the American population is African-American, they comprise over one-third of the total incarcerated population. In 2013, this meant that African-Americans had an imprisonment rate of 2,306 per 100,000, six times higher than white people. Hispanic Americans, too, are disproportionately overrepresented, but to a far lesser extent; they make up 16 per cent of the general population, and 19 per cent of the prison population.

Being young and disadvantaged also plays a part. The largest overrepresentation of black prisoners is among young men aged 18 and 19 (Wildeman 2009: 273), and those who don't finish high school are at more risk still. Black male 'high-school dropouts' born between 1975–1979 had a 70 per cent chance of spending some time in prison before reaching age 35 (Western and Wildeman 2009: 231).

Reflecting more general trends, the US incarcerates more of its young in youth training and detention centres than any other country in the world. This has been a source of controversy, with concern about overcrowding and violence, the long-term consequences of incarceration, and the prosecution of youths as adults. In 2014, the UN Human Rights Committee criticized the United States for being the only nation in the world to sentence juveniles to life imprisonment without parole (Sherrif 2015).

Many writers like Wacquant (2009), Alexander (2010) and Tonry (2011) claim that this represents a four-decade-long American neoliberal experiment in penal policy, devised from the start as a political strategy to restructure American racial and class relations. We turn to how we make sense of this claim after describing what is going on elsewhere.

England and Wales

Incarceration rates have been rising in England and Wales.[3] In 2010, the British incarceration rate was 153 people per 100,000 but in 2015 this had risen to 184 per 100,000 (ICPR 2016). This is the latest stage of a century-long trend, amounting to around a 500 per cent increase in imprisonment between 1900–2015 (Allen and Dempsey 2016: 7).

Demographically, there are no surprises. Most prisoners are young men in their twenties, who account for over 30 per cent of prisoners, while 15 to 20-year-old men account for another 10 per cent (ibid.: 11). Only 4.6 per cent of prisoners are women. As in the US, there are clear discriminatory practices at work. In 2015, approximately 25 per cent of the prison population was from a black or minority ethnic group, while they constituted around 10 per cent of the general population. The UK's Equality and Human Rights Commission argues there is now greater disproportionality in the number of black people in prisons in the UK than in the USA (Prison Reform Trust 2015).

The story of younger people is more complex. There has been a significant reduction in the total number of children and teenagers receiving some kind of youth justice sanction since the early 2000s, including a dramatic reduction in prison sentences. For example, 76 per cent fewer children in 2014 were sentenced to prison than in 1999 (Bateman 2015: 34). Similarly, there was a 79 per cent reduction in the number of children receiving sentences or pre-court decisions between 1992 (when 143,600 children were subject to them) and 2014 (29,800 children) (ibid.: 11).

This decline may reflect a decline in crime committed by young people. The *Crime Survey for England and Wales* 2013–2014, for example, documented a drop of 11 per cent in offences in a year, taking the number of crimes to the lowest level since 1981. This evidence suggests crime peaked in 1995 with the number of estimated offences falling more than 63 per cent since then. The majority of offences were trivial, such as theft and minor drug offending (Bateman 2015: 12).

The complexity comes when, while the total number of teenagers and children receiving some sort of sanction has decreased dramatically, this is not the case for black and mixed ethnicity young people. In 2104, 1.8 times as many black children came to the attention of the youth justice system than would be expected given the composition of the general youth population (Bateman 2015; 24). This overrepresentation increases with the intensity of the intervention. In 2013–2014, black and mixed ethnicity children were particularly overrepresented among those getting custodial sentences. While those two groups made up 12.9 per cent of the youth offending population, they accounted for more than 25 per cent of those receiving a custodial sentence and 38 per cent of those sentenced to more than two years (ibid.: 23–24). The latter proportion is almost six times as high as would be anticipated given the composition of the general population (ibid.). And this disproportionality is getting worse. The share of black prisoners, who now account for one in five young people locked up, has risen by 67 per cent, and that of mixed ethnicity young prisoners by 42 per cent over a 10-year period (ibid.: 24).

Many suggest that 'stop and search' police powers have helped perpetuate, even worsen, this disparity. Stop and search, an area of policing plagued by accusations of racist targeting by patrolling police officers, has seen more than 600 children under 10 years old stopped and searched in the last decade (EHRC 2014). Two types of stop and search powers are in operation in the UK: Section 1 of the Police and Criminal Evidence Act and Section 60 of the Criminal Justice and Public Order Act 1994. Race plays a significant role in determining who is searched under both; in Dorset, for example, black people were 11.7 times more likely than white people to be stopped and searched under Section 1, and in the West Midlands, black people were 29 times more likely than white people to be targeted under section 60 (ibid.).

Australia

Australia has seen equivalent increases in its prison population to those seen in the UK and USA. In the early 2000s, it had an imprisonment rate of around 154 per 100,000 of the general population, which began to edge upwards in all states and territories. By March 2016, the average daily imprisonment rate was 205. Much of this reflected a continuing increase in withholding bail and putting defendants into prison on remand: the number of unsentenced prisoners in custody increased by 21 per cent between 2014 and 2015 alone (ABS 2015).

If we scratch the surface, a more disturbing picture emerges. In March 2016, Australia's Northern Territory had an average daily imprisonment rate of 958 prisoners per 100,000 adult population, considerably higher than the US average rate (ABS 2016). Hidden in this is a more uncomfortable fact: in 2015 9,885 prisoners – 27 per cent – identified as Aboriginal and Torres Strait Islander, despite making up around 3 per cent of the population at last estimate (ABS 2014b). Their imprisonment rate is increasing, jumping 4 per cent in 2014–2015 alone (ABS 2015).

When we turn to the ways children and young people are dealt with, an even more disturbing picture emerges. Again, as in the UK, the number of young people being given prison sentences is not high. Data from 2013–2014 shows that the number of children and young people aged between 10–17 years old in detention on 'an average day' in Australia was 794, a rate of 35 per 100,000 young people in the population.[4] However the rate of indigenous children in detention was 371 per 100,000, 24 times higher than for non-indigenous children, with this pattern repeated across all states and territories. The difference is particularly marked in the state of Western Australia, where the incarceration rate for indigenous children is 751 per 100,000, 52 times higher than for non-indigenous children. To put this in an international perspective, this is far higher that the incarceration rate of African American children and young people in the US (Sickmund *et al.* 2015; AIHW 2014). The fact that incarceration rates for indigenous children are 24 times higher than for non-indigenous children across Australia, and 52 times higher in Western Australia, shockingly does not attract much attention domestically.

France

While French legislation was introduced authorizing tougher penalties, French judges remain free to use the increased sanctions or not (Roche 2007). Mandatory minimums, or 'three strikes' legislation, has never been introduced, meaning penal sentences are nowhere near as prevalent as they are in Australia, the UK and the US.[5]

The imprisonment rate held roughly steady between 1961–1987 – at 68 and 70 per 100,000 respectively – but has seen growth more recently. The rate drifted slowly upward, peaking in 1994 then peaking again in 2002 and 2004 at 99 prisoners per 100,000 of the adult population. The rate has declined a little from this comparatively low peak in the last decade.

We see a similar pattern in juvenile justice. A punitive turn should have affected children and adolescents, but in France there has been little change in the rate at which young people are imprisoned. Since the 1970s, we have seen no increase in youth incarceration rates. In fact, there has been a decrease since the early 1980s. The total number incarcerated oscillated between 800–1,000 between 1980–1989 and between 400–800 between 1990–2005 (Castaignede and Pignoux 2010). No 'adult time for adult crime' policies have yet been adopted for juveniles, which is reflected in the relatively steady and low prison rates for young people.

Understanding crime and incarceration rates

The evidence suggests there has been a significant punitive turn in the US, the UK and Australia, but little evidence of an equivalent pattern in France. Explaining this variation is complex but necessary. Below we address three problems – the need to appreciate the nuance of government; issues with definitions and counting; and an issue of reductive logic. We then turn to developing arguments around irrational decision-making and different levels of 'crazed' governance in the US, UK and Australia.

First, as we argued in earlier chapters, we need to avoid the tendency to assume that 'the state' or even 'the government' is a unitary entity possessing a single vision or will to act in a clear and specific fashion. Close attention shows governance and policy-making to be messy, unstructured processes involving multiple agencies, uncertain information, conflicting expert advice and unforeseen consequences. In the case of justice policies, there is a crazy-quilt pattern of law-making agencies like parliaments or Congress, policy-making departments and numerous law-enforcement institutions, a pattern which gets immeasurably more complex in federated states like the US and Australia. A 'singular' response to any broad policy agenda is less likely and explaining differences in the face of generalizing theories, such as the spread of neoliberalism, becomes difficult (Roche 2007: 747).

Second, there are cascading issues around how crime is counted and defined, that make cross-national comparisons and those over time complicated. Words like 'crime' or references to 'murder' or 'violence' are frequently used as if their meanings are self-evident and can be applied easily to a simple 'fact'. It is sobering, then, to find a criminologist like Fattah arguing that 'there is no universal or agreed upon definition [of crime] … It means different things to different people … all attempts to define it are doomed' (1997: 37). Conservatives and people who like to think they have common sense may well scoff at this idea. Wilson and Herrnstein, neo-conservative criminologists, promoted the idea that certain activities are intrinsically criminal (1985). They argued that some human behaviours – including homicide, incest, rape and robbery – are intrinsically and universally evil and 'condemned in all societies, and in all historical periods, by ancient tradition, moral sentiments and formal law' (Wilson and Herrnstein 1985: 22).

Yet historical and anthropological research contradicts these claims. What do we make, for example, of the legal marriages contracted between brothers and sisters in ancient Egypt, an activity usually defined as incest (Boswell 1994: 128)? To be clear, activities that are likely to make the readers – and the writers – of this book shudder – like cannibalism, incest, ritual killing of children for religious or magical purposes, and sexual relations between young people and adults – have all been normal, even admired aspects of some societies, somewhere, at some time. The stubborn fact is that 'crime' is not always obvious, objective or simple. As Wilkins noted: 'at some time or another, some form of society or another has defined almost all forms of behaviour that we now call criminal as desirable for the functioning of that form of society' (1965: 46).

Given this sociocultural slippage, what we are left with is that governments decide what is criminal. Some time ago, Michael and Adler suggested that 'the most precise and least ambiguous definition of crime is that which is prohibited by the criminal code' (1933: 2). This is why criminologists can talk about the 'crime rate' and the result can look reassuringly simple and authoritative, as we did above when we talked about crime and imprisonment rates.

This seemingly simple definition opens up further problems, however. As we suggested above, there are significant consequences to crime 'rates' if governments chose to increase the kinds of activities that are counted as criminal (Simmons and Dodd 2003: 14; Maguire 2007: 259). It also produces problems for analysis of federal countries, such as the US or Australia, where each state has their own criminal code. The same activity may or may not be criminalized on different sides of the border. For example, in one US state (Maryland), the legal age at which sexual activity was lawful was set at nine until the late 1950s while in most other states the age was 16 or 18.

Beyond definitions, the way crime is counted is potentially even more problematic. Criminologists like Maguire argue that, given 'the problematic nature of the data, concepts and categories which derive from official and institutional sources', an accurate measure of the amount of crime in a country is impossible, even if there were an objective definition (Maguire 1997: 142). Data from England and Wales, produced every year by the Home Office, highlights this perfectly. The Home Office collects data from direct police reporting as well as data from the *British Crime Survey* (BCS), which uses extensive surveys (Walker *et al.* 2006). The two data sources rarely agree, and there is a large mismatch between the number of crimes people say they are victims of in the survey and the numbers reported to police. In 2005–2006, allowing for differences in the way the categories are put together, police data suggested there had been 5.3 million crimes of violence and property offences, while the BCS data suggested there had been 11 million offences (Hoare and Robb 2006: 2–8).

It then becomes particularly difficult to explain the punitive turn in the US, UK and Australia, and its absence in France. The apparently simple idea, often voiced by politicians, is that governments have adopted a more punitive approach because there has been an increase in crime. In the 1990s, for example, Britain's then Home Secretary, Jack Straw said: 'if crime is rising, the prison population is bound to rise' (Straw, cited in Richards 1998: 27). While, for reasons outlined above, we must approach any official crime rate data with a good deal of care, there is still perhaps one thing we can say about the crime rates in UK, Australia, the US, and Spain and France: the overall volume of crime has been declining since the 1990s. This is 'evidenced' in a number of different ways. In Europe, as Table 6.1 suggests, there has been a steady decline in the number and the index rate for murders in England and Wales, France and Spain.

Using BCS data as well, it seems that since the peak year in 1995 there has been a consistent decline in crime in England and Wales (D. Brown *et al.* 2011: 19). In 2006, the BCS suggests that crime had fallen 44 per cent between 1995

Table 6.1 Murder rate 2002–2012

Country	2002		2008		2012	
	Number	*Index*	*Number*	*Index*	*Number*	*Index*
England and Wales	1,047	100	620	80	552	71
France	1,119	100	682	83	430	52
Spain	564	100	412	85	364	76

Source: Eurostat (2014a): Homicides recorded by the police, 2002–2012 YB14.

Note
Index 2002 = 100.

and 2006, with the overall risk of becoming a victim of crime decreasing from 40 per cent to just under 23 per cent (Walker *et al.* 2006: 1).

Finally, and significantly (as Table 6.2 shows), the United States has a similar story with quite a significant drop in its murder rate.

Incarceration rates are broadly up and stable in the UK, Australia and US, while crime rates are decreasing. This points to a problem.

Panic and irrational policy-making

People's beliefs about the crime rate are not necessarily aligned with the crime rate (Walker *et al.* 2006: 3). Since the 1980s, we have seen big increases in the numbers of people expressing anxiety about increasing crime, yet official research points to a measurable reduction in the total number of crimes, especially since 1995 in the UK, US and Australia. For example, the majority of British citizens continues to believe crime has risen across the country. In 2005–2006, around 63 per cent of Britons thought crime nationally increased in the previous two years, a figure that held steady a decade later in 2015 (ONS 2015a: 10). As Jansson pointed out, those who relied on tabloid newspapers were almost twice as likely as those who relied on quality media to believe that the Britain's crime rate had increased in the previous two years (Jansson 2007: 19).

This popular fear of crime has encouraged some governments, police agencies and courts to behave in increasingly authoritarian, even brutal ways. In Britain

Table 6.2 Violent crime rate and homicide rates, United States 2002–2012

	2002		2008		2012	
	No.	*Rate per 100,000*	*No.*	*Rate per 100,000*	*No.*	*Rate per 100,000*
Homicide	16,229	5.6	16,445	5.4	14,827	4.7

Source: FBI (2014) UCR Data.[6]

for example, 'public' concern about juvenile crime mobilized by the tabloid media has encouraged governmental 'solutions' – such as the Crime and Disorder Act 1998 – aimed at dealing with the apparent threat posed by 'the growing ranks' of 'marginalized', 'disaffected' and 'excluded' young people (Garland 2001; Muncie 2006).

However, we are *not* seeing the same criminal justice policies and practices in every country (Cavadino and Dignan 2006a: 346). While governments in some countries have reacted 'favourably' to 'public' pressure for tough 'law and order' policies, others have resisted this pressure. How do we make sense of this?

The larger problem we need to address is the evidence that at least in Britain, the US and Australia, governments are dedicated to showing how tough they can be on crime – especially when it involves young people – but this doesn't seem all that rational a response.

The absence of rationality, especially when directed at young people, is hardly new. The punitive response to young people has its antecedents in a long-standing tradition of social-scientific research and conservative, authoritarian and 'populist' discourses about how 'young people' are 'wild', 'undersocialized' and deviant. As Garland (1996) observed, crime has long been constituted by conventional criminologists largely as conduct associated with 'the poor' the 'urban working class' and/or 'young people'. All that remains for the criminologist is to record, catalogue, classify and report on the nature and extent of the 'crime problem'.

Throughout the twentieth century, many young people have been continually represented as juvenile delinquents, deviants, gang members, or excoriated for being part of subcultures like punks or goths. More recently, they have been represented as 'welfare dependents', 'the underclass' or simply as 'youth at risk'. As Cohen (1972) observed in his account of young people as 'folk devils', exaggeration and fabrication has played a critical role in the ways policy-makers, experts and journalists framed the problem and set policy agendas. In the US from the 1990s, for example, neoconservative experts like John Dilulio warned Americans about an epidemic of teenage crime creating what he called a 'superpredator crisis'. Dilulio was apparently worried about 'radically impulsive, [and] brutally remorseless youngsters' who were part of the 'hordes of depraved teenagers [who were about to resort] to unspeakable brutality, not tethered by conscience' (Bennett *et al.* 1996: 12).

For the record, the evidence does not support the oft-told story about troubled young people. While it may be judged to have failed against the weight of received opinion, a significant body of research by Judith and Daniel Offer (Offer 1984, 1987; Offer and Offer 1975) and others (like Larson and Lampman-Petraitis 1989) came to one conclusion: the majority of young people are normal.

Young people are not especially tumultuous, criminally inclined or troubled. As Larson and Lampman-Petraitis (1989: 1257) summarized their work they found that the 'onset of adolescence is not associated with appreciable differences in the variability of emotional states experienced during daily life'. Yet, in spite of this work, the old story about troubled teenagers continues to be told.

For example, after 9/11, states everywhere began to worry about 'terror' and the 'radicalization' of young Muslims. Governments began to expand the reach of their 'criminal justice' policies involving enhanced surveillance, regulation and various kinds of community 'integration' projects. By the beginning of the twenty-first century, the figure of the 'terrorist' had merged into the older figure of the juvenile 'folk devil'. This has sponsored the development of preventive justice policies based on the premise that the state needed to take coercive measures even though no crime had actually been committed.[7]

Neoliberal freedom, security and risk-crazed governance

Various writers have explored the link between neoliberalism and punitive penal policies and practices, as well as punitive welfare and social policies. Writers like Cavadino and Dignan (2006b), Reiner (2007) Wacquant (2009) and Brown *et al.* (2011) all point to the ways countries whose governments have embraced neoliberalism, like the US, the UK, Australia, New Zealand and South Africa, have adopted harsh penal policies. Garland (2001) and Reiner (2007: 18) both stress that rampant egotistic individualism (valued by neoliberalism) is often expressed as a lack of care for others and a willingness to punish and further exclude the 'socially excluded'. Wacquant (2009) goes so far as to argue that harsh penal policies and harsh welfare policies are intrinsic to neoliberal statecraft.

Policy-making in many countries, including those we are interested in here, has assumed a distinctly neoliberal cast but in different ways. Some neoliberal governments introduced tuition fees for higher education and loan schemes to enable students to pay their fees while others have not. Writing about France, Roche makes a general point when noting how factors like the crime rate, variations in public opinion, the role of the media, politicization and institutional arrangements including decentralization and insulation of the criminal justice system from political pressures are likely to play a role but not necessarily in ways that are coherent or that go in a single direction (2007: 474).

Making a simple link between neoliberalism and punitive policies is far too simplistic to explain all the variation (Brown *et al.* 2011: 3). Instead, subtle differences between the UK, US, Australia and France and Spain need to be recognised. The table below makes an important point. It points suggestively to an association between the extent that nations have taken the 'punitive turn' (defined here only in terms of rates of imprisonment) and their adoption of particular types of neoliberal political and policy frames.

All these countries have capitalist economies and, while neoliberalism has made policy inroads in Europe, there are still important differences in the relationships between the state, citizens and various social and economic interest groups. These differences (as we argued in Chapter 3) point to the historical evolution of different welfare states. Esping-Anderson refer to significant

Table 6.3 Rates of imprisonment for select countries

Country	Imprisonment per 100,000 population	Year
US	714	2003
England and Wales	142	2004
New Zealand	168	2005
Australia	117	2004
France	91	2004
Sweden	75	2003
Finland	71	2004

Source: Cavadino and Dignan 2006a: 447.

differences between liberal and conservative welfare states, while Cavadino and Dignan (2006a) refer to the differences between neoliberal and conservative regimes.

Rates of imprisonment suggest a significant association between different political regimes and the tendency to pursue a punitive policy. At the beginning of the twenty-first century, there are clear dividing lines between the different types of different political regimes. All the neoliberal countries have higher rates of imprisonment than all the conservative countries, which in turn are higher than the Nordic social democracies.

Freedom, security and governance

Cavadino and Dignan suggest that the association between different political regimes and differing rates of imprisonment has a lot to do with political and socio-cultural attitudes towards 'deviant' and marginalized fellow citizens (2006a: 447–448). These attitudes are *embodied* in government policy and reflect attitudes *embedded* in the wider community, producing a mutually reinforcing cycle. In particular, we see in neoliberalism a deep affinity between the apparent commitment to freedom and the seemingly contradictory commitment to measures designed to promote security that are deeply antagonistic to freedom (Neocleous 2008). The freedom/security antimony is the fault line that runs deep through liberalism and produces typical patterns of 'crazed governance' (Carlen 2008).

Security has become a major cliché of our time, linking politicians of all persuasions silently under a neoliberal umbrella. In 1994, the United Nations encouraged 'a new concept of human security' (Neocleous 2000a). Much broader than military or territorial issues, human security invited citizens of the world to move 'from nuclear security to human security' incorporating 'universal' concerns within several broad categories: economic security, food security, health security, environmental security, personal security, community security and political security (Neocleous 2000b). This broader call for security resonated in politics across the globe. Leadbetter argued that at the heart of social democracy is the one economic feature specifically and unashamedly ruled out by the resurgent free market: security (1999: 157). Social democracy offers nothing if it does not offer security. Sociologists of the 'risk society' like Giddens (1990) represented his 'third way' renewal of social democracy as the basis of a 'new security'. Yet Neocleous (2000a) observed the affinity between the preoccupation with freedom in the emergent liberal tradition that begins in the eighteenth century and the far darker interest in security.

Neocleous argues that by the eighteenth century, the category of security had already developed an intensely political meaning focused on the state. As with many concepts in this period, 'security' underwent a semantic shift re-focusing on individuals and understood in highly positive ways. In the 1780s, Bentham suggests that 'a clear idea of liberty will lead us to regard it as a branch of security' (Bentham 1843: 302). By 1861, John Stuart Mill could declare that security is 'the most vital of all interests' and that 'security of person and property ... are the first needs of society' (Mill 1972: 355). Liberty and security became more or less synonymous.

This speaks to certain liberal traditions preoccupied with security. For liberals, 'liberty' designated a range of activities which occurred *outside* the political realm shaped by the state. The role of the state, embodied in Britain's Act of Security 1704 and later revived by the US in legislation like the 1947 National Security Act, became to secure liberty by ensuring the undisturbed development of the economic lives of citizens. 'Security', for liberalism, came to refer to the liberty of secure possession; the liberty of private property. For Adam Smith, government exists 'for the security of property', presenting us with a triad of concepts which are run so closely together that they are almost conflated: 'liberty, security, property' (1979: 710, 944).

However, security is usually obtained at the cost of someone else's insecurity (Derian 1992), and all security is defined in relation to insecurity. Hobbes, a cofounder of liberalism, decried that state power exists to pursue security. Not only must any appeal to security involve a specification of the fear that engenders it (as in Hobbes), but this fear (insecurity) demands the countermeasures (security) to neutralize, eliminate or constrain the person, group, object or condition that engenders fear. Securing is, therefore, what is done to a condition that is insecure. It is only because it is shaped by insecurity that security can secure. This is what Derian describes as the *paradox of security*: 'in security we find insecurity' (1992).

The preoccupation with security encourages fear of the those who threaten 'our' security, be it the 'poor', immigrants, Muslims, the young or people of colour in predominantly white or postcolonial societies. 'Security' becomes one of the principal liberal preoccupations, designed to defend the unequal property relations and wealth constituting any society with a capitalist market. This is where the specific character of a society like America, which has a long dark history of slavery and white racism, intersects with the liberal conflation of liberty and security in which 'my' liberty and security is secured by 'your' unfreedom and insecurity.

In the name of promoting security, neoliberal regimes will exclude both those who fail in the economic marketplace and those who fail to abide by the law – in the latter case by imprisonment or, even more radically, by execution. This is no coincidence. Both types of exclusion are associated with the highly liberal, individualistic social ethos associated with and cultivated by neoliberalism. This individualistic ethos leads governments and political parties to adopt a neoliberal economy in the first place, but conversely the existence of such an economy fosters the social belief that individuals are solely responsible for looking after themselves.

At the same time, there is something else to be said about neoliberal criminal justice policy: it does not add up. The evidence cumulatively points to an essential irrationality at work in the neoliberal politics driving the punitive turn, especially in the US, the UK and Australia.

For one thing, there is no necessary connection between the crime rate and a punitive policy. In many countries, the crime rate has decreased but the punitive turn worsens. For another, increasing criminalization does not reduce crime. For example, analysis of the 'three strikes legislation' in California found that it dramatically increased the prison population, by putting away more 'criminals' for non-violent and petty crimes (Stolzenberg and D'Alessio 1997). This is not necessarily desirable.

Finally, though neoliberals claim they want to 'shrink the state', the punitive turn works against this. For example, the increase in public spending on American criminal justice over the past few decades has been astonishing. Between 1980–2010, total correctional expenditures in the US more than quadrupled, jumping from US$17 billion to US$80 billion (Hamilton Project 2014: 13). At the same time, per capita expenditures increased by 250 per cent, going from an average of $77 per US resident in 1980 to $260 in 2010. The average yearly cost of incarceration per inmate hovers around US$31,200, more than three times the average annual cost of tuition at a good university (Henrichson and Delaney 2012: 9).

This irrationality has been summed up by Carlen (2008:1) as a kind of 'imagined penalty' characterized by 'risk-crazed governance'. An essentially irrational discourse has become a deranged reality, where people inside the justice system know that the policies they enforce have no chance of working but continue to enforce them. The imagined or 'as if' penalty comes to define a criminal justice system, when neoliberal governments try to meet popular demands for tougher, punitive approaches at the same time as trying to reduce crime and spending. These things cannot happen together, but policy-makers behave 'as if' they can and are. The imaginary serves to cover up the contradictions between the demands on governance and the capacity to meet those demands, even as this 'cover up' serves to exaggerate the contradictions.

Conclusion

There is no reason to assume that governments make policies on a rational basis (that is, based on facts) or in ways that are that are morally defensible. The defence offered for the Kentucky policeman's actions in brutally handcuffing an eight-year-old child points to a less than rational basis and suggests some form of 'wilful blindness' (Heffernan 2011) or 'preferred ignorance' (Haas and Vogt 2014). In the decision to use CS gas on six boys in Australia's Northern Territory, we see brutal mindlessness, made more evident when one of the prison officials asks the officer in charge 'you going to gas the lot of them?' to which the officer in charge replies 'mate, I don't mind how much chemical you use, we gotta get him [the one child who was distressed] out' (Children's Commissioner 2015: 20). In both cases, we might be concerned about the inability or unwillingness to acknowledge when state-sponsored violence is being committed against children and young people (Giroux 2015).

More generally, the criminal justice systems of the UK, America and Australia added further injury to the injurious effects of decades of neoliberal policy-making. Young people, disadvantaged people and people of colour, already diminished by decades of neoliberal cutbacks to school, welfare, health and other public goods, are being rounded up and punitively sentenced for relatively trivial offences, further damaging lives that need care and respect – not more punishment.

Notes

1 The legislators' intention was also to increase the age of criminal responsibility from 12 to between 14 and 18, meaning fewer young people would be in contact with the court. This was in stark contrast to the UK, where the age of criminal responsibility was *reduced* from 12 to 10 in 1998 (Alberola and Molina 2007: 327).

2 The privatization of American prisons, which also began in the 1980s, raises interesting if complex possibilities. In 2013, private companies were responsible for 141,900 prisoners, but the majority of inmates – approximately 91 per cent – were housed in government-run prisons (Galik and Gilroy 2015). (Around 40 per cent of the nation's *juvenile* inmates are housed in private, for-profit institutions). More interesting is the way many states have legalized the use of prison labour by private corporations within state-run prisons (Pelaez 2014:1). The pay rates enable huge profits. One suggestion frequently made is this practice leads to longer jail time as companies and prison managements have an incentive to keep inmates in for longer periods of time (ibid.).

3 Scotland maintains its own criminal justice system.

4 The upper limit for being treated as a young person in the justice system is 17 everywhere in Australia, except in Queensland, where it is 16.

5 Roche points out that the evidentiary base for claims about the French criminal justice system like this need to be considered carefully (Roche 2007: 476). He notes this is because the collection of criminal justice data in France is not sophisticated or done well, a problem reflecting the fact that criminology is not as well developed a social science as it is in the UK, US and Australia.

6 Presenting a sequence of tables like this implies something we need to be careful about. Some have compared the crime rates in the UK and the US, noting that in the UK there are 2,034 violent crimes per 100,000 people while the US has a violent crime rate of (only) 466 [violent] crimes per 100,000 residents. However, the definitions of violent crime are different and make direct comparisons difficult. The FBI defines violent crime as one of four specific offences: murder and nonnegligent manslaughter, forcible rape, robbery, and aggravated assault. The British Home Office, by contrast, has a substantially different definition of violent crime. The British definition includes all 'crimes against the person,' including simple assaults, all robberies, and all 'sexual offences'.

7 It is worth recalling the German state pioneered the use of 'preventive justice' after 1933 (Best 1940: 31–33).
8 The third kind of regime is '*social democratic*' corporatism, such as in Sweden. This is more egalitarian and secular than conservative '*corporatism*'. Social policy is informed to a greater degree by the trade union movement, committed to the principle of 'universalism', and by a willingness on the part of employers to accept high levels of investment in return for wage restraint by the unions. The state undertakes a commitment to promote full employment, the pursuit of profit, the funding of generous welfare provision and an active labour market programme that seeks to minimise the disruptive effects of deindustrialization and changes in economic conditions (Cavadino and Dignan 2006a: 445). This produces a corporatism with an egalitarian ethos and generous universal welfare benefits.

7   Young people making sense of it

Anclaudys Rivas is a 24-year-old college student living in New York. On hearing we were writing this book, he sent us a short piece about his life. He speaks about the judgements others make of young people, about the broader political economy, the pending ecological issues and technology and how all this is defining the spirit of his generation.

> The last time I read about my generation, the millennials, I did not hear very nice things. We are often regarded as self-centred and lazy. We have been referred to as the most entitled generation ever, even by some of our own kind. During instances in which we are not being criticized or pathologized, we are often regarded as helpless victims of an inevitable doom. But to be honest, being a millennial has not been that bad.
>
> You see, we have one of the greatest inventions of all times – the internet. This allows us to access almost any piece of information we desire. The internet not only nurtures the consumer in us, but it also has the power to efficiently nurture the inner philosopher, the inner musician, the inner seeker of entertainment, the inner scientist, the inner crafter, and of course, the inner procrastinator in all of us. Yet, most notably, the internet has displayed the ability to nurture our inner truth seeker.
>
> (When I was younger) I was a very ignorant and misguided truth seeker, (but) I was still a truth seeker. I soon realized that there was nothing special about me. A lot of people of my generation were also truth seekers in one way or another. As far as I can see, a lot of us broke free from the dogmatism and conservatism of the generations that raised us via this exposure of endless information. An evangelical pastor of one of the churches that my parents used to go to even referred to it as Satan. I suspect it is because it challenged some of the misinformation that was being shoved into our heads.
>
> The internet is not the only thing responsible for the millennials' concerns about the world around them. The increasing level of income inequality, the increasing average global temperature, the threat of world war, corporate greed, and the instability of the market, are obvious tangible threats to our near future.

Most millennials I personally know are not leading half the lives their parents did. Jobs with benefits are not as common as we expected them to be, and most of us are working at jobs that are irrelevant to our fields of expertise. An alarming number of millennials seem to have postponed or given up on achieving common milestones of life. To add violent injury to this blatant insult, we have come to the realization that the future of most life rests in the hands of humans and that the way we live our lives leads us precisely to its end.

For an average educated millennial, who is more or less aware of all of this, it takes a great degree of cynicism or rationalization to simply go on with daily life and strive to achieve the American dream, which was largely founded upon this unstable system. It is no longer our grandchildren, no longer our children, but we ourselves who are beginning to suffer the consequences of our actions. At this point, activism, and involvement transformative action is no longer reserved for 'those political people over there'. With such knowledge, comes great moral responsibility. Even if we do not partake in any form of action, deep in our minds we know this system is not right and it is making us very uneasy.

My personal involvement in activism has been with the Stop Shopping Choir ... a diverse community with members ranging from different economic backgrounds and races. The choir's main objective is to promote anti-consumerism, and to tackle corporate greed, racism, and climate change through singing and satirically proselytizing our message, as if we were hardcore evangelicals....

The satire element of the Stop Shopping Choir has been therapeutic for me. Growing up, I used to be one of those Devil's children who would ask too many questions and would never have the Holy Spirit touch them during intense church services. I just never prayed hard enough. Sometimes, I just simply did not believe hard enough. In the Stop Shopping Choir, I not only felt liberated from the devaluations of the type of churches I grew up around, but I had actually felt emotionally connected to the Earth Spirit which took place of the ever-elusive Holy Spirit.... Most importantly, this is a great general platform to get involved in all kinds of actions with a wide range of issues.

As I had mentioned previously, I really do not believe that I am special for being involved in activism. I full heartedly believe that most of us, at the very least, would like to be involved in some sort of way to change the world, especially with our current level of awareness and urgency. For these reasons, although our situation is worrying I am very optimistic of what my generation can accomplish, if the rest of the world allows it.

While this offers an eminently clear account of one person's take on some of the issues this book addresses it could also become grist for a quite heated debate by those doing research about how we can best interpret and understand young people's various experiences and understandings of what is happening.

Many people work in youth studies, sociology, politics and criminology with much to say about young people. They use words like choice, reflexivity, consciousness, and there is talk about an 'epistemological fallacy' (Furlong and Cartmel 2007). As we noted in Chapter 2, this discussion about how young people make sense of their world began when Beck argued that traditional 'social structures' were dissolving in the face of a 'surge of individualization' (1992: 87). According to Beck, this is rearranging young people's lives and enabling increasing choice about studies, careers, housing and sense of self.[1] While much of the initial research exploring 'choice-biographies' highlighted the enhanced capacities of affluent young people to make themselves up (du Bois-Reymond 1998), other research on low-income children and young people also emphasized the agency and creativity they exercise, highlighting the extent to which they author their own lives (Ridge 2002; Attree 2006; Redmond 2008). It seemed the 'surge of individualization' left young people more responsible for shaping their own lives than was ever possible for 'baby boomers' or 'Gen X'.

Others did not agree. In their critique of 'choice biographies', Furlong and Cartmel argued that young people 'may not be as aware of the existence of constraints as they are of their attempts at personal intervention' (1997: 7). They said the story about individual 'self-making' and 'choice' obscured the actual and continuing role 'structure' plays in the lives of young people, especially those who are socially disadvantaged. Furlong and Cartmel argued that a neoliberal political discourse encouraged young people to believe they have more 'choice' and 'opportunity' than they do, creating an 'epistemological fallacy' (2006). The epistemological fallacy refers to the gap that Furlong and Cartmel see between a neoliberal discourse of individualism and choice, and the stark reality that most young people face persistent structural inequalities that restrict the array of options in their actual lives. They argued for a return to structure.

Another line of argument was advanced by Côté in his 'new political economy of youth', based on the idea of 'youth-as-a-class' (2014: 528). Brannan and Nilsen summed up the conundrum as young people telling 'stories' about the choices in their lives even when the evidence says otherwise:

> a young person will typically be optimistic and will say that he/she is in control of his/her life course and that occupational success is largely based on individual effort, while there may be a whole mass of data and theory [pointing to structural effects].
>
> (Brannan and Nilsen 2005: 423)[2]

These discussions have promoted a lot of discussion about 'conscious' and 'unconscious' thought and young people's 'reflexivity'.[3]

Much of this debate is not primarily about the evidence that young people are increasingly disadvantaged. As we documented in Chapter 2, plenty of evidence exists attesting to the ways young people under 35 in America, France, Australia, Spain and Britain are systematically disadvantaged socially and economically. The point of contention is about *how to interpret what is happening*. One implication of this is that we need to establish how young people make sense of their own lives.

As we argued, a political economy of generation that connects the political and economic dimensions of continuing generational inequality can help to understand what is happening. It does this by avoiding the trap of the structure versus agency frame. It also provides a framework to explore how young people themselves experience and make sense of their world.

In this chapter, we consider the various ways young people understand themselves and their world. The political economy of generations offers a non-reductive relational account of young people's practices and relations in the world. One implication of is that we cannot expect a simple large general answer to a question like 'how do young people understand their world', whether this be in one country or a number of them. Another implication is that it allows for the possibility that people can explain themselves and understand their world in ways that may be reflexive and accurate, and confused or contradictory, at the same time. As we argue later, the study of ignorance implies there is no particular reason to believe that young people will exhibit any greater capacity for being able to see clearly what is taking place than any other group (Gross and McGoey 2015). This does not, however, require that a binary choice between 'false consciousness' or 'truth' must be made.

In what follows, we listen to the ways young people reflect on their lives. We acknowledge their capacity to think as insightfully as other people do about how decisions by government policy-makers and other power elites have affected their lives. A political economy of generations highlights the complexity of the social spaces and relations young people find themselves, and the complex ways young people make sense of their world.

A political economy of generations, and the stories young people tell

A political economy of generations acknowledges that we can and should talk about a generation of young people. Following Mannheim, we argue that generations are 'a temporal unit of history of intellectual evolution' that can be used for appraising a given time (Mannheim 1952: 282). A generation can be 'defined' because large-scale historical events shape the lives of that generation, although not in a singular or deterministic way. Like Mannheim, Bourdieu (1977, 1987) sees the societies we live in as spaces marked by inequality and persistent contest over the distribution of valued social resources in which government policy can affect a whole generation.

As we argued earlier, those who draw on the structure versus agency frame tend to emphasise the likelihood that young people will be afflicted with 'false consciousness'. For Côté (2014: 538) this means the 'young are unaware of their manipulation and disadvantaged position in the political economy'.[4] We agree with France and Threadgold (2009: 209) who also draw on Bourdieu that making a case for false consciousness is unhelpful. As much research shows, many young people, including the most disadvantaged, are quite aware of their status (France and Haddon 2014; Threadgold and Nilan 2009). This is not to say, as Côté's critics note, that young people like people more generally 'do not always act in their own best interests or often seem to do things that are actually against their own interest' (France and Threadgold 2016: 619). As we argue, young people who are well able to work out where they sit in the order of things, may still be unclear about the precise role government policy plays in disadvantaging them, or that some may explain what is going on by blaming Muslims, refugees, immigrants or welfare recipients. This does raise an issue about how young people can become 'reflexive' in the way Bourdieu understands reflexivity as an epistemic capacity oriented to truth.

A brief discussion pinpoints the key problem. As Wacquant explained: 'If there is a single feature that makes Bourdieu stand out in the landscape of contemporary social theory, it is his signature obsession with reflexivity' (1992: 36). Reflexivity, alas, is not easy to achieve. Bourdieu claims this is because we are all relationally positioned in specific fields, with each person drawing on various forms of capital to develop situated viewpoints of the practices in each of the fields we find ourselves in. We engage in practice (habitus) in the various fields, using it while adding to it; however, our habitus is largely 'unknown' to us. We have only a partial view of the fields and the larger social space in which we act. It's this characteristic of habitus and the partial view we form of the various fields we inhabit that help explain why it is very hard to achieve reflexivity.

What does this imply for how young people understand their own lives and achieve reflexivity?

Bourdieu's political economy treats us as strategic improvisers whose practice draws unknowingly on deeply ingrained *and* embodied past experience. Because habitus implies that we mostly act 'unknowingly', it seems that habitus forecloses the possibility of reflexivity because it is unconscious or unknowing. Bourdieu's texts are littered with references to the 'unconscious' and how actions are 'not conscious' (1977: 78–79). Given this, it might seem that Bourdieu is better at explaining why change is difficult rather than how it is possible. As Burkitt asks, is Bourdieu explaining how we are so often resistant to change, how we are invariably so stubborn in letting go or, in many cases, afraid to do so?

> Even when it is an outright call to rebellion ... it is hard for critical reflexivity alone to reshape the many varieties of habitus, let alone the various social fields that formed them.
>
> (Burkitt 1997: 195)

Under what circumstances can and do people become reflexive? For Bourdieu, critical reflexivity is clearly possible. He points to several 'sources of reflexivity', which highlight the value of being positioned as an 'outsider'.

First, certain groups (academics, in particular) engage in the 'intellectual project of codification' (Bourdieu 1977). This refers to various kinds of scientific research that identify internal rules and conventions of a social practice. This indicates the possibility of the reflexive understanding of practices that are embedded in the habitus into explicitly codified rules, laws and regularities. As Bourdieu says, 'in societies where the work of codification is not very advanced, the habitus is the principle of most modes of practice' (1990a: 65). This implies that, where the social sciences are active, the habitus is not the only means of orientation in social fields: there are other, more 'conscious' and intellectual modes of practice that are bound by rules, rituals or customs.

Second, Bourdieu recognises how some people become critics as a result of 'alienation', or simply by being an outsider. Being an outsider is a critical enabler of reflexivity. This is what anthropologists do as 'outsiders' looking 'into' a society.

Third, Bourdieu claims that a crisis within a given field can become a source of critical reflexivity. This is what makes politics possible:

> Politics begins ... with the denunciation of this tacit contract of adherence to the established order which defines the original *doxa* [or collective common sense] in other words, political subversion presupposes cognitive subversion.
>
> (Bourdieu 1991: 127–128)

Breaking with the established order becomes possible when a crisis that is too big or obvious to avoid erupts, and people already disposed to be critical seize on it. Consider, for example, how the 2008 recession encouraged a critique of neoliberalism that may have caused others to query the disparities between promises made by proponents of neoliberalism and the ways things actually were, thus causing some to suspend their adherence to the established order.

To this we add a fourth possibility for critical reflexivity. Because generations coexist, the dimension of time itself comes to play a role in creating critical reflexivity, especially in the field of family. Because young people can only have their own experiences, the experience of previous generations can help them see how things were once different, and may be different again. In this way, the coexistence of generations in the family field can plays an important role as a site of difference/otherness in ways that are central to the possibility of critical reflexivity.

As we argue later in this chapter, the transmission of stories and narratives is a central aspect of the fields of family, education and work. Intergenerational and parental stories play a vital role in the ways cultural capital is transmitted between generations. This is especially pertinent in families when 'parents have strong political persuasions and/or discuss socially important issues in the family' (Jennings *et al.* 2009: 795). In these ways, young people can draw on the stories and memories of older generations to add to their own cultural capital and inform their own habitus (Vollebergh *et al.* 2001: 1196). It provides a further opportunity for young people to become reflexively aware of themselves, their place in the larger social space and a sense of belonging to a generation.

In what follows, we canvas evidence for several claims. First, many young people born since the early 1980s broadly identify as a generation. Second, while young people are often represented as naïve and ignorant about political issues, many understand the impact of policies that adversely affect them when compared with earlier generations. This leads some to become disenchanted with conventional politics and even to actively seek redress and promote change, albeit in different ways. Third, as we will see, young people understand what is going on. Like everyone, they do so in ways that are often fragmented, complex, and even seem contradictory, or at least that their ideas don't always fit together in coherent ways. In what follows, we offer a severely constrained account of some of the views and experiences of young people in the UK, Australia, Spain and America.

Young people understand they belong to a generation that is systematically disadvantaged

Do people see themselves as a generation who share a collective fate? According to American research by the Pew Research Center, young people (aged 18–36) do not see themselves as a single generation (2015b). While there are problems with the substantialist assumption that underpins such research, the characteristic paradoxes resulting from this assumption (and how research is done) raises several questions.[5]

Using mail and online surveys, Pew (2015d) asked people whether they see themselves as belonging to a given generation. A majority of respondents (aged 18–34) said they did not consider themselves part of the 'millennial generation', with 40 per cent of that age group saying they were. Another 33 per cent, mostly 'older millennials', said they were part of Generation X. Only 27 per cent thought the millennial label applied to them.[6] Generational identity was strongest among the Boomers: 79 per cent of those 51–69 considered themselves part of the Baby-Boom generation. Among those 35–50, the age range for Gen X at the time, 58 per cent considered themselves part of Generation X.

However, although most respondents age 18–34 did not think of themselves generationally, they were nonetheless willing and able to generalize about their generation. Pew asked whether they thought their generation exhibited certain positive and negative traits (e.g. hardworking, patriotic, self-reliant etc.). Very few respondents who identified as millennial believe the terms 'responsible' (24 per cent) and 'hard-working' (36 per cent) applied to them, although a large majority of Boomers believe those qualities applied to their generation. Only one-quarter of those who saw themselves as millennial thought their generation was 'self-reliant', and Gen X (35–50 year olds) weren't too far ahead (37 per cent).

Conversely, self-identified millennials stood out for their willingness to ascribe negative stereotypes to their own generation. They were more critical of their generation than older age cohorts were of theirs. Fifty nine per cent of respondents aged 18–34 described the members of their generation as self-absorbed, compared to 30 per cent of Gen Xers, and 20 per cent of Boomers.

Just 36 per cent of millennials said their generation was hard working, while 54 per cent of Gen Xers said they were. The negative stereotypes continued: 49 per cent of those aged 18–34 said they were wasteful and 43 per cent described them as greedy. Given the real differences in life experience, the results are hardly surprising. Given their experience of insecure employment, for example, it is perhaps easier to see why younger people would not see themselves as self-reliant.

However, we argue that even if they reject the label, many young people can and do understand that the issues they are experiencing are collective and affect their age cohort specifically. For example, in March 2016, an Australian essay magazine, *The Monthly*, published an article criticizing the impact that state legislation to close Sydney's bars earlier would have on young people (Cooke 2016). While, on the surface, it was an unlikely topic to cause a stir, the premise of the article – that baby boomers had yet again wielded their power to lock young people out of recreational spheres, just like they'd locked them out of housing, careers and politics – struck a chord. As one journalist described it, 'the Boomer Supremacy' was possibly *The Monthly*'s most popular ever article (Triple J 2016), and caused a storm on social media sites and online forums.

Examining this online discussion gives us a glimpse of how young people understood the issue of inequality as a generational issue. We analysed freely available discussion threads on *the Monthly* website itself, its social media sites, threads on Australia's national youth broadcaster Triple J's sites related to the article, and discussions on an Australian housing forum to explore young people's understandings.

It is worth noting that the concept of generation appeared to provide a useful category of explanation to frame the discussion. While this may seem obvious for discussions relating to an article about intergenerational inequality, it is worth noting as it confirms an earlier argument about the usefulness of the concept and challenges the Pew idea that people aged 18–34 uniquely reject the label at all times. Both young and older participants, in all of the discussion forums analysed, were able to use the construct of generation to explain and develop their own arguments. They used generation to describe their social place in the world, and develop a shared concept that facilitated rational debate.

Moreover, having engaged the generational concept and claimed a label (the Gen Y or millennial) in this sphere, all young participants described 'their generation's' situation as more difficult than their parents' generation in one main area: housing. Despite the initial article focusing on recreational constraints, the limitations imposed on young people by failures in the housing market dominated the discussion, presumably influenced by the emerging housing crisis in Australia. Housing was an easy way to use the concept of generation, because it comes at a cost that is simple to quantify.

The vast majority of respondents who mentioned housing were keen to reiterate a point made in the article, that in the 1970s, roughly when they felt their 30-year-old boomer parents would have been purchasing their first house, the average house price in Sydney was around four times the average Sydneysider's annual income, with similar multiples around the country. Come 2015, the multiple had grown to 12 times the average income in Sydney. The huge disparity between what baby boomers paid to climb on the property ladder, compared to what Gen Y will have to pay made the point. As one young respondent explained:

> [to previous older respondent] your comments are completely inaccurate. Fact is $23,000 was the average house price in 1974. The annual wage in 1974 was $7,300. This make the house price 3 times the annual wage. Current average wage is $59,540, current average house price is $612,100. This is 10.2 times the annual wage. That means that houses are 3.4 times more unaffordable now than back in your day regardless of the trimmings and location.... Oddly it is your generation and foreign investment mainly from Chinese who are holding us out of the market with your real estate investment portfolios. You may have been underpaid in 1978 but so are many people today. The figures don't lie. Things are harder now on average. Maybe not for [former respondent] but on average they are.
>
> (McCormack 2016)

Comments from older participants tended to take one of two forms. They blamed young people themselves for being locked out of the housing market, and other symptoms of inequality. Some maintained that reduced home ownership among the young was a result of poor spending choices, or a lack of work ethic among millennials. This often took the form of blaming the young:

> Gen Y want to live in the city, have a good job, party on the weekends, refuse to change their social life, and own a house when they are 30.
> No sacrifices made, No stepping stones taken.
> Here is some advice.... Join the army, move to a less competitive city/ town where there are more jobs, walk from jobsite to jobsite asking builders for work or an apprentice[ship].
> The stories of your mothers and fathers are something to learn from. A self-entitled generation with their hands out, that think because they applied for 20 jobs on SEEK [an Australian job seeker website] this week or that they work 30 hours a week at a coffee shop and can't get anywhere, that they are hard done by and oppressed. Get off the computer, get off your iPhone and get out there.
>
> (Ibid.)

Others refused to acknowledge there was a real and problematic difference in the material situations of the young today when compared to previous generations. This generally took the form of 'in my day' it was tough too, writing previous generations into the story of equal suffering, often combined with a blanket denial that there were systemic issues at play:

> I know there are advantages and disadvantages for all generations. It is not productive to assume the victimhood status that the article takes and simply say all your problems are caused by someone else and have zero introspectivity (*sic*).'
>
> (Cited in Cooke 2016)

The posts that fell into blaming young individuals and/or implying there wasn't a systemic issue were mainly refuted in the conversations, and were discussed as 'proof' that older people really did not understand the socio-historic situation of Gen Y. Instead, these kinds of reactions were described as a new form of 'blaming the victim' or a new phenomenon of 'Boomersplaining' (Cooke 2016).

The use of the '-splaining' suffix draws on the neologism 'mansplaining', used to describe a phenomenon where a male patronisingly explains something to a woman (Rothman 2012). The idea that older baby boomers were explaining what it really took to get access the housing market to younger people was thus treated as like a man describing how to break through the glass-ceiling to women.

The young people involved in these discussions rejected these critiques, sometimes mockingly, but often calling them out for being over-simplistic. As one young person responded:

> I think he may have trudged 20 kms on horseback in the snow to get to school too, every generation seems to think their generation was so well-behaved!! Let's just all admit there are some serious issues and work together for policies that are fairer to all!
>
> (Cited in Cooke 2016)

What is revealing about this is how the concept of generation was so easily used to refer to people and to describe the predicaments they face. Just as women are understood to be a heterogeneous social category who face common discriminations and difficulties, those born since the 1980s understood themselves as a diverse social group united by their unique and troubled socio-historic positioning in this world. As one commentator observed:

> I'm sorry but my parents' generation didn't have to join the army and buy a house at the back of Bourke [Australian slang for 'the back of beyond']. Talk about sacrifices for Gen Y, how about a house, a decent wage, free education, unionized full-time employment, holiday pay, weekend rates and being trapped in a rent cycle all so baby boomers can have a real estate investment portfolio which holds us out of the housing market, buy a Winnebago and go on river cruises.
>
> (McCormack 2016)

Research in Spain, as part of the MYPLACE project, likewise reinforces the idea that young people well understood the generational impact of the 2008 recession.[7] They understood this in terms of increased unemployment and employment insecurity:

> I believe that what affects people the most is not finding a stable place in their life, on a work level as well as in finding a relationship or a job. I mean a job, a relationship and having a house or a place to live.
>
> (Isabel, aged 21, cited in Ferrer *et al.* 2013: 21)

They also pointed to increased education charges:

> [I] paid €5,000 after this year's rise. Finishing your Bachelor's degree and knowing that you can spend many years not getting paid for your work, I mean, they tell you, 'come, work, you'll learn a lot, but we won't be able to pay you', and I'm doing just that, I'm working at three different places ... for free, but of course, it will be useful for my CV [ironic tone].... And it's going to stay the same; and probably spend many years working our hands to the bone without getting paid or ... and that's because of the crisis.
>
> (Paula, aged 22, cited in ibid.: 22)

In short, such evidence suggests these young people indeed understand that they face particular issues as a generation in ways that did not burden previous generations. It is to this aspect that we now turn.

Young people's awareness of the role policy plays in their lives

Before we explore young people's understanding of policy in their lives, we need an account of understanding that does not buy into the binary of 'false consciousness' versus 'scientific truth'.[8] Truth can have multiple origins. Gross and McGoey (2015), for example, suggest two ways scientifically inaccurate truths can become 'real'. First, people can adopt beliefs that aren't 'scientifically true' when embracing scientific truth would be too painful. Second, people often create their own truths when they rely on 'common sense' that is actually inaccurate.[9] Common sense often trumps scientific truth because, in many fields, knowledge is valued less for its truth, and more for its social capital, such as its ability to advance elite interests. Where common sense protects the status quo, it is more often accepted than radical scientific truth.

Given the complexity of truth and the relations that construct it, many people legitimately hold contradictory views about themselves and their social contexts. The reliance on the different kinds of acquired capital will mean we hold views that, to the eyes of external observers, are at odds with each other or contradictory. This is why some young people may be critical of policy, while at the same time understanding themselves and the world around them by drawing on internalized forms of policy discourses or *doxa* (Farrugia 2013a; Threadgold 2011).

Between 2010–2014, one of us carried out research with young people, aged 11–18 and living in low-income neighbourhoods across England to develop youth-authored anti-poverty strategies.[10] The complexity and contradiction of 'truth' was evident in the way these young people understood their lives. The discussions among the young people provide compelling evidence that these young people were not suffering from any 'epistemological fallacy', were able to understand their own lives and the effect of neoliberal government policies on them, and they wanted redress. It also, however, showed the ways they had embraced parts of the neoliberal mind-set despite broadly challenging it.

In discussions about their lives they frequently used phrases like 'it's your own fault' or 'make yourself', echoing the responsibilization discourse of neo-liberalism. As one young woman put it: 'we're responsible for everything because it's us and if we're doing it so we're responsible, you can't just blame it on someone else, all right?'

They believed strongly in self-making and choice.

For example, one young person who had just left state care talked about suicide as a matter of choice. The conversation began with Tammy talking to Keila about a newspaper article that said people who live in her area had a sig-nificantly shorter life expectancy than people from richer neighbourhoods:

TAMMY: It says like how poor we are and like how we grow up like…
KEILA: Like little feral kids.
TAMMY: Like we've got nothing, like, lost in our own. But like every kid in care makes their own decisions. Like if Keila decides to commit suicide 'cause of her life in care, like in 10 years. That does not affect me, like, doing what I wanna do. She just chooses to be, like wallow in self-pity, isn't it?
KEILA: Exactly. Basically.

At the same time these young people understood that government policies and agendas were shaping the choices that were available to them. While discussing career ambitions and the ways young Muslim women in London's East End would deal with the recession, policy was not overlooked:

MODERATOR: What about your career? Do you guys feel that you are going to be able to choose what you want to be in the future?
SABA: No, there's no jobs about now, so if there ain't none now, then they won't even have it a few years later. Unless the government actually made plans.

Talking about being able to make yourself in the modern world did not neces-sarily mean accepting the totality of a neoliberal framework. For example, while they sometimes seemed close to accepting the totality of a neoliberal framework when they talked about 'lazy' people choosing to 'sit on their bums' and take government benefits, they did not advocate a punitive neoliberal policy frame-work to punish those lazy people who made 'poor choices'. In fact, despite 'lazi-ness' and 'choice' being factors in their understandings, they argued for more generous benefits and the collective provision of basic social goods and services so people had better options to make different choices. In this respect, they believed simultaneously in individual choice and self-making *and* social policies that involved public investment in housing, free education and social security benefits that helped everyone live a decent life.

When the young people in the project considered anti-poverty strategies, they emphasized and prioritized public issues like housing. The most pressing issue they had to deal with was poor quality and overcrowded housing. Their concerns were in stark contrast with the then Conservative government's anti-poverty strategy. While the official policy and the young people's own policy ostensibly addressed the same issue – poverty of children and young people – they were radically different in how they described the problem and the solutions.

The neoliberal worldview outlined in earlier chapters overwhelmingly shaped the Cameron government's Child Poverty Strategy 2014–2017 (HM Government 2014). It was a strategy that prioritized investment in human capital, arguing for the need to tackle poverty at the 'source', which ostensibly meant starting with education and specifically in schools (ibid.: 6). Schools, it argued, are 'the critical site for poverty reduction' (ibid.: 9). It continues describing low incomes as the product of an intergenerational 'cycle' that is best 'broken' by education (ibid.: 36).

It also focused on 'individual responsibility' and the need to avoid behaviours and characteristics deemed 'risky', which appear to echo the voices of young people when they spoke of choice and self-making. In the Cameron government's anti-poverty strategy, the 'causes' of poverty were identified as 'family breakdown, educational failure, addiction, debt, and worklessness' (ibid.: 6). In this way, the problem was squarely located within 'the risky family' and its various dysfunctions, like addiction or lack of character. Blaming the victim is a time-honoured practice that censures and blames the victims while working to divert attention away from more important explanatory factors (Ryan 1976).

Government policy and its blaming the victim strategy has been central to neoliberalism's punitive welfare policy. In this case, the government's anti-poverty strategy blamed the lack of 'character' among the young as a cause of future poverty (HM Government 2014:43). 'Character' was defined in terms of 'non-cognitive skills such as social skills, self-esteem, resilience and self control' (ibid.), and the government proposed three solutions to improve young people's 'character':

- Funding more military cadet programmes in school;
- Removing red tape to enable expeditions and work experience;
- Extending school days, so children from low-incomes can take drama, debating, chess and sport (ibid.).

The Cameron government never made clear how military training or playing chess would assist low-income young people to escape poverty, rather relying on 'common sense' to imply that building character through these activities would naturally convert to poverty reduction.

Not surprisingly, the young people in the policy research project did not share this 'official' view that expeditions and drama classes would alleviate the poverty that plagued their communities. In the strategy that they developed, 'character' did not get a single mention. Moreover, these young people did not reiterate the neoliberal faith in individualism and choice. Despite their own declared belief in agency-choice, they rejected a neoliberal framing. They described this framing – evident in the government's Child Poverty Strategy 2014–2017 (HM Government 2014: 43) – as both 'manipulative' and judgemental. The issues they wanted to address were not about bad families, but quality housing and education. In their view the government was giving too much credence to anecdotal evidence pedalled by shock-jocks like Jeremy Kyle who were recycling socially harmful prejudices (see for example Nicholas and Appleyard 2008).[11]

The young people's belief in self-making and choice is part of their own complex understanding of their lives. They understood that while the choices they made and the actions they took would affect their lives, the options they had were limited and they certainly did not have the resources needed to create the kind of lives they wanted. In the various focus groups, they discussed how different people could end up 'in the same place', like being homeless or dependent on benefits, despite doing 'all the right things' and making great efforts. These young people understood clearly how the state was shaping their lives.

In Britain, neoliberal austerity policies have continued to systematically increase intergenerational income inequality in the UK. As a consequence, young

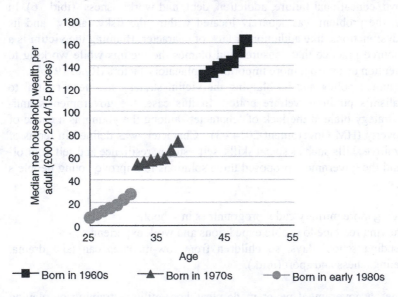

Figure 7.1 The median wealth of households by age cohort.

Source: based on data from Cribb, J., Hood, A. and Joyce, R. 2016 *The Economic Circumstances of Different Generations: The Latest Picture*. IFS Briefing Note BN187 online (www.ifs.org.uk/uploads/publications/bns/bn187.pdf) accessed 10 November 2016.

Britons born in the early 1980s have around half the wealth in their early 30s than those born in the early 1970s (Cribb *et al.* 2016). Recent budgets passed by the Coalition government (2010–2015) and the Conservative government (2015–) are perfect examples of how this gap emerged, as expenditure cuts directly targeting young people (Wilson 2014). In April 2013, for example, the Cameron government cut low-income young people's access to housing support at the same time as increasing old age benefits via a 'pension triple lock', which means it will rise in real terms for forever after. One recent estimate suggests that the cumulative impact of the 'austerity' drive over the next parliament entails a £1.7 billion cut in the incomes of young people, contrasted with a net £1.2 billion increase in the incomes of baby boomers getting old-age pensions (Gardiner 2016: 46).

While the young people participating in the policy research project, and others like them, may not be across details like this, many are aware of the general thrust of government policy. As Humaira Garasia, a young woman from London, involved in earlier research, argued:

> I think it (austerity) is harming the young more than the old. We are the future of this country, yet, we are being held back. The old, they have had support systems and structure throughout that helped them with life, but, the young? We are being prevented, we are excluded because of the cuts and changes. Impacting our chances to flourish, especially when you are a young person from a working-class family.
>
> (Farthing 2015: 113)

Harry McMullen, a young man from Liverpool, confirmed this when he said:

> Young people absolutely have borne the brunt of the austerity measures in the UK.... With the rise in fees and cuts to student aid leaving less than 75 per cent of students progressing to higher education. It's harder today for young people to get on the property ladder than ever before. 10 per cent of 15–19 year olds are classified as NEETs while mandatory retirement ages creep up.

While young people are aware of what governments are doing to them, some are making sense of their world in ways that can have serious social and political consequences. In Britain, for example, many young unemployed working-class people interviewed in 2012[12] drew connections between their economic and social status and the presence of Muslim immigrants. Many parents and young people living in communities with significant unemployment tended to blame immigrants and/or Muslims for unemployment, the perceived decline in communal solidarities and, ironically, the rise of racism. At the same time, they were suspicious of, even hostile to government and politicians because they thought the political elites did not care about their kind of communities. This led to expressions of frustration with mainstream political parties by some young people and an interest in radical anti-establishment movements like the English Defence League (Popov 2014: 103).

In Spain, we observe similar dispositions to blame immigrants and especially Muslims. In Catalonia, anti-immigrant/Muslim sentiment has been actively promoted by the Plataforma par Catalunya whose slogan '*primers els de casa*' translates to 'first those from here'. This anti-Muslim prejudice was reflected especially by those experiencing unemployment. One young woman pointed to what she described as 'pro-Muslim discrimination':

> And they didn't give it (a job) to her and they gave it to her friend who is Moroccan. And his father's driving a Mercedes, and you are like: did you just give it to him because he's Moroccan? Does this man have undeclared stuff? How does it work? I mean … look close and … people see all this and if everyone, if it was the same for everyone that would be it, because … because a local might have less money than an immigrant, it can happen. That's how it is.
>
> (Silvia, age 20, in Ferrer *et al.* 2013: 29)

A young unemployed man had a similar complaint:

> Right now, I'm unemployed: if I ask for one of these social benefits, they won't give it to me, because I'm living with my parents. That's unfair: they [Muslims] live together and they each get a payment. These things are unfair. And then there's an eviction and what happens, happens: if it's a foreigner they pay for a social housing flat for him, which are about 150–200 euro, the State pays for it. But, when it happens to people from Vic, long-term residents, they kick us out, the police come to evict us, and no one helps us. And when you see these injustices then you start thinking … you get pissed off.
>
> (Xavi, age 23, in Ferrer *et al.* 2013: 29)

This raises real questions around how angry and disillusioned young people are and who they are actually upset and annoyed with. How much do young people want change and how will they promote the change they want? Although we address this more thoroughly in the next chapter we can suggest here that many young people are less wedded to conventional politics than older people.

Young people and politics

A large survey by the research group Pew (2014) points to significant generational political polarization in America. Using a set of 10 political values questions on issues such as the role of government, the environment and business, just 15 per cent of young people aged 18–34 expressed consistently or mostly conservative views compared with 44 per cent who espoused a mix of liberal and conservative views, while 41 per cent expressed consistently or mostly liberal views. By comparison, more Gen Xers (25 per cent), baby boomers (33 per cent) express consistently or mostly conservative views (Pew Research Center 2014).

Another study (Pew Research Center 2015e) found a significant flight by young people (18–34) away from identifying with the two main parties in America, the Democrats and Republicans. Nearly half of those young people (48 per cent) identified as independents, higher than any other age range, usually on the 'liberal' side of the spectrum (ibid.). Determining whether, or how, these findings relate to the way people use media is not so clear.

In 2014, the Pew Research Center surveyed 2,901 online respondents of various generations using Facebook for news and political news. The results look to be paradoxical until we recall the reliance on a conventional notion of politics and the media. On the one hand, 18–34 year olds expressed less interest in political news, with only a quarter of them (26 per cent) selecting politics and government as one of the three topics they are most interested in (from a list of nine). This was less than 'Gen Xers' (34 per cent) and baby boomers (45 per cent) (Pew Research Center 2014). Equally while about half (49 per cent) of baby boomers said they talk about politics and government at least a few times a week, just 35 per cent of 'millennials' reported doing this. However, those aged 18–43 stood out for seeing more political content on Facebook. Approximately a quarter (24 per cent) of respondents age 18–34 who use Facebook say at least half the posts they see on the site relate to government and politics, which was higher than Gen Xers' (18 per cent) and baby boomers' (16 per cent) response to the same question (ibid.). In effect, social media like Facebook has become the local TV of the younger groups. Sixty one per cent of respondents age 18–34 reported getting their political news from Facebook in a given week, a much larger percentage than any other news sources like TV or print media.

Yet the obvious should not escape us. Families are a site of intergenerational relationships, and considerable research points to the role parental memories and familial experience have in shaping the habitus of young people. In 2012, Popov (2012) ran focus groups in England with 14 young people (18–24) mostly 'white' and homeless residing in Coventry, five young (16–21) middle-class young activists in Nuneaton, and four young non-white people with 'ethnic backgrounds'.

He later interviewed three families whose younger members were activists on the 'left' and one who identified with the far-right English Defence League. They were all originally working-class families who experienced various kinds of upward and downwards social mobility: the far-right were affected by intergenerational unemployment while the others were using education to move upwards. Popov suggested that his discussions with families revealed the active role family memories, stories and myths played in shaping these young people's life views (Popov and Deák 2013).

Popov's research established that the daily life of families (along with other forms of popular culture like films, TV, and music) were the main means by which young people interpreted the past and connected it to their understandings of the present. The family field, and popular culture, were more important than what they learned at school or university. In particular, older family members often shaped attitudes and political disposition through expressions of nostalgic regard for a 'lost age' of secure well-paid jobs, affluence and state welfare in an

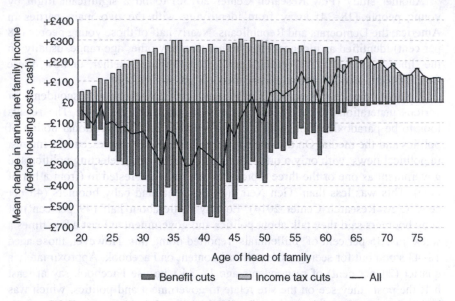

Figure 7.2 Key tax and benefit policy being implemented in this parliament, by age: UK 2020–2021.

Source: RF analysis based on OBR, *Economic and Fiscal Outlook*, March 2016, using IPPR tax-benefit model.

Notes
Income tax cuts based on 2015 Conservative Manifesto commitments to a £12,500 Personal Tax Allowance and £50,000 Higher Rate Threshold (compared to a scenario in which both rise in line with CPI inflation from their 2016–2017 values); benefit cuts include freezes to the value of various working age benefits and cuts to Universal Credit, assuming half the UC population are new or changed claims and half benefit from transitional protection at this point (compared to a scenario in which UC cuts are reversed and benefits rise in line with CPI inflation form their 2016–2017 values).

age of perceived decline and austerity. They could also supply the political inter-pretation of key local historical events such as the 1986 Miners' Strike, de-industrialization and unemployment.

The effect of parental stories is evident in an interview with Martin, a 19-year-old working-class man. Martin's ideas about the kinds of policies that would help young people make transition from education to employment are influenced to a great extent by the stories his father and grandfather told about their employment histories:

INTERVIEWER: Was it easy for [your dad] to find [a] job at that time?
MARTIN: I think it was, because I can, I've never been told he had a hard time finding a job, so, I think it was a bit easier then, 'cause like my grandad was still working then. So, he was be able, yeah, he was being able [*sic*] to get like links for him to get a job (Popov 2013: 82).

The effect of parental stories is also clear later in the interview with Martin:

INTERVIEWER: You mention Tony Blair as [prime minister], and his sort of period then the country became [a] mix, mess, [a] big mess basically. What make[s] you think about this? What do you think happened at that time?

MARTIN: I don't know, I'm not really sure how it all went downhill, that's, I've been told, that's what my mum told me, she said it was Tony Blair that wrecked the country so that's what …

INTERVIEWER: Oh really, it's from your mum?

MARTIN: Yeah, that's what I've always thought. I guess it's a bit of everything, isn't it, that's making everything go downhill (ibid.: 81).

Although Martin claimed to be disinterested in politics, he nonetheless expressed strong views about youth (un)employment and education, albeit in ways that seem to some extent influenced by the memories about 'the golden age' communicated by his grandparents. This informed Martin's belief about what should be done:

> children in schools should be fixed up with, every child, like they should all have apprenticeships straight from when they leave school because it's the easy way to get, like, [an] education as well as earning money. And I think like all children should have like an apprenticeship set up before they finish school so, but in order to do that there'd need to be loads more apprenticeships out there.
>
> (Ibid.: 82)

Conclusion

Bourdieu's notion of generations suggests that what is represented as generational conflict is often simply about people from different age groups who had different experiences and who derived different benefits over time. Using the education system as his primary example of how 'benefits' are divided, he argued that intergeneration conflict 'is not between the young and the old but between two states of the education system, two states of the differential rarity of qualifications' (Bourdieu 1993: 100). In this respect, he argues 'beyond all class differences, young people do have collective generational interests' (ibid.: 101). The research we drew on here suggests that young people are aware of the different benefits and experiences they are having as a result of their age, and the way that neoliberal policies are quickly turning this difference into inequality.

It is also the case that many young people see themselves and others in their generation in far more complex ways than many people give them credit for doing.

Notes

1 See, for example, Giddens (1990); du Bois-Reymond (1998); Wyn and Dwyer (1999); European Group for Integrated Social Research (2001); and Walther (2006).
2 See also Rudd and Evans (1998); Tulloch and Lupton (2003); Lehmann (2004); Roberts (2003); Ball *et al.* (2000); MacDonald and Marsh (2004); Gunter and Watt (2009); and Farthing (2016).
3 See, for example, Farrugia (2012); Roberts (2010); Threadgold (2011); Woodman (2009;) and Woodman and Threadgold (2014).
4 We note also the misreadings of Bourdieu. Akram, for example, says Bourdieu had no explicit ontology (which is wrong) even as Akram relies on a structure versus agency frame and a substantialist ontology (2013: 56). She argues that the dialectical approach advocated in her paper sees 'agents' and 'structures' as 'independent and autonomous' which is far from being a relationalist or dialectical approach (ibid.).
5 The Pew Research Center created the American Trends Panel (ATP) (N = 3, 147), which was drawn from a much larger sample of 10,013 people. This is a national representative panel of randomly selected US adults living in households. The ATP relied on interviews. This research is an example of substantialist framing of traits (age) that are seen as a variable and designed to predict differences in attitudes and behaviours in a process referred to as 'empirical research', which sees generation as an 'age cohort' (Pew Research Center 2015c).
6 Generational identity was strongest among the boomers: 79 per cent of those 51–69 considered themselves part of the baby boom generation. Among those 35–50 (the age range for Gen X), 58 per cent considered themselves part of Generation X.
7 This research included 60 in-depth interviews conducted with young people in Vic and Sant Cugat (both municipalities in Barcelona province, Catalonia region).
8 The binary choice between 'false consciousness' and 'scientific truth' relies on the 'structure determines consciousness' logic found in determinist Marxism. It is self-negating because it presumes there are interests within structure (class or gender) that generate false consciousness, and conversely a privileged structure exists that generates truth. Bourdieu's non-reductionist account of knowledge as cultural capital dissolves this logic. The question of how 'truth' can be promoted requires a different understanding, which Bourdieu's account of reflexivity offers.
9 Gross and McGoey's (2015) account refers to the way 'ignorance' shadows knowledge. While it is a powerful explanatory tool, we have chosen to omit their original language of 'ignorance'. Acknowledging the relations at play between young people and academics, we do not choose to claim 'ignorance' because of the cultural and social power embodied in the word.
10 The research involved running repeated focus groups with young people from five neighbourhoods with high levels of child poverty. A full discussion of the methodology can be found in Farthing (2014).
11 Nicholas and Appleyard (2008) provide a near-perfect example of far-right delusional claims about the 'cushy life' unemployed people enjoy by living on welfare benefits. The journalists tell a story about a family of 10 people who they say 'boast' three generations of adults who are not working.
12 As part of the MYPLACE project (Ferrer *et al.* 2013).

8   Taking action

Young people and politics

On 10 May 2008, a 15-year old boy attended a peaceful rally in front of a Church of Scientology building in London carrying a sign that read: 'Scientology is not a religion, it is a dangerous cult'. The police told him to take the placard down, but displaying grace under fire he refused, referring to a 1984 United Kingdom High Court ruling describing Scientology as a 'cult' that was 'corrupt, sinister and dangerous'. The police seized the placard and issued the boy with a court summons referring to Section Five of the Public Order Act 1986. This young person was part of a global campaign against Scientology mounted by the online 'collective' Anonymous using the website 4chan (Gleick 2014: 36–38). Anonymous launched 'Project Chanology' against the Scientology 'cult' on 12 January 2008. The campaign included distributed denial of service action, a form of direct action or a 'virtual sit-in' that slows down or causes a website to crash. Social media was also used to mobilize traditional forms of street-based protest activity against Scientology. Police later abandoned their prosecution of the boy after Anonymous mounted further protests in support of free speech (Dawar 2008).

Since the Paris attacks of 13 November 2015, organized by the militant group so-called Islamic State (ISIS), Anonymous mounted a digital attack on thousands of Twitter accounts linked to ISIS. In late 2015, a 4chan user mockingly changed the battle cry of ISIS soldiers from 'Allahu Akbar' ('God is the greatest') to 'Allahu Quackbar'. It was then suggested they replace 'the faces on all the propaganda photos with little yellow bath ducks'. Users began Photoshopping images of rubber bath ducks onto images of ISIS militants. People associated with Anonymous followed suit by hacking into an ISIS website so visitors to the website encountered messages like: 'Too much ISIS'.

Both incidents reveal how some people are engaged in political action even as it raises questions about the nature of that engagement. As we demonstrate, some people have trouble recognizing Anonymous as a political project.

Interest in young people's politics has been revived, especially since the late 1990s, when extensive public discussion and research began addressing the 'youth–politics relationship' (Benedicto 2012). A cursory survey of this large and growing body of work indicates that this work tends to fall into a clearly defined binary about young people being political, or not political (Bessant

2014).[1] On the one hand, there is research offering a pessimistic account accompanied by 'alarmist diagnoses' of the apparent rise in political disengagement among young people (Benedicto 2012: 719).[2] Numerous surveys of youth political attitudes and behaviour appear to confirm this. Some point to declining electoral participation by young people and, more generally, to decreasing interest in political issues (Kimberlee 2002; Print *et al.* 2004). Others indicate that participation in political processes is rare among young people, especially when it comes to traditional or conventional forms of political participation (Galston 2004; Martin 2012: 485). Indeed, a considerable body of research points to low rates of electoral turnout among young people. In the 2009 European Parliament elections, 50 per cent of those over 55 voted while only 29 per cent of 18–24 year olds voted. The Australian Electoral Commission (2013) found that, in mid-2013, only 60 per cent of 18 and 19 year olds were enrolled.[3]

On the other hand, a no-less substantial body of research exists that says young people are politically engaged, and the harbingers of new kinds of politics.[4] Some observe 'an explosive growth in studies examining relationships between social media use and political engagement', much of it focusing on young people (Vromen *et al.* 2014: 151). According to this research, young people are using new information and communication technologies in ways that are reviving the public sphere and democracy and fostering new forms of citizenship. Increasing online participation is interpreted as evidence of major shifts in young people's political engagement (Lewis 2006; Livingstone *et al.* 2005). Much of this literature is optimistic about the long-term effects, exemplified when Carlisle and Patton (2013: 3) claim that social media is 'taking it one step further to provide the individual greater flexibility to actively engage in the public sphere' (also Zuniga *et al.* 2012).

Thus it seems we are left hanging on the horns of a binary. Young people are either being chastized as the apolitical heralds of a 'crisis of democracy' (Furlong and Cartmel 2007), or seen as the progenitors of a new, sophisticated, technologically-mediated form of online politics (Coleman 2014). Our view is that what is happening is more complex than binaries allow. In this chapter, we focus on young people's relationship with contemporary politics, and identify some of the assumptions relied on in descriptions of their activity as either political or as some other kind of activity.[5]

Using the political economy of generations outlined in Chapter 2, it becomes apparent that those representing young people as politically disengaged are unreflexively contributing to the symbolic violence against the young. They do this by saying some actions are legitimate and political – often the actions of older people – while others are not – most often the action of young activists. Many conventional political scientists and other experts refuse to acknowledge actions like the campaigns by Anonymous against Scientology as political expressions. Nor, for example, do they acknowledge that the UK riots of 2011 were political.

A political economy of generations avoids this binary. It means we don't have to make an either/or choice in the form of structure versus agency or, in this case, between political participation versus disengagement.

Here we continue developing the political economy of generations. A political economy of generations appreciates that young people by and large do not have the kinds of capitals that provide access to the traditional political field, and will largely be excluded from it. Given they have been excluded, it's likely many will take heterodox or critical positions, such as engaging in 'unconventional' political activity. We should not be surprised to find that when young people engage in political activity, much of it will be outside the political centre. We build on discussions in the previous chapter about young people's understandings to address how young people now engage in political activities using four vignettes. We use these impressionistic, evocative accounts to provide insight into the ideas, settings and activities of these young people.

Politics and a political economy of generation

Mainstream political science offers a largely unreflexive account of politics. More than most other social sciences, modern political science seems content to 'pass' on discussing what it studies. How politics is defined significantly influences both what we look for and how we research politics (Leftwich 2004: 2), and the lack of agreement about its definition hollows out analysis. Yet as Leftwich (2004) notes, the absence of an agreed understanding has not stopped political science developing many styles or traditions of inquiry that rely on tacit or implied understandings of 'politics'.

Although overly simplified, Leftwich points to three types of political science.

1   An older political science tradition focused on the rules, procedures and formal organization of government. This 'institutionalism' uses research methods akin to those used in law and history and privileges research around a narrow range of formal institutions and practices (Heywood 2013: 17).
2   Political 'behavioural science' co-opts the methods of the natural sciences to create quantitative accounts of voting behaviour, the behaviour of legislators, etc.
3   'New institutionalism' is concerned primarily with 'formal' political reasoning (Downs 1957, Becker 1976). It includes ideas like rational-choice theory and public-choice theory (Dunleavy 1991).

Each type of political science is underpinned by an implicit understanding of what is 'political'. To be counted as a political action, each tradition required first, that the motivation for an action is expressed in recognized political language; second, that this language must be rationally articulated; and finally, it should be articulated through 'legitimate' institutional means such as political parties, or parliaments. Such narrowly constrained framings affect young people: any action sitting outside this schema simply doesn't count as 'political'. Given young people's general exclusion from formal politics and their engagement in other modes of action, they are doomed to be classed as apolitical and inactive.

Replacing this inadequate political science standpoint, the account of young people's politics that we offer builds on the political economy of generations. From Bourdieu, we have the idea of 'generation' explaining how time affects different fields. Different trajectories through time can produce unequal access to capitals. This makes a relational understanding of generations inherently political; they are inextricably linked to the unequal distributions of resources and capitals (Bourdieu 1993: 94). From Mannheim, we see the effects of large-scale historical events on people born at a particular time. This opens a different, but complementary, way of understanding generations. We can understand a generation as a social phenomenon based on the relationship between those born in a particular time and the socio-political events that affect their lives (McMullin *et al.* 2007: 299–300). Each generation, according to Mannheim (1952), has its own a distinctive historical consciousness that is shaped by the historical events of that time. One of the major events shaping millennials' experiences is the advent of a neoliberalism.

A political economy of generations has a particular view of the 'political' that draws on Bourdieu's theory of politics.[6] Bourdieu's theory of politics *(le politique)* sees the political field as a specific, structured space enabling 'traditional' politics-as-practice. His focus is on relations – and contests – over various capitals within this space. The political field is 'both as a field of forces and as a field of struggles aimed at transforming the relation of forces which confers on this field its structure at a given moment' (Bourdieu 1991: 171).

Powerful 'producers' monopolize the production of political goods offered on the political marketplace, while 'ordinary citizens' are reduced to the role of consumers outside this political field, except for elections. Theoretically, consumers have equal access to political goods; however, in practice, multiple factors limit this access, such as reduced social, cultural and symbolic capital. Those with access to these resources become knowledgeable consumers while those lacking them have no alternatives, and either abstain in elections or passively accept what their political representatives say. Those with significant symbolic and cultural capital will therefore serve as gatekeepers and boundary riders, establishing the boundaries of the field and who is allowed to play within it.

Political capital is a deeply fought over combination of symbolic and cultural capital. Once acquired, this political capital becomes form of symbolic capital in its own right:

credit founded on *credence* or belief and recognition or, more precisely, on the innumerable operations of credit by which agents confer on a person (or on an object) the very powers that they recognize in him (or it).

(Bourdieu 1991: 231)

Individuals are distributed throughout the political field according to the volume of capital they possess. Those who accumulate the most political capital tend to dominate, while those with the least will be dominated. This means that those who possess abundant symbolic and cultural capital in the political field are *the ones who get to say what the political is*.

Like most social fields, the political opinions of the dominant come to be seen as 'common sense', as the powerful come to be seen as having good political judgement. What might appear good political judgement (or technical competence) is actually an endowment of a certain habitus, arising from a mixture of symbolic and cultural capital. The domination, in turn, shapes the ideas that become common sense in the political field. The value of any political idea, from 'liberty' to 'austerity', depends less on its truth-value and more on the political capital of its proponents. Those with political capital will be able to present it as common sense and mobilise people around it.

Variations in this capital depend less on knowledge of politics, but on the social competence that translates to the feeling of having a 'right' to have a political opinion. Because the ability to formulate and articulate political opinions is unequally distributed, those with more resources are more likely to have the sense of entitlement to formulate and express a political opinion than those with little or none. As Bourdieu explained:

> The probability of producing a political response to a politically constituted question rises as one moves up the social hierarchy (and the hierarchy of incomes and qualifications).
>
> (Bourdieu 1984: 427)

The political field has its own autonomous logic. For Bourdieu, the object of politics is knowledge of the social world; the struggle over who gets to exercise authority in defining reality; and preserving the social order or promoting change. The last of these objectives is organized around two poles – those who are promoting order and those proposing change (e.g. conservatives or progressives). This binary logic supplies an orientation for political parties and ideologies that shapes the political field as a whole. The tension between order and change is ever present.

Bourdieu's political economy offers six insights into understanding young people's politics.

First, young people are largely excluded from the normal political field because they have not accumulated sufficient capital. Exclusionary processes range from legislative minimum voting ages, to just not being taken seriously.

Second, such exclusion from the political field may provoke reactions against the dominant bipartisan political consensus, which usually has a neoliberal frame. This reaction is likely to be stronger because of the many ways, documented in earlier chapters, that neoliberal policy-making has hurt the young; from housing market exclusion, to increasingly punitive welfare and criminal justice policies.

Third, this politics of consensus presents young people with an alienating choice between Tweedledum and Tweedledee. As we outline below, many young people will no longer accept this choice. The politics of many traditionally politically inclined young people will be neither centrist nor mainstream. Other young people will eschew the traditional political field altogether, and embrace alternate ways of mobilizing for change. Alternatives include campaigns like the anti-austerity Occupy movements in the US and UK, Spain's Indignados movements, anti-racist campaigns like 'Black Lives Matter' in the US, and anti-immigration movements like 'Reclaim Australia' and the English Defence League in the UK. All of these approaches are anathema to traditional politics and its neoliberal centre.

Fourth, it is worth noting that exclusion from the mainstream political field has unexpected advantages. It gives young people opportunities to develop new styles of political practice drawing on the expressive and technical affordances of new technologies. New technology, including social media, opens up access to new ways of mobilizing support and shaping public opinion, which do not depend on participation in the traditional political field.

Finally, it highlights that we should still expect young people's politics to be dismissed by traditionalists. Participants in the traditional political field, such as politicians and journalists, will still promote (and wield) the dominant forms of capital needed to monopolise political opinion. They have the power to define young people's new fields as 'not political', instead deriding them as a failure to participate 'properly', or as constituting various forms of deviance or criminality.

Politics online: distributed denial of service actions and hacking

Distributed denial of service action (DDoS) has become a popular form of online political activism. It involves making a computer network temporarily or indefinitely unavailable using digital technology. Typically, it entails calling on people to target a website at a particular time, flooding the website with requests and overloading systems. The result is that the targeted website can only respond slowly, or not at all, to the incoming traffic. This action does not normally damage files or data, or put security at risk. In many ways, DDoS activism is the digital equivalent to traditional protests like sit-ins, that involve people crowding into a space and creating bottlenecks in ways that cause disruption (Sauter 2014). This analogy encouraged Anonymous in 2013 to post a petition on the US White House website asking that DDoS actions be recognized as a legal form of protest similar to the Occupy Wall Street campaign (Jauregui 2013). However, many governments have criminalized DDoS, even as those governments use DDoS actions themselves (Zuckerman *et al.* 2010; see also Nazario 2009). In the US, for example, DDoS 'attacks' are a federal crime under the Computer Fraud and Abuse Act, while Britain outlawed DDoS and set a maximum penalty of 10 years in prison under its Police and Justice Act 2006.

Many high-profile campaigns, involving thousands of people, have been initiated by collectives like Lulzec and Anonymous. Many governments, including the US, Britain, China, Russia, Israel and Australia have been subject to DDoS actions, and campaigns have been mounted against the FBI and the CIA, as well as terrorist organisations like so-called Islamic State (Bessant 2016). It has also been used against corporations like Sony and Nintendo; and, as discussed above, organisations like Scientology. DDoS was central to highly organized protests against the US Congress when it was considering legislating its Stop Online Piracy legislation in 2011 and 2012. Stop Online Piracy legislation targeted people downloading free music, film and video. In this case, DDoS action involving approximately 9,000 people who targeted the FBI and Department of Justice was instrumental in persuading Congress not to proceed with the legislation (Bessant 2014; Bessant 2016: 1–17).

Beyond simple DDoS, hacktivist collectives like NullCrew engage in online political activism specifically targeting organisations they consider corrupt and involved in socially harmful behaviour. In 2012, they targeted the World Health Organization, protesting against poor health care systems. NullCrew, pointed to:

> the pathetic health-care. It's been decades and our Health Care system has never been what it should be. Thousands of people are dying just because of this. Either waiting in waiting rooms for too long, or not being able to pay the extreme amounts to be cared for. We deserve better. Now NullCrew has taken one step forward to fight for our proper rights.
>
> (NullCrew 2013)

NullCrew took similar action against a major South African internet service provider's online directory (ispdirectory.co.za) because they objected to reports of child-abuse and their reliance on child labour in sweatshops (Softpedia 2012).

NullCrew identifies itself as a defender of 'online innovation' and internet freedom. They protested against the Cambodian government after it arrested a Pirate Bay founder and joined campaigns against the US Congress online piracy bill, among others (Fuchs 2013). In the campaign against online piracy legislation, they accessed Time-Warner's website, defacing it for a few hours before adding an image of a gorilla. They declared this action was in support of open and free access, freedom of information, and against moves to detect and punish subscribers who use copyrighted content (Softpedia 2013).

When Coleman (2014) asked why those who were engaged in this kind of online action actually did it, she reported how they referred to the fun (the 'lulz') and the excitement that comes from 'straddling serious political protest and carnivalesque shenanigans'. While some spoke of 'the fun and thrill of it all', most identified an interest in democratic values like public accountability, the right to freedom of information, speech, and privacy, as well as ideas like fairness and justice. Others referred to a mixture of political and moral emotions, like outrage and indignation at the privileges claimed by organisations like Scientology or governments (Coleman 2014).

As predicted by a Bourdieun account, DDoS and hacking are often regarded as not 'real' politics. They are criticized as 'slactivism'/'clicktivism', a kind of 'lazy' politics which discourages traditional 'active' forms of politics like door knocking or joining political parties. Dismissing hacking as not political adds to the broader gloomy prospect that many political scientists are describing.[7] Some writers refer to an emerging democratic deficit among the young, while others talk about a youthful fear of politics, all the while dismissing actions like these and their prospects for reinvigorating our political culture.[8] Furedi (2005) and Mouffe (2005a) argue that the modern political consensus represents any diversity of political views as inefficient, dysfunctional and potentially dangerous, a tendency we particularly see when it comes to hacking.

These writers suggest we can reconceptualize 'the political' in ways that bypass the tacit consensus of what traditional politics is. Critchley (2007) and Unger (2014) argue that the preference for consensus over conflict subverts the democratic politics we actually need, which ought to embrace a genuine diversity of opinion, debate and action. According to Mouffe (2005b: 3) a democratic politics is one that aim to create a vibrant 'agonistic'[9] public sphere of contestation 'where different hegemonic political projects can be confronted'.

Apart from rejecting the fake consensus of neoliberal political cultures, these actions emphasise the role of 'non-rational' elements like emotion, morality, creativity, play and imagination. Critchley (2004:1), for example, emphasises the ethical ground of politics, offering a conception of politics that requires 'an experience of empowerment that is irreducibly *ethical*'. This entails a:

> ... disturbance of the political *status quo*, a meta-political disturbance of established politics for the sake of politics, that is, for the sake of a politics that does not close over into itself, becoming a whole, a state, the fantasy of the One, or what Levinas will call a totality.
>
> (Ibid.)

Framed by this body of political theory, the motivations and the consequences of hacking and DDoS actions look to be authentically political. DDoS, hacking and other digitally mediated protests are political in that they are motivated by a willingness to engage with matters of public interest in ways that enhance political participation and expand the public sphere.

Street politics: the English riots, 2011

In the summer of 2011, protesters took to the streets of London and 66 other sites across England. The catalyst was the police killing of Mark Duggan, a 29-year-old black man in the London suburb of Tottenham on 4 August. On 6 August, a peaceful protest in his community turned into 'riots', triggering further protests across London, Bristol, Manchester, Birmingham and Liverpool (Riots Communities and Victims Panel 2012: 3). For the next four days, England experienced one of the most widespread instances of public disorder in recent history (Bridges 2012:1). An estimated 15,000 people protested (Riots Communities and Victims Panel 2012: 3). Five people lost their lives, there was extensive looting and 3,975 people were arrested (Guardian/London School of Economics 2011). The damage was estimated to cost approximately half a billion pounds (Riots Communities and Victims Panel 2012).[10]

The 2011 protests began 15 months after the election of the Cameron Conservative-Liberal coalition government. The unrest caught the recently-elected government off-guard. Prime Minister Cameron was on vacation at the time and did not return to London until 9 August, the day before the riots ended (Watt 2011). One immediate and predictable response was that the riots were treated as an outbreak of criminality and hooliganism. Cameron dismissed the action as 'criminality, pure and simple' stating that those 'old enough to commit these crimes (were) old enough to face the punishment' (Sparrow 2011). The mainstream media concurred initially at least, framing the protests of August 2011 as 'youth in revolt'. Cameron picked up and ran with this theme, arguing that a 'lack of values' explained the riots. Here we see how representing the protest as a 'problem of juvenile deviance' drew on and reinforced a longstanding vocabulary of images, categories and narratives about 'delinquent teenagers' and 'dangerous thugs', which generations of social science experts had developed since the 1880s (Cohen 1972; Pearson 1983). Cohen's 'moral panic model' has some heuristic capacity to explain this response (1972).

A different response was advanced by some sociologists and criminologists when they said that these were 'shopping riots', a perspective picked up by politicians like the Conservative, Kenneth Clarke (2011), who said the riots were a product of frustrated consumerism created by a 'feral underclass, cut off from the mainstream in everything *but its materialism*'.

The idea these were 'shopping riots', seems to have originated with a journalist (Williams 2011), but others quickly joined in, interpreting it as the extreme image of neoliberalism. Big-hitting sociologists like Bauman (2011) pronounced they were riots of 'defective and disqualified consumers', and Zizek (2011) declared it was a case of violent consumerism, with the rioters declaring: 'you call on us to consume while simultaneously depriving us of the means to do it properly – so here we are doing it the only way we can'. According to Harvey (2012), the protesters 'are only doing what everyone else is doing, though in a different way – more blatantly and visibly, in the streets. They mimic, on the streets of London, what corporate capital is doing to planet earth'. For Treadwell *et al.* (2013: 14) the riots were not a response to widening social inequality, but an effect of

> the ruling ideology: grab what you can, look out for 'number one' and transform the self into a winner in advanced capitalism's interminable competition over the ability to acquire and display symbolically charged consumer goods.

Meanwhile, the 2011 riots seem to have been overlooked by British political science. A survey of British political science journals for 2011 to 2015 indicates there were no research publication addressing the 2011 riots published in the major political science journals, including the *Journal of Political Science, Political Studies, Political Studies Review* and *British Journal of Politics and International Relations.* A few criminologists, however, made the point the 2011 riots were political (Akram 2014; Newburn 2015; Newburn *et al.* 2015).

Bourdieu's point about the symbolic violence of experts, who deploy their cultural capital to draw the boundaries of the political field, is not lost on us nor a handful of other academics. Younge (2011), for example, points out that framing the riots as criminality or frustrated consumerism 'as though that alone explains their motivation, and [that] the context is irrelevant, is fatuous'. He explains:

> To stress criminality does not deny the political nature of what took place, it simply chooses to only partially describe it…. When a group of people join forces to flout both law and social convention, they are acting politically.
>
> (Younge Guardian/LSE 2011)

Newburn (2015: 60) made a similar point that, while some commentators saw the street protests as an exercise in violent consumerism, 'the danger in so doing is that the "political" and protest elements of the riots become marginalized'. They observed how commentary that focused on the looting as the distinguishing feature of the protests ran the risk of 'reducing the complexity' of the event to looting while 'ignoring other elements of the disorder, particularly the politics elements of the protest' (Newburn *et al.* 2015: 987).

One of the most compelling arguments for understanding street protests as political action was made by Martin Luther King, leader of the American civil rights movement before his murder in 1968. Speaking about 'riots' he said:

> It is not enough for me to stand before you tonight and condemn riots. It would be morally irresponsible for me to do that without, at the same time, condemning the contingent, intolerable conditions that exist in our society. These conditions are the things that cause individuals to feel that they have no other alternative than to engage in violent rebellions to get attention. And I must say tonight that a riot is the language of the unheard.
>
> (King 1968)

Research and analysis of demonstrations and disorder have long underscored King's point that protest and disorder are political. Many historians explored the political character of disorder caused by agricultural and industrial workers in the eighteenth and nineteenth centuries (Hammond and Hammond 1912; Thompson 1971; Rude and Hobsbawm 1973; Horspool 2009; and Bohstedt 2010). This historical insight encourages us to look beyond 'the immediate conditions in which such disorder occurs' and toward the legitimizing ideas or events that underpin them – namely their 'moral economy' (Newburn 2015: 48).

To understand this, Newburn developed a 'flashpoints' heuristic frame for identifying and analysing 'riots and disorder':

1 The structural (material circumstances of different social groups, their relationship with the state and how such factors relate to conflict)
2 Political/ideological (relationship between dissenting groups to political and ideological institutions and how dissenting groups are treated by those institutions)
3 Cultural (how different social groups understand the social world and their place in it)
4 Context (the long-term and immediate backdrop to relationships – for example between particular groups and police – within which disorder occurs)
5 Situational (the spatial and social determinants of disorder)
6 The interactional (the dynamics of interaction between police and protesters) (ibid.).

Using this heuristic approach, Newburn *et al.* pointed to certain commonalities between the British 2011 protests and a string of earlier protests that had threaded through the Thatcher years (1979–1990), the early years of New Labour (1997–2007) and into the Conservative Cameron–May administration (2010–) (Newburn 2015; Newburn *et al.* 2015). The major 'outbreaks' in 2011 tended to occur in sites of earlier riots, that is, urban inner-city communities with high concentrations of black young people in the early to mid-1980s, such as Brixton in 1981; in predominantly white working-class housing estates in the urban periphery in the early 1990s, such as Meadowell 1991; and in north of England mill-towns in 2001, like Bradford.

All these protests, including the 2011 protests, occurred during periods of economic downturn and relatively high levels of unemployment. They were presided over by a combination of right-wing and centrist Labour governments driving a radical neoliberal policy agenda, whose leaders were indifferent to increasing evidence of social inequality.

A further commonality was ethnicity, an issue that informed most protest actions in post-war Britain (Newburn *et al.* 2011). According to the *Guardian/* London School of Economics (2011) survey of those who participated in the 2011 protests across the country:

a significant factor in sparking the disturbances was the humiliation, unjust suspicion, lack of respect and targeting that characterises the way rioters felt the police carry out stop and search.... The complaint of harassment by those interviewed on the receiving end of stop and search was made in every city the research took place in and by interviewees from different racial groups and ages.

Reicher and Stott (2011) likewise argued the 2011 riots were responses to racialized policing. In the three months to the end of June 2011, there were 6,894 police stop and searches in the one local borough of Haringey, with only 87 of these resulting in an arrest (Reicher and Stott 2011: 47). They also noted how 'stop and searches' had increased steadily and were directed disproportionately at young black and Asian people.

Researchers established that participants in the 2011 riots found themselves on the streets for a variety of reasons. Some went to see what was happening, some went to participate in the excitement and others went to protest (*Guardian/ LSE* 2011; Newburn *et al.* 2015). Yet much of the research carried out in the wake of those protests reveals that many who took part had a history of bad relations with police, many lived in poverty and were angry about government attempts to introduce 'austerity' policies (Guardian/LSE 2011: 11). Others referred to the absence of employment opportunities for young people, and a failing justice system (Riots Communities and Victims Panel 2012: 3). While the 2011 protests were unplanned, they enabled the spontaneous expression of people feeling suddenly freed from everyday constraints.

Other street-based protest actions – like the 2005 French protests, the 2006 French anti-discriminatory labour laws protests, the Occupy protests (2011–), the *Indignados* or 15-M Spanish protests, the US 'Black Lives Matter' movement and the recent French *Nuit Debout* (Rise-up All Night) protest action (2016) – were moved by a parallel sense of 'situated injustice', by concerns about inequality, and anger about the unwillingness of governments to deal with 'the big issues'. As Jocelyn, a 26 year old participating in the 2016 *Nuit Debout* protest, reported:

> The idea is to let everyone speak out. People are really sick and tired and that feeling has been building for years. Everything Hollande once promised for the left but gave up on really gets me down. Personally, it's the state of emergency, the new surveillance laws, the changes to the justice system and the security crackdown.
>
> (In Chrisafis 2016)

Cecile, a French law student also engaged in *Nuit Debout* agreed:

> I don't agree with the state society is in today. To me, politics feels broken. This movement appeals in terms of citizen action. I come here after class and I intend to keep coming back. I hope it lasts.
>
> (Ibid.)

Politics as laughter: Catalan satire

Facu Díaz, a 23-year-old Spanish comedian produced a video satire titled 'The Popular Party is Dissolved'. On 29 October 2014, it was broadcast on the Spanish 'Tuerka', an internet news program, before spilling out onto social media. The skit lasted three minutes. It begins with Díaz sitting at a desk, facing the camera wearing a distinctive black balaclava like those worn by the Basque separatist group Euskadi Ta Askatasuna (ETA).[11] On the wall behind him were logos resembling those of the ruling conservative Christian 'Popular Party' (PP).

On the desk was a photo of Francisco Granados, former Minister in the Popular Party who was sentenced to prison on charges of corruption in late 2014.[12] Díaz read a statement, supposedly from the 'People's Party', in a style caricaturing statements issued by ETA before announcing the People's Party was collapsing and being disbanded. The party, he announced, would end their 'armed activity' and 'surrender' their 'weapons'. This was a reference to the arrests of many People's Party politicians and their associates on corruption charges. Pretending to be a spokesperson for People's Party, Díaz called for a 'ceasefire from far left-wing political group'. It was a reference to the relatively new and increasingly popular party Podemos ('We Can').

The satire used remixes to create official sounding announcements. One statement referred to People's Party corruption prisoners, (a reference to politicians now prisoners). The statement called for the prisoners' relocation to jails 'closer to … where 'the food is good', a barbed reference to ETA's earlier demands that their imprisoned members be relocated to their Basque homeland. Díaz then carried out a mock interview, asking himself what he will do as a comedian if the People's Party closes its doors under the weight of the corruption scandals. He answers himself saying he would lose a rich source of material and inspiration for his satires. He then reverted to being a People's Party official, announcing that several wayward members of that party would be integrated back into political life through the newly created right wing Christian Popular Party, breakaway party 'VOX' (Voice) and the anti-separatist UPyD.

To understand what then happened we need to recall that many Spaniards were still suffering from the hardship triggered by the 2008 recession. The hardship was aggravated by government decisions to implement austerity policies, described as adjustments necessary to stabilise the economy. These policies included cuts to public spending, such as public sector salary and job cuts, increased taxes and charges for basic amenities like electricity, and cuts to welfare.

Any reference to high-level corruption that drew links between elite corruption and Basque terrorism was likely to elicit a strong reaction. Díaz was not to be disappointed, and his skit infuriated elite powerbrokers. They encouraged a group calling themselves the Victims of Terror Support Group (Dignity & Justice) to allege that Diaz had humiliated victims of terrorism. Pablo Iglesia, the Secretary General of *Podemos,* Spain's new left-wing party, defended Díaz on Twitter. This produced an immediate response from the ruling People's Party government. A government spokesman repeated the claim that Díaz was ridiculing victims of 'ETA terrorism': 'we cannot support those who make mockery of the 'victims of terror' (Barreda 2015). Díaz replied that his satire was directed at the 'People's Party' and not victims of ETA:

> I can come to understand that the [People's Party] offense, because it gives an exaggerated context the issue, but … to say I'm laughing at the victims, if at any time you see the video none of you will see a reference to the victims.
>
> (Díaz 2014)

However it became clear that Díaz would face a trial. On 8 January 2015, one day after the murderous attack by Islamist radicals on the Paris office of the satirical magazine *Charlie Hebdo*, the Spanish High Court charged Díaz with 'humiliating victims of terrorism' in his comedy sketch. The Spanish Popular Party introduced new Citizens Security Laws, and 'gag laws' to outlaw this kind of critique. These laws were subsequently described as presenting the biggest threat to democratic rights since General Francisco Franco. In Spain, large numbers of people rallied online and on the streets to support the satirist (Facu Díaz of #YoconFacu – 'I'm with you Facu'). Díaz's trial began as millions of people mobilized across Europe in support of freedom of the press in the wake of the *Charlie Hebdo* attack. The irony was not lost on Díaz and his supporters.

On 15 January 2015 Díaz found himself before the Spanish High Court on a charge of 'glorifying terrorism'. The charge carried a maximum penalty of two years' imprisonment. During the proceedings, he answered questions about his 'mocking tone'. However, the magistrate, Javier Gomez Bermudez, terminated the case, concluding that Díaz had not contravened the law and that his satire was not humiliating for victims of terrorism. As he explained: 'Like it or not, it [the satire] does not discredit or humiliate the victims' (Europa Press 2015).

Ranciere (2010) and Critchley (2012) provide accounts of politics that recognise the role of moral emotions, the value of dissent, and is inclusive of practices like satire and other comedic performance. According to Critchley (2012), satire and humour help bring about change. Satire creates humour by pointing to the incongruities or disjunctures between the ways things are represented, what is actually happening, and what should or could be.

Humour and play energise and renew democratic practice. They entail expressions of emotions including moral emotions (outrage, righteous anger, a sense of injustice) and ethical responses to situated injustices (Critchley 2012). In this way, the arts, and satire, in particular, work as a binding influence in politics and achieve this in ways that are missing from deliberative practices understood as communicative, rational, directed towards consensus-based decision-making processes. It's an understanding quite different to mainstream notions of politics as devoid of emotion, play and ethics.

For the Russian literary theorist Bakhtin (1984), folk-humour, which includes satire, formed a critical part of ancient and medieval European carnival and served important public functions like comic relief from the grind of daily life. It also offered a glimpse into alternative social relations and opportunities to question the established order. As Bakhtin argued, the carnival,

> celebrated temporary liberation from the prevailing truth and from the established order; it marked the suspension of all hierarchical rank, privileges, norms, and prohibitions. Carnival was the true feast of time, the feast of becoming, change, and renewal.
>
> (Bakhtin 1984: 10)

Carnival provided abrupt and brief moments in time when normality was placed on to hold make way for festivity, indulgence, and freedoms and when everything was turned upside down. Carnivals created eccentric social spaces constrained by few limitations. Normal rules of law, and regulation that governed daily life, were suspended, giving way to creative energies. They were inclusive communal pageants characterized by the inversion of conventional hierarchies that demarcated castes and cultures. In these short-lived moments, the powerless assumed powerful identities, peasants became kings, royalty was dethroned and everyone transgressed from one to another through costume, mask, music, dance and festivity. For a short time, the idea of social equality and collaboration reigned.

These communal performances inverted the traditional social order. They replaced the mono-logical flow of single authoritative voice with 'dialogue'; a rare open space of interacting and contesting voices (Bakhtin 1992). 'The powerful' and 'respected' became objects of satire, and serious weighty matters became objects of playful subversion. Soon after normality returned, traditional power relations were re-inscribed and order restored. It served as a reminder that things change, that the norms that govern our lives and the power operating within the world is historically specific, made up and will, in time, change. Protests deploying 'the carnivalesque' and other critical art practices are important forms of contemporary political expressivity. Drawing on Bakhtin's (1984) account of carnival, certain forms of contemporary humour are beginning to rearrange political space. Bakhtin (ibid.) appreciates how satire works to create upside-down worlds while Appiah (2010) reminds us how moral revolutions begin in laughter and mockery. Humour and ridicule challenges the idea the status quo is natural and inevitable by highlighting its contingency and fragility in the face of laughter and ridicule.

In these ways, we see the generative capacity of new media in creating political action in the form of satire and other kinds of absurdity, jesting and comedic critique. While Bahktin (1984) maintained that carnival had gone into decline in the eighteenth century, we see courtesy of digital media, a rebirth, of a carnivalesque spirit evident, for example, in the popularity of contemporary satire, parody and other forms of political comedy. If we take the case of Facu Díaz as an example of the kind of satire now populating the internet and more traditional media, it becomes evident that carnivalesque imaginary and practice is alive and well.

Contemporary moral philosophers like Nussbaum (2015) also observe how emotions are central to our cognitive and evaluative capacities. Moral emotions that evoke laughter, indignation or outrage are not simply irrational acts or impulses that obstruct 'proper' 'cool-headed' political deliberation. As Nussbaum argues, emotions including those of love are central to a conception of justice. They help ground our understandings of experience and inform our judgements. They can be part of our reaction and ethical response to injustice like corruption, or unfairness. While saying this, it's also worth remembering how emotions like pride in one's country and fear can inform a politics that promotes violence and hate.

Politics of the ultra-right in Australia

Alongside a growth of left-wing or progressive youth politics, is a growing network of young, radical ultra-right and 'patriotic' movements. Australia is one of many countries now home to an assemblage of far-right, para-military, ultra-nationalist, anti-Semitic, anti-Islamic, neo-Nazi movements, which are attractive to young activists (Liddington 2015). The medley of loosely associated ultra-right wing nationalists and neo-Nazi groups include Reclaim Australia, the Patriotic Youth League, the Australian Defence League, True Blue Crew, and the National Democratic Party of Australia to name but a few. There are also Australian branches of international ultra-right groups like the English Defence League and the Greek neo-Nazi Golden Dawn party.

Their politics share common features to the European and American far-right, including overt white racism, xenophobia, and social conservatism aimed at bolstering male values and privilege. They understand themselves as Australian patriots preserving and protecting a white, Anglo-Saxon heritage against particular groups, including Muslims, Jews, immigrants, and indigenous Australians. There is a strong anti-globalization framework. There is also considerable antagonism directed at internationalist agencies like the UN and its human rights project, which these groups see as a direct threat to 'Australian sovereignty'. There is a tendency to claim a historical link with earlier far-right movements. Blair Cottrell, Chairman of Australia's United Patriots Front (UPF), has a Facebook page with images of Hitler and argues that pictures of Hitler need to be hung on the walls of all Australian schools (Cotrell, cited in Bachelard and McMahon 2015).

Like other political movements, the mostly young male members of UPF rely on a combination of traditional political action (protests, street marches etc.) and new social media as a medium for expressing opinions and mobilising support. Members of the UPF use all available social networks (Twitter, Instagram) to market themselves. Much of the content they share is self-promotion, featuring images of 'on the street actions' alongside interviews of members detailing their rationale for joining UPF. Promotional stunts for rallies also become content for YouTube videos, like footage of 'Tommy' waving a national flag over a freeway bridge on a Friday evening at peak hour. He explained to the camera what was happening:

> all these working class people driving home from work on a Friday arvo are tooting in support of Australian nationalism. Maybe they are not a big fan of equalitarianism (*sic*) and internationalism after all ...
>
> (Sewell nd)

A dominant and persistent theme in their publicity is what they see as evidence of the Muslim takeover of Australia. Films like *The Unholy Quran* illustrate their message and style. Set against a musical backdrop of hard punk, the film opens with images of the Qur'an, graphic pictures of injured and bloody children, images of Osama bin Laden and ISIS 'warriors threatening infidels' ... all designed to represent Islam as a direct and immediate threat to Australia (United Patriots Front 2016).

The use of bloody violence to denote the threat is a common theme in UPF promotions. In October 2015, members of the UPF gathered outside council offices in the regional city of Bendigo to protest plans to build a mosque. Part of the protests involved cutting the head off a dummy and spraying fake blood on the steps outside the council. These groups deploy violence as a political strategy online as well (Arzheimer and Carter 2006; Pilkington 2014).

According to UPF member Chris Shortis, ultra-right groups are victims of discriminatory treatment by police because when they engage in violence, there is a zero-tolerance response compared with the 'soft treatment' anti-fascists receive when they act violently. As Shortis explains, indigenous people get away with violence when they 'assault police and destroy government buildings. (Then) it's called protests, when the UPF does things like this there are serious consequences' (Shortis nd).

Thomas Sewell, member of the UPF, describes his political commitments as rational. He rejects allegations that he is irrational or Islamophobic because he says the threat of 'the enemy' is real. For Sewell (2015), those who insist on 'political correctness' are the irrational and foolish ones because they don't appreciate the danger:

> we currently have a 17-year-old in custody for making homemade bombs. This is all for a plot to kill Australians on mother's day.... It is not the Australian people who have voted for this Islamic nature that is growing in our country.... A lot of people say that this kind of language is Islamophobic, and what I'm saying is against this rule of political correctness and how we are meant to talk.... Islamophobia is the irrational fear of Islam. Does it seem irrational to you when today we have the incident of a 17-year-old being arrested for making a homemade bomb?

Likewise, while participating in a march in Brunswick, Melbourne, one young man from a similar far-right group – Reclaim Australia – argued a 'rational' case for what he saw as justice in the electoral system:

> we've got to look at how we can make changes in parliament.... We can highlight the problem on the street, and we can bring more people to a movement on the street, but we need to make changes in parliament itself. So we've got to bring more patriotic Australians into these marches, wake more people up, get more people voting differently. Liberal and Labor are poison are treasonous, they do nothing but sell our country out to foreign investors. They ... open up the borders and allow a flood of Islamic immigration into this country.
>
> (DyslexicCBeanie 2016)

Anti-globalization and anti-foreigner sentiments permeate much of the rhetoric of the ultra-right. As Cottrell (2016) explained on Facebook: 'People are waking up all over the world. No longer will the people be silenced. No longer shall we submit to foreign globalism'.

He then made a call to arms to 'fight for your country' 'so you can preserve your nation which is you and your children and the future of your people'. He seems committed to the idea that he is serving 'a greater purpose', and is willing to make a sacrifice for the greater good:

> We are all here for a greater purpose. We are here to fight and protect what we love … and government these days it gets around as if it created us.
>
> (Ibid.)

These insider accounts provide insight into why some young people join or sympathise with protest action against Islam and immigration and why they promote ultra-right ideas through the social media and other means. As unpalatable as it seems, many of those committed to these ultra-right groups think the ideas and arguments they espouse are perfectly reasonable.

When a young man identifying as a 'patriot' talks of national security and the need to be proud of 'our culture' to protect 'our heritage', he espouses sentiments and powerful political emotions like loyalty and pride that many other people feel. Such sentiments and views also resonate with many working in mainstream media and with some politicians as they justify the need for war or the need to suspend certain civil rights to ensure national safety against the threat of terrorism. Membership of ultra-right groups also offers friendship and comradeship as well as a novelty, and the chance to be a 'hero'. It is attractive because it provides a 'noble' mission, a sense of purpose combined with ideas about duty, self-sacrifice and honour.

Neil Erikson, now 31 and a former neo-Nazi, says he 'started out in the neo-Nazi movement when [he] was about 16…. If you want to show pride in Australia, there was no other place to go' (Toohey 2016). He went on to explain the attraction to such groups and why he stayed:

> In hindsight, it's appealing to join something like that. But there are darker sides to neo-Nazis – lost kids, lost people. Until this patriotic rise of Reclaim last year, there was no one to hang out with apart from neo-Nazis.
>
> (Ibid.)

It is also helpful to pay attention to the semiotics of the rallies and marches. The clothes, the tattoos, the iconic memorabilia including flags, 'white pride' banners, masks and 'Aussie digger' (soldier) tags are strongly associated with Australian identity and patriotism. As young 'fighters', the uniform, paraphernalia and gestures like salutes of ultra-right groups is important part of their self-proclamations of who they are. So too are catchphrases ('Rise Without fear') and chants like the football chant: 'Aussie Aussie Aussie oi oi oi' regularly 'performed' at rallies and protests to energize the group, express their solidarity and enthusiasm for 'the cause'.

Conclusion

The political economy of generations suggests that the political field (which includes politicians, policy-makers, journalists and academics) tends to exclude young people. One form of exclusion is denying the legitimacy of their concerns about the consequences of neoliberal policy, like inequality and hikes in tertiary fees. Another, often connected, form of exclusion is to deny that their responses to this are political, by instead labelling them lazy, delinquent or criminal. These denials are often effective because they resonate with and affirm long-standing and influential discourses of young people as 'inherently troubled and troublesome'.

Instead, we have argued that DDoS actions, hacking, satire and street protects are 'political' in ways that expand the repertoire of the political beyond the traditional framework.[13] This challenge has potential consequences for 'producers' who currently monopolise the political field: legitimizing other fields challenges their domination. On this point, we would like to note the current preoccupation with national security has become so dominant that it is undermining core features of liberal democracies, particularly civil liberties and the rule of law. Given this context, the emergence of alternative politics and a challenge to the status quo is timely.

Finally as we demonstrated here, and as a growing body of research confirms, young people are drawing on the affordances of new media to engage in politics. They are recreating the fields of politics in novel, but legitimate, ways.

Notes

1 See Collin (2007, 2008); Middaugh (2012); and Phelps (2012).
2 See Kimberlee (2002); Henn *et al.* (2005); Henn and Weinstein (2006); Edwards (2007); and Furlong and Cartmel (2012).
3 While this seems comparatively high, voting is compulsory in Australia – legally, it should be 100 per cent enrolment.
4 See variously Vromen and Collin (2010); Vesnic-Alujevic (2012); Soler-i-Marti (2012); Sloan (2014); and Vromen *et al.* (2014).
5 See also Bessant (2004, 2014); Manning (2009); Harris *et al.* (2010a), Farthing (2010); and Gordon and Taft (2011).
6 Kauppi (2002) suggests there are three aspects of Bourdieu's thinking about politics: a general analysis of the social aspects of the political (*la politique*), a specific analysis of politics (*le politique*), and the political practice he developed at the end of his career (Bourdieu 1998). We engage largely the first.
7 See, for example, Mouffe (2005a, 2005b); Critchley (2007); Zizek (2014); and Unger (2014).
8 Those who talk of a crisis of democracy include Norris (1999), Bauman (1999), Posner (2010) and Graeber (2013); while others speak of a 'fear of politics', like Furedi (2005); Hay (2007); Ginsborg (2009); and Hay and Stoker (2009).
9 *Agonism* refers to a 'we' relationship in which the conflicting parties declare commitments to shared ethical-political principles. It is not to be confused with *antagonism,* a 'we-they' relationship where those involved are 'enemies' and do not share common ground.
10 Some saw in the 2011 protests a pattern evident in history. Dilmot (2012) suggested that roughly every decade in summer, England appears to riot, from the 1981 English race riots, to the 1990 Poll Tax riots.

11 The Spanish government claims ETA is responsible for killing 829 people, injuring thousands and undertaking dozens of kidnappings. The EU has designated it a terrorist group.
12 Granados belonged to syndicates of political elites who had been receiving kickbacks of 2–3 per cent on government contracts worth €250 million.
13 In making this case we do not deny there were criminal acts in political actions such as, for example, the 2011 riots, although this needs to also acknowledge the power of the state to constitute the 'criminal'.

9   A new intergenerational contract

We live in a world being radically reshaped by the convergence of two tectonic plates bumping up against each other, producing increasingly serious 'creative disruptions'. One is the consequence of decades of neoliberal policy-making involving deregulation, privatization and fiscal austerity. While neoliberal policy-makers said we would all benefit from the combination of globalization, deregulation and privatization, these policies were actually intended to serve the needs and interests of a small but powerful set of financial institutions and economic interests. The 2008 recession epitomized the damage done over those decades.

The other is the transformation now underway involving the displacement of an industrial, work-based social and economic order. We are seeing the disappearance of an industrial work-based order courtesy of what is variously called the 'Information Society' (Fuchs 2014), the 'Digital Transformation' (Brown *et al.* 2011) or the 'Fourth Revolution' (Micklethwait and Wooldridge 2014). New forms of digital labour, information capital and robotic technologies are steadily displacing both high- and low-skill labour. This is a transformation on a scale paralleled only by a few periods of radical change like the agricultural revolution (around 11,000 BCE), or more recently what Polanyi (2001) called the 'Great Transformation' of Europe between 1600–1800. Unlike those earlier epochal transformations, this period of change promises to be both more rapid and more radical. Both processes are already bearing down on young people. Young people born since 1980 are already experiencing significant generational disadvantage.

While what is meant by an intergenerational contract is open to interpretation, the current circumstances involve a significant breach of an intergenerational contract on two grounds. One understanding of an intergenerational contract is the idea that each generation will not be worse off than the previous generation. This is not the case for many young people today. Another version of an implied intergenerational contract is the promise that young people will benefit if they agree to spend more time in secondary and higher education. Their investment in human capital would be rewarded with secure jobs, higher incomes and 'a good life'. That promise has also been broken.

The time is ripe to think about repairing the breach and to prepare for the digital disruption. One way of doing this is to imagine what a new intergenerational contract might look like.

In this chapter, we identify some principles that might inform such a project. We have in mind an intergenerational contract that includes young people in its making and benefits young people – and everyone else. In what follows we outline what we understand by an intergenerational contract, then point to certain prejudices that have impacted negatively on young people. We then identify some considerations that might inform a revised intergenerational contract. In doing so we draw on the work of Sen, Nussbaum and Unger as well as on the political economy of generations outlined earlier in this book.

An intergenerational contract

Many people have explored the idea of an intergenerational contract and the related idea of intergenerational justice. For Laslett and Fishkin (1992) intergenerational justice was couched in terms of the rights of persons not yet born. Accordingly, intergenerational justice requires that people today recognize

> the rights of all future persons regardless of geographical position or temporal position. No generation is at liberty to ransack the environment or to overload the earth with more people than can be supported ... or to act in such a way as to ensure that the human race will disappear.
>
> (Laslett and Fishkin 1992: 14–15)

Yet Laslett and Fishkin also acknowledge serious difficulties with treating the 'intergenerational contract' as a legal process because it forces us to consider the utility of describing rights and duties across generations as a 'contract' (ibid.: 62–63). While we acknowledge these challenges, we suggest there are some basic considerations worth remembering.

The notion of an intergenerational contract is an old idea and does not need to be understood in a legal or contractual way. The eighteenth-century writer and politician Edmund Burke offered a helpful non-legal conception of such a contract when he said 'Society is indeed a contract.... The state ... is ... a partnership not only between those who are living, but between those who are living, those who are dead, and those who are to be born' (Burke 2001: 261). For Burke, it was a partnership understood in political terms that established a relationship of duties and rights *over time*:

> You will observe that, from the *Magna Carta* to the Declaration of Right, it has been the uniform policy of our constitution to claim and assert our liberties, as an *entailed inheritance* delivered to us from our forefathers, and to be transmitted to our prosperity ...
>
> (Burke 1812: 59–60)

According to Burke, 'we receive, we hold, we transmit our government and our privileges, in the same manner in which we enjoy and transmit our property and our lives' (ibid.: 12).

Burke was suggesting that passing on political traditions has the same permanence and solidity as bequeathing an acre of land to our children, or when we transmit some part of ourselves by sexual procreation in the embodied form of a child. We also transmit cultural capital like literature, music, art works, stories, myths, or scientific knowledge to our children in the family, in schools and other cultural spaces. In each case, there is an understanding that doing these things is intrinsically valuable and that if we engage in these intergenerational transfers well, then the living, the dead, and those not yet born will all benefit.

Yet intergenerational justice is not just about what is transmitted to people not-yet-born in some imagined future. The wellbeing of older people in America, Australia and Europe has been privileged at the expense of younger people. As we argued, a neoliberal political project has hijacked the conception of intergenerational justice. Claiming to be concerned about the fairness of bequeathing fiscal obligations to young people and those not yet born, neoliberals promoted exercises in generational accounting ostensibly to achieve fiscal sustainability, but ignoring contemporary intergenerational equity. This failure parallels the larger refusal of 'welfare states' to assess or address intergenerational equity (Tapper 2002). This matters because intergenerational justice is *also about the degree of fairness of intergenerational relations right now*.

Developing a new intergenerational contract is a project that can be assisted by understanding the failure to think about intergenerational justice. Several things explain that failure. As we noted in Chapter 4, they include the absence of a defensible account of justice. Another issue is the absence of young people from the political and policy-making processes, an absenteeism often justified by certain prejudicial beliefs about young people. In what follows we address these factors while making the case that young people need to be involved in making a new intergenerational contract that encompasses an understanding of justice and certain minimal political principles.

Prejudices about young people

The unwillingness to acknowledge or address the problem of contemporary intergenerational unfairness relies on several unhelpful and deep-seated age-based prejudices (Young-Bruehl 2012). If progress is to be made in developing an intergenerational contract, these prejudices require acknowledgment before they can be overturned. To develop a generational contract, obstacles like the belief that young people lack the moral competence or cognitive abilities to make ethically informed or rational choices that adults presumably possess need to be put to rest.

A widespread and common-sense set of ideas exists that young people and children are insufficiently cognitively capable or ethically developed to participate in the deliberative processes needed to inform a defensible intergenerational contact. This common sense reflects long-standing paternalist assumptions grounded in the view that young people and children lack certain features of adult competency or defining aspects of humanity. This view, in turn, underpinned exclusionary political, legal, educational and social practices designed to protect young people from adult practices.

Across the twentieth century, experts developed, reproduced and confirmed this commonsense. It was given authoritative form by the influential psychologist Jean Piaget, who concluded that children and young people were rationally inferior to adults by drawing a direct analogy between 'savages' and children (1932). Piaget said 'early man' and all children shared what he called 'pre-operational thought', which meant they could not engage in 'hypothetico-deductive reasoning'. Like Piaget, the anthropologist Charles Hallpike argued that children and 'primitives' think alike because they are 'pre-literate' (1979). Similarly, Kohlberg's (1981) account of moral development drew on Piaget's claim that rational thought and morality develop through constructive stages. For Kohlberg, the process of moral development related to justice (defined in Kantian terms) because it relied on universal ethical principles and reasoning. Kohlberg described six developmental stages, each more adequate at responding to moral dilemmas than its predecessor. His work assumed humans learn to argue as they evolve across stages of moral reasoning.

Talking about freedom and young people in the same breath tends to elicit deeply entrenched and naturalized age-based prejudices. After all, don't we all 'know' that young people lack the moral or intellectual capacity to exercise such freedom, *and the younger a person is, the less their capacity* (Bessant 2014a). Not only has this prejudice drawn on and entered into various political, philosophical and psychological disciplines and allied fields of practice, ironically it has entered into the very tradition of inquiry we draw on to develop ideas for an intergenerational contract.

Kohlberg's work influenced political philosophers like Habermas, who thinks young people should not be asked to do things they cannot 'naturally' do, like engage in deliberative and rational practices needed for engagement in the 'public sphere' (2004: 10). As we argue, other major theorists and defenders of democracy, like Arendt, Sen and Nussbaum, also argue that young people should not, or cannot exercise substantive freedom – and thus engage in any kind of adult political practice requiring deliberation.

Arendt made this point in her account of the role Elizabeth Eckford, a 15-year-old African-American girl, played in a political conflict involving a newly racially desegregated school in Little Rock, Arkansas in 1957. Arendt was fervently opposed to what took place. 'No one,' Arendt said

> will find it easy to forget the photograph reproduced ... throughout the country, showing a Negro girl [Elizabeth Eckford], accompanied by a white friend of her father, walking away from school, persecuted and followed into bodily proximity by a jeering and grimacing mob of youngsters.
>
> (Arendt 1959: 50)

Arendt's concern was that Elizabeth Eckford was required to be a 'hero' for a political cause that 'neither her absent father nor the equally absent representatives of the 'National Association for the Advanced of Colored People (NAACP) felt called upon to be' (ibid.). 'Have we now come to the point,' Arendt asks, 'where it is the children who are being asked to change or improve the world? And do we intend to have our political battles fought out in the schoolyards?' (ibid.).

For Arendt, politics is adult business and not the place for young people. Arendt's view depends on her distinctions between 'the private' and 'the public' and between 'the social' and 'the political', and on her understanding that schools are institutions designed to support the child's move from home and family (the social) to the public life of the world (the political). The school therefore is a non-political space. According to this view, young people like 15-year-old Elizabeth Eckford can only have limited positive freedom.

Even proponents of the capabilities theory of justice-as-freedom give credence to this idea. Sen and Nussbaum argue that the younger a person the more restricted their freedom ought to be because it can adversely impact their future 'adult-freedom'. Sen accepts the view that older people are best placed and qualified to decide for young people for when they 'grow up [they] must have more freedom, so when you are considering a child, you have to consider not only the child's freedom now, but also the child's freedom in the future' (Sen, cited in Saito 2003: 25). If, for example, a young person chooses to withdraw from studying mathematics they will lose the freedom later in life to choose to pursue career options that require mathematics. Nussbaum warns against this, describing it as 'capability-destruction', arguing that it 'is a particularly grave matter and as such should be off limits' (2011: 27). A young person can only make minor decisions and ought therefore to be restricted to minor decision-making. The concern here is with the future, when: 'they will actually exercise some freedom' (Sen, cited in Saito 2003: 26).

A three-day-old baby or a three-year-old child cannot choose to make substantive decisions. Equally, they will at some point acquire the capacity to make these choices. The question is when. Our political economy of generations understands that many social fields including schools are political spaces. Many young people experience this field as a critical site of political contest where important goods or social harms are at stake and where young people can pursue redress (Nakata 2008). Indeed, it is because young people are directly affected by a range of other policies (including education), that their political agency needs to be recognized and supported rather than denied on a priori grounds.

We argue that young people can, and ought to, exercise political agency as soon as they express that intention. As we explain later in this chapter, expression of that interest is the point when their capability to do so ought to be recognized. This is one reason why a capabilities framework should be used to inform a new intergenerational contract.

This matters because if exercising freedom is critical for a good life, it is then just as important for young people as it for their elders. Moreover, we assume the purpose of public and private interventions, like education, is to help ensure that a young person's capacity to make choices becomes a real ability. The question this raises is how will young people develop their capacity for political agency, a question central to the task of developing a defensible intergenerational contract.

Accordingly, we turn to the task of saying why and how an intergenerational contract needs to be informed by ideas about a good life and justice, and then consider the kind of political principles that might inform an intergenerational contract. What ethical considerations are pertinent? To clarify the core aspects of the good life we need to engage in ethical or practical deliberation centering on ideas about a just society and a good life. We begin by drawing on the political economy of generation approach offered in this book. The relational political economy of generations outlined in this book points to the purpose of developing an intergenerational contract based on what Bourdieu calls an ethics of recognition in terms of the relations within a generation and between different generations. We argue that certain affinities exist between a political economy of generations and Sen and Nussbaum's capabilities approach to justice.

If the ethical refers to a good life, then the political refers to ways of organizing our lives to articulate and achieve a good life. This means asking how we should and can organize policies and practices to promote the obligations identified.

Because the processes in developing an intergenerational contract ought to be deliberative, we are not overly prescriptive or pre-emptive. The political dimensions of an intergenerational contract also entail not speaking on behalf of others, a practice young people have been subjected to too often. This is why we cannot offer a list of '20 things to do' to address the problem of intergenerational unfairness. Our focus is on the considerations that might lead to such process of working out the content.

Thinking about ethics

How does a political economy of generations help in clarifying the ethical issues? Doesn't a political economy see ethical ideas as the product of our social and political arrangements designed to justify the interests of the powerful?

For a long time social scientists thought so. In the nineteenth century, Marx argued the ruling classes produced ethical ideas to justify their unfair and unequal share of wealth and their oppression of the working class. This implies that ethical ideas simply reflect class structures and powerful interests. Through the twentieth century, many argued that ethical ideas are products of social structures like class, ethnicity and gender and so are best understood as social constructs that serve various social functions. From this perspective, ethics as something valuable in itself is not only futile, but potentially dangerous; and ethical ideas are best understood as 'ideologies' and something to be un-masked (Sayer 2005). Isn't Bourdieu, who is in some ways a 'Marxist', likely to treat ethical ideas as a mask for 'real' political interests? This implies he reduces ethics to being an effect of power, because powerful people use ethical language and ideas to disguise their actions or to justify their power. A close reading of his work, however, reveals a more complex story.

In his early career Bourdieu certainly saw ethics as a mask used by powerful interests, and thus understood ethics as the effect of power (Pellandini-Simanyi 2014). In his theory of practice-as-habitus he argued that people incorporate into themselves different conditions of existence and moral frameworks, which model what it is to be a proper person. This is 'inculcated in the earliest years of life' until it becomes a 'permanent disposition, embedded in the agents' bodies in the form of mental dispositions, schemes of perception and thought (1977: 15). At the same time, Bourdieu also saw ethics as part of the unconscious competitive strategies we use to maintain and advance social position and to acquire and legitimate power or 'symbolic power'. Using and adding to our symbolic power is central to our social life because life is a struggle:

> to win everything which, in the social world, is of the order of belief, credit and discredit, perception and appreciation, knowledge and recognition – name, renown, prestige, honor, glory, authority, everything which constitutes symbolic power as recognized power.
>
> (Bourdieu 1984: 251)

From the 1980s Bourdieu moved on from this reductionist approach to ethics. For one thing, he began speaking publicly about certain harmful aspects of social life, like neoliberalism, social inequality and injustice. It was then he began thinking about ethics without treating it simply as an effect of power. For example, he began to criticize the:

> sceptical or cynical rejection of any form of belief in the universal, in the values of truth, emancipation ... of any affirmation of universal truths and values, in the name of an elementary form of relativism which regards all universalistic manifestos as pharisaical tricks intended to perpetuate a hegemony.
>
> (Bourdieu 2000: 71)

Bourdieu began arguing that the capacity for reflexivity in the social sciences made it possible to affirm the universal value of ethical ideas (1990a: 178).

Bourdieu relied on the idea of 'recognition' as an ethical reality. He first saw the pursuit of recognition as a social process among children. As children develop in the field of the family they move from 'narcissistic self-love' to discovering themselves as an 'object of others and start to seek their approval'. For Bourdieu the process of the search for recognition is the anthropological root of all symbolic capital (glory, honour, credit, reputation, fame) (Bourdieu 2000: 166). This begins to articulate his 'ethics of recognition':

> The social world gives what is rarest, recognition, consideration, in other words, ... reasons for being. It is capable of giving meaning to life.... One of the most unequal of all distributions, and probably, in any case, the most cruel, is the distribution of symbolic capital, that is of social importance and

of reasons for living.... Conversely, there is no worse dispossession, no
worse privation, perhaps, than that of the losers in the symbolic struggle for
recognition, for access to a socially recognized social being, in a word, to
humanity.

(Ibid.: 240–241)

Like Bourdieu, we argue that our ethical ideas are part of our social world, but
also have an autonomy and truth-value that is not reducible to an effect of social
power. We cannot offer here a full account of the argument that ethical claims
are neither simply relative to a given social order nor just expressions of personal preference. Charles Taylor argued that ethical principles can be tested for
their truth-value. An idea is ethical because it is independent from personal incli-
nation – and different from preferences – because it represents a way of living or
being that is true as opposed to being more desirable (Dworkin 2012). As Taylor
explains: 'We sense in the very experience of being moved by some higher good
that we are moved by what is good in it, rather than that it is valuable because of
our reaction' (Taylor 1989: 74).

Contemporary politics and policy-making is characterized by the absence of a
credible account of what constitutes a good life. While neoliberalism provides an
'ethical orientation', it describes what is valuable using only market categories.
Neoliberalism, like its alter ego Marxism, is economically reductionist. Everything is reduced to the monetary value of buying and selling. Thus we are
encouraged to worship the market as a goddess to be appeased so we might be
granted the bounties promised. A new intergenerational contract requires a more
complex account of the good life.

Our political economy of generations provides a point of departure that can
inform a new intergenerational contract. The political economy of generations
manifests a number of key principles. It is non-reductionist, non-determinist and
pluralist in that it accepts that no one social resource or capital plays a more
important role than any other. It is relational in the way it emphasizes that 'generation' is less a thing and more a relation *and* a process among people within a
generation as well as between different generations. It helps to detail a defensible account of how we might develop a descriptive *and* normative assessment
of the extent to which a society now or in the future can promote intergenerational fairness. It recognizes the value of critique and reflexivity for identifying
suffering and oppression, and an understanding of why such pain is harmful.

Implicitly, such an ethical framework points to the conditions that a just
society promotes. In what follows we offer a pluralistic account of the human
goods that might be discussed, elaborated and negotiated as part of an intergenerational contract. It draws on the capabilities theory of justice developed by Sen
(2009) and Nussbaum (2001): a non-reductionist, non-determinist and pluralist
project features that parallels our political economy.

Intergenerational contract: freedom-as-justice

Around 2,500 years ago, the ancient Greek poet Pindar wrote about what a young person needs to grow well. 'Human excellence' he said 'is like a young plant: something growing in the world, slender, fragile, in constant need of food from without' (cited in Nussbaum 2003: 1). Paraphrasing Pindar, Nussbaum adds that 'we need to be born with adequate capacities'. We also need 'fostering weather (gentle dew and rain, the absence of sudden frosts and harsh winds), as well as the care of concerned intelligent keepers.' We need fostering natural and social conditions to avoid catastrophes and 'to develop affirming relations with other human beings' (ibid.). While much has changed in 2,500 years, what it means to thrive and to enjoy a good life has not. One way of asking what we need to live a good life is to imagine a just society as a space where people are free to choose that life and are enabled to live it. This is what Sen and Nussbaum argue.

Sen and Nussbaum reject the dominant commitment to an ethical tradition that says happiness defines the good. This utilitarian tradition informs neo-liberalism, modern economics and Anglo-American ethical philosophy (Sen 2009: 317–319). They say happiness ('utility') will not help to when trying to define a good life nor can we reduce a good life to the amount of income or wealth a person owns. We can certainly measure the income benefits of education but will that tell us much about whether a person is living a good life or whether the community they are part of is fair and just? In short, the value of a good life cannot be reduced to a measure like money. The values used to determine a good life do not have the same common qualities or 'units' from which comparisons can be made. For this reason they cannot be compared or measured against each other (Nussbaum 2011: 239). This 'incommensurability' highlights the diversity of valued ends that inform a good life.

For Sen 'wealth is evidently not the good we are seeking, for it is merely useful and for the sake of something else' (2009: 253). It is more fruitful to identify the 'opportunities of living' well, rather than the '*means* of living' (ibid.: 233). Like other liberal philosophers, they say there are multiple and incommensurable ways of determining what a good life looks like. Having both the freedom to choose *and* the ability to make real choices is justice. Sen and Nussbaum say that justice is the freedom to choose what a person values to do and be, and then to have the ability to realize those choices. In this way, their account of justice expands the classical liberal idea of freedom.

This ethical and analytic framework is summarized in their work on 'functionings' and 'capabilities'. For Sen it is important to ask what people are able to choose to be and do. Sen illustrates his point about our capacity to achieve what we choose with the example of a bicycle (1983: 160). A person may choose the good of mobility or 'transportation'. A bicycle promises that good, but whether it actually provides the transportation depends on certain characteristics of the person trying to use the bike. The bicycle will work for most people who have full use of their legs or who have access to roads or paths, or who live close enough to their destination. A bicycle is useless, however, for a person without legs, who lives where there are no paths or who lives too far from where they need to go. The capability approach focuses on the quality of life that people are actually able to choose and achieve. This is analyzed in terms of two ideas: 'functionings' and 'capabilities'.

For Sen, *functionings* are the substantive goods that define a good life that resembles Aristotle's virtue ethics. Functionings are states of 'being and doing' like being healthy or being loved, or enjoying beautiful things. They are distinct from the resources or *capabilities* needed to achieve those goods.

This raises questions about the 'functionings' needed for a good life, and how we work out which ones matter. On this last question Sen and Nussbaum disagree. Nussbaum says we can and should stipulate the aspects of a good life. Sen says we should not do so because this denies people the opportunity to choose freely what they value and want to be and it denies the value of a democratic political process (Sen 2004). Philosophers and social researchers can provide helpful ideas, evidence and arguments, but the only legitimate source of decisions about the nature of the life we have reason to value must come from the people concerned. It's a principle that looks much like the key idea associated with deliberative democracy, that is, people affected by a decision should be involved in making it. While we agree with Sen, later in this chapter we draw on Nussbaum to develop some ideas about the goods needed for a good life.

Capabilities refers to the abilities we have to make choices that become real. Framed in terms of a political economy they are economic, cultural, social, symbolic and political capitals. They are the abilities (or powers) a person has to pursue certain goods or functionings. Our capacity to access goods depends, for example, on bodily endowments like health, illness, physical (dis)abilities, age or gender. There are also resources or conditions that relate to where we live, such as climate, geography, the presence or absence of epidemic diseases, or pollution. Added to this are social conditions, like public services (education, health and welfare), as well as the effects of class, gender, generational or ethnic differences. Tradition and culture also affect our abilities to make effective choices like ideas about marriage, dress standards, and so on. Finally, there may be gender and generational rules in families that determine things like the allocation of food and health-care between children and adults, males and females. In short, a person's capability (to live a good life) points to their freedom to choose between different functioning (states of being and doing) that they value. Sen proposes a social-choice model involving public reasoning and democratic procedures of decision-making.

In this account of freedom, Sen and Nussbaum see a *plurality of valued ends* or goods as necessary for a good life. Justice involves freedom to make choices about what we value (to do and be) and to have the ability to pursue those choices. A comprehensive account of freedom entails a self-determination or ability to choose between different ends (i.e. between various goods) that we value and to lead the life we value, which involves being supported to realize that life (Sen 2009: 233).

Nussbaum argues a basic threshold level of capability exists that we all need just to function, beneath which life becomes so impoverished as not to be a human life (Nussbaum 2000; Sen 2009). There is also a second threshold: anyone who lacks one or more of the capabilities needed to meet this threshold falls short of living a good life. We live, but in a fashion that is not a *good* human life. According to Nussbaum, moving from a 'bare minimum life of sub-sistence' to a 'good human life' involves becoming more 'self-reliant' by acquir-ing 'practical reason' through education or by abolishing oppressive forms of work or traditional gender relations that render women subservient to men.

A person's capability never depends just on their natural constitution like being born tall or short. It certainly depends on social relations and institutions like the kind of family one is born into, government policies or what is available in an economy (Nussbaum 2011: 33–34).

Nussbaum's list of functionings or goods is outlined below as one example of the considerations that *might* inform the development of an intergenerational contract.

1 *Life.*
   Being able to live to the end of a human life of normal length; not dying prematurely, or before one's life is so reduced as to be not worth living.
2 *Bodily Health.*
   Having good health, including reproductive health, to be adequately nour-ished, and to have adequate shelter.
3 *Bodily Integrity.*
   Being able to move freely, to be secure against violent assault, (including sexual assault and domestic violence), having opportunities for sexual satis-faction and choice in matters of reproduction.
4 *Senses, Imagination, and Thought.*
   Being able to use our senses, to imagine, think and reason – in ways informed and cultivated by an adequate education. Being able to exercise our imagination and thought in connection with experiencing and producing works and events of one's own choice, (religious, literary, musical etc.). Being able to use one's mind in ways protected by guarantees of freedom of expression with respect to political and artistic speech, and freedom of reli-gious exercise. Being able to have pleasurable experiences and to avoid non-beneficial pain.
5 *Emotions.*
   Being able to have attachments to things, people and other animals outside ourselves; to love those who love and care for us, to grieve at their absence; in general, to love, to grieve, to experience longing, gratitude, and justified anger. Not having one's emotional development blighted by fear and anxiety.
6 *Practical Reason.*
   Being able to form a conception of the good, being able to exercise good judgement and to engage in critical reflection about the planning of one's

life. (It entails protection for the liberty of conscience and religious observance.)

7   *Affiliation.*

A   Being able to live with and toward others, to recognize and show concern for other human beings, to engage in various forms of social interaction; to imagine the situation of another. (Protecting this capability means protecting institutions that constitute and nourish such affiliations, and protecting freedom of assembly and political speech.)

B   Having the social bases of self-respect and non-humiliation; being treated as a dignified being whose worth is equal to that of others. This entails nondiscrimination on the basis of race, sex, sexual orientation, ethnicity, caste, religion, national origin.

8   *Other Species.*

Being able to live with and express care and concern for and in relation to animals, plants, and the world of nature.

9   *Play.*

Being able to laugh, to play, to enjoy recreational activities.

10   *Control Over One's Environment.*

A   Political. Being able to participate effectively in political choices that govern one's life; having the right of political participation, protections of free speech and association.

B   Material. Being able to hold property (land and movable goods), and having property rights on an equal basis with others; having the right to seek employment on an equal basis with others; having the freedom from unwarranted search and seizure. In work, being able to work as a human being, exercising practical reason, and entering into meaningful relationships of mutual recognition with other workers.

Sen's non-prescriptive approach and Nussbaum's more prescriptive approach provide a valuable evaluative heuristic for assessing a range of social provision. (We also note that Nussbaum provides a useful heuristic for assessing a range of policies and practices). It has important implications for the kind of politics that can inform an intergenerational contract involving young people in far more comprehensive and inclusive ways than are currently considered desirable or possible.

Intergenerational contract: political principles

Young people are largely missing from formal policy and political debates regarding matters of public interest and issues of direct interest to them. Paradoxically this occurs in a context of pervasive official rhetoric extolling the virtues of greater 'youth participation'. Youth participation, we are told, is needed if we want to address 'the democratic crisis'. Yet despite this and concerns about intergenerational inequity, most young people continue to have little, if any say (Bessant 2004).

The inclusion of young people in deliberative democratic processes about such matters is critical. This raises questions about the nature of the public sphere and what we might appeal to for ensuring young people have access to the deliberative processes that constitute a public sphere. An orientation to equality, non-domination and freedom are political principles that should inform an intergenerational contract. A case for this as an extrapolation of the capabilities approach has been made by Anderson (1999) and Robeyns (2009).

Equality and non-domination in the public sphere

For Anderson equality in relationships is critical for a theory of justice. Equality needs to be analyzed in terms of the social conditions supporting it as a capability (Anderson 1999). If the social conditions needed to secure everyone's freedom are to mean anything, everyone should stand in a relationship of fundamental equality, including equal respect, such that all have freedom to participate in democratic self-government. In seeking the construction of a community of equals, democratic equality integrates principles of distribution with demands of equal respect. In such a state, citizens make claims on one another in virtue of their equality, not their inferiority to others. Because the aim of citizens in constructing a state is to secure everyone's freedom, democratic equality's principles of distribution don't presume to tell people how to use their opportunities nor to judge how responsible people are for choices that lead to unfortunate outcomes. While Anderson's primary concern is for equality of democratic citizenship, she argues this has extensive egalitarian implications for society as a whole, because other capabilities (e.g. health, education, personal autonomy and self-respect, and economic fairness) are required as supporting conditions to realize equal citizenship (ibid.: 317).

In a parallel argument, Alexander proposes a capability theory based on the Republican tradition and its commitment to freedom-as-non-domination (2008). Alexander argues the capability approach should go further to elaborate the commitment to freedom as it is understood in the Republican tradition. From this perspective, it is important that one is able to achieve certain functionings, (such as mobility), and that achieving those functionings is not conditional on the favour or goodwill of other people or the broader *context*. Armstrong argues that the objectives of the capability theory will be achieved when the state and citizens attend to capabilities but also seek to promote a context of non-domination (Armstrong 2010: 24). Both of these considerations are vital for how we think about the public sphere.

The space long-recognized as critical for deliberative democracy is the 'public sphere'. Writers like Habermas (1989) and critics like Fraser (1995) understand this as a single, all-inclusive space directed to the formation of rational deliberation, consensus-making and public opinion, processes deemed vital to a functioning democracy. Currently many young people are excluded from it. For these reasons the public sphere is pertinent for developing a new generational contract.

As a design principle for developing a new generational contract we argue for a significantly revised version of the traditional public sphere. Instead of a single, all-inclusive site in which rational debate occurs for the purpose of consensus-making, as Habermas promotes (1989), we argue for a network of multiple and competing publics (Fraser 1995; Bessant 2014). This is preferable because it would be more welcoming of and more inclusive of young people, enabling more participatory parity, and so help mitigate the problem of inequality between participants.

While it is assumed that equal social access is a condition necessary for deliberative practice in the public sphere, that is not and never has been the reality. Inequalities of various kinds have shaped the public sphere in ways that too often ensure the views and interests of dominant groups dominate deliberative processes. We have tended to manage the disparity between the requirement for equity and the reality by 'bracketing' the power or status differentials in the public sphere, and acting 'as-if' all participants are social equals. It's a practice that sends the message that equality is not really critical for democratic deliberation and that we can just act 'as-if' equality really exists when it does not (Fraser 1995). Yet for most young people, power disparities due to experience and access to resources that come with age, in combination with age discrimination, are usually significant enough to make a difference to their ability to engage in democratic practices on a relatively equal footing.

This situation has been alleviated somewhat by the development of new, multiple spaces created and populated by young people drawing on the affordances of new technologies. This can also have immediate practical benefits because it entails recognizing all the ways young people have already created new public spaces, set the agenda and engaged in deliberative and creative practices on their own terms. The establishment of multiple sites has created the dramatic expansion of a much more fragmented public sphere. As Fraser argues, a plurality of public spheres can better promote participatory parity. This means that new kinds of political expressivity are evolving through means other than by rational deliberation or consensus-making.

This can help cast an intergenerational contract in ways that are different to that shaped within a more traditional public sphere where more powerful and typically older groups tend to dominate and set the agenda.

All this is not to suggest that we relegate young people to deliberation in a multiplicity of cyber public spheres and informal modes of political expression, but that they open new public spheres that be added to more traditional deliberative sites in which they *also* participate.

Political agency and age

Young people have the capacity 'to critique, re-imagine and reconstruct their world for themselves with and for the communities to which, through so acting, they would, it was believed, experience a greater sense of belonging and therefore continued commitment.' (Ward cited in Burke 2014). Young people also have a moral entitlement to exercise political agency derived from the fact they are a person.

Claiming that young people can and should exercise political agency raises questions about the age at which a young person can exercise substantive freedom. To this question we have three answers.

First, the age at which a person ought to exercise substantive freedom is *the age at which a person expresses an interest in doing so.*

The expression of that interest is the point when their capability to exercise freedom ought to be recognized. When a person expresses an interest in exercising freedom about the issues like the learning they value, who they want to be, or in the kind of government they want in office, is when elders need to hear and respond to that interest, to support them by offering relevant resources about the options and to assist them in making good judgements in exercising choice about what they value (Bessant 2014a).

Second, while we say young people ought to be accorded the same moral consideration as adults this does not mean they should be regarded in the same ways as their elders. As Sen has argued, this is because people differ in their ability to render what it is they value when converting resources (or capitals) into 'beings' or into 'doings'. If we apply this reasoning to young people, it follows that because some may be less able because they are physically smaller or less experienced than their elders, then any difference that implies they need help places an obligation on others who are more able and better resourced to ensure the young person is supported to exercise that political agency.

This places the onus on older people as parents, teachers and community elders to make good judgements about the kind of information and guidance that is appropriate for the young people they have relations with. Any process involved in developing an intergenerational contract ought to ask how relations between older and young people can work so that good judgements are made about when a young person – and indeed an older person – can be *supported to exercise the freedom* to choose what they value to be and do (Young-Bruehl 2012). This involved making good judgements about how and when that material is best used and how a young person can learn to make good decisions themselves. In short, it entails the exercise of good judgement to determine where the shifting 'middle-ground' lies between denying freedom (by assuming an overly paternalistic position), and a libertarian, free-for-all approach.

Third, saying that young people have the moral status of any person regardless of age or abilities does not mean that they should be left 'to go it alone'. If we value freedom as Richard Sennett (2003) argues we should, this should not come at the expense of devaluing care and dependency. He says no-one ought to be left to cope on their own as neoliberal individualism encourages: it is ethically valuable to depend on others and to be involved in relations of care.

Fourth, we recognize too that sometimes different choices, or judgements about how freedoms are best exercised simply reflect legitimate differences and are not evidence that one of the participants is in some way defective in their capacity to make those decisions. It is the case that many young people make excellent judgements that are different from and sometimes opposed to the views of their elders. They have a legitimate right to dissent and have genuinely alternative views.

To summarize, we do not suggest that very young people ought to or indeed can, enjoy unfettered freedom. The issue of age matters because it is generally assumed by many that it provides a reliable marker of when we are able to exercise comprehensive freedom. Using age in this way is problematic, however, because it rests on essentialist and/or prejudicial assumptions. We each age differently in diverse social contexts and develop capacities at different times and not always in the linear, progressive ways developmentalism would like us to think we do.

Dissent, deep freedom and forbearance

Political theorists like Mouffe (2005a, 2005b), Ranciere (2010), and Critchley (2012) drew attention to the ways the neoliberal project promoted the collapse of modern political culture. Furedi argues that a 'fear of politics fed by a politics of fear' is the consequence of the rush by major political interests in many western political systems to claim the centre ground (2005). This has fed a deep fear of dissent and the active discouragement of political alternatives to the dominant neoliberal agenda while feeding increasing disengagement by many people from the democratic system itself.

The mark of a democratic free society is dissensus, understood as a genuine recognition of the value and prospect of reconfiguring the status quo by challenging conventional or common-sense stories and expectations and not simply as the mundane conflict between interests, opinions, or values (Mouffe 2005a; Ranciere 2010). Here we recognize the point of a commitment to what Unger (2014) calls 'deep freedom'. As Unger argued, deep freedom is the capacity to entertain a plurality of views and ways of living as well as being free to express different – even oppositional views – as a critical 'instrument of vision' (2014: 301).

Unger says we now have a shallow freedom that sees 'equality' and 'liberty' in a constrained fashion imposed by prevailing institutional settlements that secure 'equality' and 'liberty' as narrow and false alternatives. To promote deep freedom, we need to break through this false binary and challenge the institutions that compromise it (Unger 2014: 215). This requires major change, as we need to address questions that will not be tackled while governments and other power elites remain wedded to the neoliberal agenda and obsessions like 'cutting public debt'. It will require a commitment to experimentation. If Bourdieu is right about the power of habitus and inertia (and the role these dispositions play in securing the interests of elites) then Unger is surely correct to stress the importance of experimentation.

Informing the conception and design of a new generational contract ought to be a deliberate commitment to experimentation. In designing an intergenerational contract, we need to open and hospitable to collective experimentation with alternate forms of free society, as we struggle towards an alternative social future (Unger 2014). We will need new organizations, institutions and policies that are adequate to the ambitions of the challenges we face.

Another way to pursue and promote intergenerational contract and participation is by encouraging forbearance. It's an attitude or practice requiring older people to be willing and able to listen, and to relinquish certain interests (their status, power …). It requires a capacity to overcome self-centredness and to exercise restraint when expressing one's views so others have the space to think, to feel, deliberate and articulate their concepts and views. It also implies an interest in what students have to say and in gaining insight into their inner worlds (Unger 2014: 374). As Unger explains,

> Forebearance requires the marriage of self-denial with imagination; insight into the inner world of other people. A generosity bereft of such insight is in fact a form of cruelty or subjugation …
>
> (Ibid.)

This can have immediate practical benefits because it entails recognizing all the ways young people are already engaging in deliberative practices, in digital sites, in user-generated satire, in social movements and in their art of music. Such a principle therefore makes available a rich repertoire of political actions conventionally ignored within the public sphere.

As mentioned, taking this idea seriously necessitates revising a conception of the public sphere as a space of communicative action stipulating that deliberation ought to be directed towards consensus-making or cooperation by invoking principles of 'good reasoning' (Habermas 1996). We need to value diversity of opinion where contrarians are not censured and people are not sanctioned for raising taboo topics or expressing 'outrageous ideas' (Keane 1995). This includes transcending the censorious animus directed against ideas that transgress the 'politically correct' frames of people conventionally defined as 'right-wing' or 'left-wing'.

Distributive justice

Unger argues that in developing ideas for a good life we need to move beyond a political binary in which progressives seek more equality via state-sponsored redistribution and regulatory policies, while conservatives prioritize freedom by letting the market rip – meaning reduced regulation and economic redistribution – while promoting individual initiative and self-determination free from the state (Unger 2014: 316).

Unger is right to say 'these are false options' based on limited views that narrow the scope of politics by reconciling economic flexibility and social protection. We should not accept the dichotomy of 'more market – less state'. More is required than corrective redistribution and regulation that leaves the market and political infrastructure untouched (ibid.: 318). As he argues, we can do better than 'compensatory redistribution' by tax and transfer and other means, more is needed than 'resource transfer' (ibid.). Change that influences the primary distribution of wealth and income might take us closer to a just intergenerational contract.

In a context already being shaped by the radical reconfiguration of human labour courtesy of new technologies that are disrupting the traditional nexus between labour and income, how can we provide adequate social protection and income across all ages and particularly for those who have a greater need or who are more are vulnerable because they are young or very old?

One option is 'basic income', or a system of protection and endowments. This is the idea that every citizen receives as a right and without conditions, a regular income at a level agreed on by the community set against a minimum standard of living (Pettit 2007; Richardson 2013; Standing 2014). Such a system of income support would enable people to move easily between employment and other valued kinds of social activity like care work and education. It acknowledges that wage work, including the standard working week we have long taken for granted, is becoming less available. If the distribution of paid employment becomes less equal than it already is, this will exacerbate the suffering and hurt experienced by those people already trapped in existing and often punitive welfare systems.

Strengthened economic security and educational and cultural endowments, can assist communities experiment with new ways of living. Labour-saving technologies can also support such an arrangement (Unger 2014: 330). At the least a basic income scheme would do much to avert a climate of fear and the associated reluctance to innovate or be open to transformation. At best, it increases the likelihood that people will be able to 'thrive in the midst of instability' as well as being 'more hospitable to innovation' than they would otherwise be (ibid.).

Forgiveness

Often when bad things happen relations are damaged. While many people talk of 'generational war', we suggest this is not helpful and that the idea of restitution may be more helpful in forging a way ahead. How we might address what has happened since the late 1970s under the reign of neoliberal policy? What are the next steps to be taken? What would this look like if we used the lens of restitution? Does it mean getting back something of what was lost for young people? Can harm and damage done be repaired? Can there be redress of some of the wrongs?

One way of moving in this direction of restitution and forgiveness could come in the form of a policy of debt jubilee or debt forgiveness, which would go some way towards alleviating the debt many young people have incurred to pay for their own post-secondary education, be it higher or vocational education.

While large-scale student debt is a new problem, debt forgiveness is an old idea. It can be found, for example, in the Old Testament's Book of Deuteronomy, which stipulates a rest day every seventh day and a sabbath year every seven years. In that seventh year, people do not work and on the year after seven of those sabbatical years (that is, on the 50th year) there is to be jubilee year. During that year slaves are to be emancipated and all obligations, including debts, would be forgiven.

It's an idea that has become an important moral and religious issue informing political and economic and moral campaigns designed to address global poverty and debt. There are also good economic arguments for a contemporary debt jubilee: if education debts are forgiven, governments and citizens alike could spend the money currently devoted to interest and principal repayments on other things that would increase economic demand and encourage growth, and eventually take the world economy out of constant crisis.

The weightier argument is ethical. As we argued, young people have been persuaded to borrow heavily for their education so that they can reap benefits that have not transpired. In the US, student debt now exceeds US$1 trillion while in Australia it exceeds AU$34 billion. By 2025–2026 it is estimated that Australian university students' education loans will rise more than fivefold to $185.2 billion, amounting to 46.3 per cent of the nation's public debt (Commonwealth of Australia 2016).

There is also good reason to consider this option because some alternative 'solutions' to student debt are deeply concerning. One of these, floated by the Australian government, is that the government bundles up or 'securitizes' all the bad debt it has accumulated and sells it on the private market. According to the Australian Parliamentary Budget Office this would raise around $133 billion, still a major loss, but less than carrying $185.2 billion (Commonwealth of Australia 2016). Not only is the economics of this 'solution' a concern, it is worrying on ethical grounds that a government would consider this option, particularly given it was precisely this kind of practice that lead to the American housing crash and the 2008 recession. Our question is whether we learn from such global catastrophes. The suggestion we bundle and sell off student debt to unsuspecting citizens as a way of solving the student debt problem makes a jubilee a sound option.

In response to claims that not paying debt or debt forgiveness is immoral, we note it is already widely practised. For example, there is the modern practice of declaring bankruptcy, whereby a court decides how much if anything is repaid to creditors. Governments also forgive their own indebtedness by declaring they will default on their debt repayments; it is a practice that has long been used by governments big and small.

Student debt forgiveness would be a small but important gesture that might go some way towards restoring intergenerational fairness, and help set things right in a quite practical way.

Conclusion

The conception of justice-as-freedom in Sen and Nussbaum's account of capabilities begins to help us imagine the ways a new intergenerational contract might work to enhance the capacity of people in different generations to live good lives and to deal with an exciting but uncertain future.

The capabilities approach has a number of desirable features that map well with the political economy approach. It is not prescriptive but has a clear moral frame. It acknowledges that the world and social reality are complex and that any evaluation should reflect that complexity rather than preemptively exclude various ideas and values from consideration in advance. It is pluralist and doesn't make the utilitarian criterion of utility (happiness) the only criteria used when evaluating the purpose of a policy. This means that evaluating how well people are doing must seek to be as open-minded as possible.

It is because we cannot fully anticipate such a process or the content of such an intergenerational contract that we restricted ourselves to identifying the design principles that might best inform such a dialogue, and some of the substantive issues we believe ought to be canvassed. We cannot be too prescriptive or preemptive given the development of such a contract needs to be a deliberative and inclusive intergenerational process. It is especially important we avoid the trap of subverting the principles we believe ought to inform such a contract. An authentic intergenerational contract involves dialogue. It involves young people and elders listening to each other in conversation. It ought to be a continual, deliberative, experimental process of talking, listening, learning, and making judgements based on a clear view of what constitutes a good life and what is required to sustain such a life. It requires coming to some degree of consensus about processes and content as well as disagreement.

Conclusion

When we first drafted the proposal for this book we had in mind the title: *Eating Our Young: How policy-makers generate disadvantage among young people – and what can be done about it.* The idea of eating our own young is not new.

Adults eating children has been the subject of countless classical stories and fairy tales. Ancient Greek myths in Hesiod's *Theogyny* tell of Kronos, a Greek Titan, who pioneered intergenerational violence. Hating his own father so much, Kronos castrated him. Kronos then ate five of his own children as they were being born to prevent them from turning against him. This story inspired paintings like Reuben's *Saturn Devouring his Children* (1636) or Goya's *Saturn Devouring His Son* (c.1820). Shakespeare's play *Titus Andronicus* climaxes when the Roman General Titus feeds 'Tamora', Queen of the Goths, her own two sons baked in a pie (Titus Andronicus 5.3.59–60).[1] There are also German fairy tales like Hansel and Gretel, a story of two children deliberately abandoned in the woods by their father who are then lured to a gingerbread house by an old crone who fattens them up before cooking them in a cauldron and eating them for supper.

Somewhere along the way our book's title changed, mainly at the behest of a prospective publisher concerned that when readers, librarians and prospective readers put this title into a search engine they would be referred to cookbooks, or even books on cannibalism.

Yet if the title has changed, the key message has remained the same. Most young people born since the early 1980s (with the exception of children in families in the top two deciles of income), in contrast with earlier generations, are unlikely to be better off than their parents' generation. The result is a seriously broken intergenerational contract. While much could be said about what is meant by an 'intergenerational contract', we said two things.

First, one version of the implied intergenerational contract is that each generation will be better off than its predecessors. Second, and more recently, the implied intergenerational contract promised that young people would accrue enormous benefits if only they agreed to spend more and more time in secondary and higher education. This investment in human capital would then be rewarded with secure jobs, higher incomes and 'the good life'. Both versions of the promise implied in the contract have been breached.

One explanation for this is the role played by neoliberal policies, which have contributed in so many ways to the generational disadvantage experienced by young people born since 1980. The gap between promise and achievement is a product of neoliberal policies that began to be adopted in the 1980s, generating the unemployment, underemployment and precarious employment that now defines the labour markets most young people are now struggling to enter. This circumstance, which now includes significant graduate unemployment, is unlikely to improve in the near-to-medium-term, chiefly as a consequence of the digital disruption reshaping the labour markets of most western and developing societies alike and across all skill levels (Brown *et al.* 2011).

Again as a consequence of neoliberal policies, the incomes available to young people are now significantly less in real and nominal terms than was the case for their parents' generation at an equivalent time in their experience. In Britain, Willetts points out that young people will have earned £8,000 less during their twenties than their parents' generation and their opportunities now appear limited by a 'low-mobility, low-training jobs market'. Getting a house of their own is more difficult than ever: their parents were 50 per cent more likely to own their home at 30 than are their children (Willetts 2010). Neoliberal taxation and deregulatory policies also encouraged a significant return to the levels of income and wealth distribution last seen in the west in the 1920s (Piketty 2014). For the most disadvantaged, neoliberal governments, especially in Britain, America and Australia, took a 'punitive turn' in their welfare policies and in their criminal justice policies and systems. The result is high levels of stigmatization, and the incarceration in holding pens of vast numbers of people unfortunate enough to be burdened with psychiatric, drug and alcohol problems or by skin colour that excites the animus of many 'white folk'. These policies serve to exclude and punish people already marginalized by virtue of their ethnicity, gender and long-term economic and cultural disadvantage.

Set against a backdrop of lively debate in sociology and youth studies about how best to establish what is happening and how to interpret it, we argued for a 'political economy of generations' in Chapter 2. We argued we can and should use the generational category in ways Karl Mannheim foreshadowed. We then drew on the non-reductionist, non-determinist and relational theory of practice developed by Bourdieu. Bourdieu's theory addresses the politics at play in people's lives as well as the unequal distribution of and competition for valued social–economic resources (or 'capitals') in a variety of social fields.

We argued that Bourdieu's work is valuable because it sidesteps the problems that arise from the structure or agency dichotomy. As a philosophically inclined anthropologist, Bourdieu understood the complexity of people's lives. He understood how the language we use to make sense of our lives is relationally connected to those lives and to the political struggle over cultural and symbolic capital. His theory appreciates the value of reflexivity and the extreme difficulty involved in achieving it. Bourdieu's theory also enables us to recognize different kinds of capitals without engaging in a determinist reduction of one form of capital to another. We used this 'political economy of generations' to do several things.

As we argued in Chapters 3 through 6, that 'political economy of generations' helps identify and understand the politics of neoliberalism and how it has produced significant generational disadvantage. One effect of the politics of neoliberalism is the claim made by neoliberal apologists that young people are the victims of a generational war waged against them by greedy baby boomers. To be clear, the fact that older generations tend to be doing better, and sometimes even at the expense of people under 35, in no way justifies the use of a metaphor like 'generational war'.

The metaphor of generational war has been used by some neoliberals to argue that baby boomers are unwilling to make the needed sacrifice of reducing the high costs of maintaining their health and welfare services. In this way, they directly contribute to a crisis of 'excessive public debt'. This serves the neoliberal interest in seeing excessive public debt as the gravest economic, political and moral problem of our time as well as creating a lasting and crushing burden of intergenerational injustice. This is why neoliberal commentators like Freedman (1999) or Fishman (2010) talk up the idea of a generational war to influence and justify decisions to cut spending on health care, aged pensions and welfare benefits now, ostensibly to prevent piling increasing debt onto the shoulders of young people and especially those not yet born.

We saw this approach used in the attack by Mario Draghi, Director of the European Central Bank, in 2002 on the 'European social model'. Draghi argued that more austerity was the only option for economic renewal in Europe. Yet, as Lorenza Antonucci observes, Draghi's view 'epitomizes a widespread position in European politics, where cutting welfare state provision is perceived as a way of making government 'young people-friendly' She then pointed to the basic paradox:

> [While] welfare states have been very generous with baby-boomers, [they] have essentially failed with young people ... [However policy-makers argue] we now need to address the economic deficit by cutting these inefficient machines (welfare states) which penalize young people.... The mythology of austerity ... implies that young people will ultimately benefit from public cuts as austerity increases the competitiveness of European economies and will eventually reduce youth unemployment – even though the evidence seems to show the opposite.
>
> (Antonucci 2016 : 4)

Then, as we argued in Chapters 7 and 8, a political economy of generations also helps in understanding how people born since 1980 interpret what is going on. A political economy of generations indicates how working out what is happening may on occasions be straightforward and clear and sometimes muddled and even confused. Yet this is true for most of us as we struggle to see what is happening and to make sense of the world. We also drew on that political economy to comment on the ways many young people engage in various kinds of political activity that dominant players in the political field may not wish to acknowledge as political. Again we acknowledged the complexity that is politics.

We have now arrived at a social and political version of what climate scientists call a 'tipping point'. Once having crossed this threshold we will encounter abrupt and irreversible change. We are at such a tipping point. Metaphorically this can be represented as the convergence of two social-political-economic tectonic plates bumping up against each other, producing increasingly serious 'creative disruptions'.

One is the result of decades of neoliberal policy-making involving deregulation, privatization and other policies designed with the needs and interests of a narrow range of elite institutions and interests. The 2008 recession epitomized the damaging effects of those decades.

The other radical shift taking place relates to the long-standing relationship between humans and technology. Historically we designed technology to augment our own productive and creative abilities. Yet the new generations of artificial intelligence capabilities, networked digitalized, algorithim-driven and robotic technologies are steadily displacing and changing all low-skill work and high-level professional activities and processes in ways that also promise to transform our relationship with technology itself. We are witnessing a dramatic reconfiguration in human work and a far-reaching redefinition of the relationship between productivity and the social resources (or capitals) that hitherto provided the basis of and rewards for human endeavour and struggle. Exactly what all this means, however, is less clear. The only thing clear right now is that these processes will change how we conduct our lives.

It is apparent, for example, that the 'new technologies' are enabling 'higher forms of cooperation' that enhance economic and other activities and that can create new ways of doing things like the 'sharing economy'. It will certainly radicalize competitive selection. Innovations in our institutions and in social relations alike will also create opportunities for alternative regimes of contract and property, different ways of organizing and decentralizing access to resources of production. The last few decades indicate how 'platforms' of various kinds can be used to give voice to and enable multiple 'stakeholders' and ensure the capacity of 'entrepreneurs' of ideas, new services and technologies to move beyond traditional business practices and conventional ideas. While mindful of warnings from T.W. Adorno and others about the unintended consequences of technology, optimistically we may see here opportunities to develop new forms of collective and cooperative practices in ways that transfer power away from financial or industrial capital (Unger 2014).

While the question of new technologies and employment is fraught with uncertainty, it may be that new jobs are created as significant numbers of older jobs disappear. It's a shift that has implications for the source, scale and distribution of income and the nexus between income and social inequality.

Moreover, given the long-term links between education and employment framed by the human capital model there has been too little discussion about the implications of this transformation for education.

Having arrived at this 'tipping point' we face questions about which changes are desirable and which are not.

We argue for the need to cultivate our capacity to be alive to what is happening rather than adopting a head in the sand approach. We have choices to make and we can design our own social world even if they are constrained. One crucial point of reference in this process relates to the shape a new intergenerational contract takes. Hopefully it will be one that enables a just society and a good life for all.

Note

1 Her sons raped and murdered Titus's daughter.

References

ABS (2012) *Prisoners in Australia, 2012.* Cat. No. 4517.0. www.abs.gov.au/ausstats/abs@.nsf/Products/5087123B0CCE48C1CA257B3C000DC7CE?

ABS (2014a) *Employee Earnings and Hours, Australia, May 2014* www.abs.gov.au/ausstats/abs@.nsf/mf/6306.0/.

ABS (2014b) *Estimate and Projections, Aboriginal and Torres Strait Islander Australians* ABS www.ausstats.abs.gov.au/ausstats/subscriber.nsf/0/375E740A54DFB6AFCA257CC900143F09/$File/32380.pdf.

ABS (2015) *Prisoners in Australia, 2015*, ABS Cat No. 4517.0. Canberra: ABS.

ABS (2016a) *Corrective Services, Australia, March Quarter 2016.* ABS Cat No. 4512.0. Canberra: ABS.

ABS (2016b) *Labour force Australia 2016 6202.0*, www.abs.gov.au/AUSSTATS/abs@.nsf/mf/6202.0.

ACCC (2016a) *ACCCount: A Report of the Australian Competition and Consumer Commission's* activities, www.accc.gov.au/system/files/ACCCount%20%20January%20to%20March%202016.pdf.

ACCC (2016b) *Careers Australia undertakes to repay Commonwealth for VET FEE-HELP diploma courses*, ACCC www.accc.gov.au/media-release/careers-australia-undertakes-to-repay-commonwealth-for-vet-fee-help-diploma-courses.

ACLU (2015) 'School-to-prison-pipeline,' *ACLU Issues*, 5 August 2015. www.aclu.org/issues/racial-justice/race-and-inequality-education/school-prison-pipeline.

Adema, W., and Ladaique, M. (2009) 'How Expensive is the Welfare State? Gross and Net Indicators in the OECD Social Expenditure Database (SOCX)', *OECD Social, Employment and Migration Working Papers*, No. 92, Paris: OECD, www.oecd-ilibrary.org/social-issues-migration-health/how-expensive-is-the-welfare-state_220615515052.

AIHW (2014) *Youth detention population in Australia 2014.* Juvenile justice series 16. Cat. no. JUV 53. Canberra: AIHW. www.aihw.gov.au/publication-detail/?id=60129549676&tab=3.

Akram, S. (2013) 'Fully Unconscious and Prone to Habit: The Characteristics of Agency in the Structure and Agency Dialectic', *Journal for the Theory of Social Behaviour*, 43(1), pp. 45–65. doi: 10.1111/jtsb.12002.

Akram, S. (2014) 'Recognizing the 2011 United Kingdom riots as political protest: a theoretical framework based on agency, habitus and the preconscious', *British Journal of Criminology*, 54(3), pp. 375–92.

Alakeson, V. (2011) 'Making a rented house a home: housing solutions for "generation rent"', *The Resolution Foundation*, www.resolutionfoundation.org/publications/making-rented-house-home-housing-solutions-generation-rent/

Alberola, C., and Molina, E. (2007) 'Continuity and change in the Spanish juvenile justice system', in J. Junger-Tas, and S. Decker (eds) *International Handbook of Juvenile Justice*. London: Springer, pp. 325–348.

Alexander, J. (2008) *Capabilities and Social Justice*. Abingdon: Routledge.

Alexander, M. (2010) *The New Jim Crow: Mass Incarceration in the Age of Colorblindness*. New York: The New Press.

Allahar, A., and Côté, J. (1998) *Richer and Poorer: The Structure of Inequality in Canada*. Toronto: Lorimer.

Allen, G., and Dempsey, N. (2016) 'Prison Population Statistics', *House of Commons Library*, Briefing Paper SN/SG/04334, 4 July 2016.

Alvaredo, F., Atkinson, A.B., Piketty, T., and Saez, E. (2013) 'The top 1 per cent in international and historical perspective', *Journal of Economic Perspectives, 27*, pp. 3–20.

American Association of Physical Anthropology (1996) 'AAPA statement on biological aspects of race', *American Journal of Physical Anthropology, 101*, pp. 569–570.

Anderson, D., and Vervoorn, A. (1983) *Access to Privilege: Patterns of Participation in Australian Post-Secondary Education*. Canberra: ANU.

Anderson, E. (1999) 'What is the point of equality?', *Ethics, 109*(2), pp. 287–337.

Andres, L., and Wyn, J. (2010) *The Making of a Generation: The Children of the 1970s in Adulthood*. Toronto: University of Toronto Press.

Antonucci, L. (2016) *Student Lives in Crisis: Deepening Inequality in Times of Austerity*. Bristol: Policy Press.

Appiah, K. (2010) *The Honor Code: How Moral Revolutions Happen*. New York: W.W. Norton.

Arendt, H. (1959) 'Reflections on Little Rock', *Dissent, 6*(1), pp. 45–56.

Arestis, P., and Sawyer, M. (2007) (eds) *A Handbook of Alternative Monetary Economics*. Cheltenham: Elgar.

Arzheimer, K., and Carter, E. (2006) 'Political opportunity structures and right-wing extremist party success', *European Journal of Political Research, 45*, pp. 419–443.

Atkinson, A. (2014) *Inequality: What Can Be Done?* Cambridge: Harvard University Press.

Atkinson, A.B., and Morelli, S. (2015) *Chartbook of Economic Inequality* [Website]. www.chartbookofeconomicinequality.com/.

Attree, P. (2006) 'The social costs of child poverty: A systematic review of the qualitative evidence', *Children & Society, 20*(1), pp. 54–66.

Auerbach, A.J., and Gale, W.G. (1999) 'Does the budget surplus justify a large-scale tax cut?', *Tax Notes*, 22 March 1999, pp. 1827–1850.

Auerbach, A.J., Gokhale, J., and Kotlikoff, L. (1991) 'Generational accounts: A meaningful alternative to deficit accounting', in D. Bradford (ed.) *Tax Policy and the Economy*, 5th edn. Cambridge: MIT Press.

Auerbach, A.J., Kotlikoff, L., Hagemans, R., and Nicoletti, G. (2004) *The Economic Dynamics of an Ageing Population, The Case of Four OECD countries*. Paris: OECD.

Augustine, A., and Nash-Stacey, B. (2016) 'The generational opportunity index: The state of millennials', *BBVA Research: US Economic Watch* https://externalcontent.blob.core. windows.net/pdfs/160809_US_MillennialsOpportunityIndex.pdf.

Australian Council of Social Service (ACOSS) (2010) *Submission to the independent review of the Job Seeker Compliance Review*. Sydney: ACOSS. http://acoss.org.au/ images/uploads/ACOSS_compliance_review_submission_2010.pdf.

Australian Electoral Commission (2013) *Annual Report 2012–13* http://annualreport.aec. gov.au/2013/contents/files/aec-annual-report-12-13.pdf.

Australian Government Productivity Commission (2016) *Digital Disruption: What do governments need to do? Research Paper?* www.pc.gov.au/research/completed/digital-disruption.

Australian National Audit Office (2007) *Administration of the Work for the Dole Program.* Department of Employment and Workplace Relations, Australian National Audit Office.

Australian Taxation Office (2016) *Tax Expenditures Statement 2015*, Canberra: Australian Taxation Office http://apo.org.au/files/Resource/document.pdf.

Ayers, D.F. (2005) 'Neoliberal ideology in community college mission statements: A critical discourse analysis', *The Review of Higher Education,* 28(4), pp. 527–549.

Ayton, P. (2012) 'Judgment and decision-making', in N. Braisby, and A. Gellately (eds) *Cognitive Psychology.* Florence: Oxford University Press, pp. 298–394.

Bacchi, C. (2009) *Analyzing Policy: What's the Problem Represented to be?* Melbourne: Pearson.

Bachelard, M. and McMahon, L. (2015) 'Blair Cottrell, rising anti-Islam movement leader, wanted Hitler in the classroom', *Sydney Morning Herald,* 17 October 2015.

Baker, J. (2008) 'Revisiting the Explosive Growth of Federal Crimes' *Heritage Foundation,* www.heritage.org/research/reports/2008/06/revisiting-the-explosive-growth-of-federal-crimes.

Bakhtin, M. (1984) *Rabelais and His World* (trans. H. Iswolsky). Bloomington: Indiana University Press.

Bakhtin, M. (1992) *The Dialogic Imagination: Four Essays.* Austin: University of Texas Press.

Ball, S., Maguire, M., and Macrae, S. (2000) *Choice, Pathways and Transitions, Post-16.* London: Routledge Falmer.

Baller, S., Dutta, S., and Lanvin, B. (2016) (eds) *The Global Information Technology Report 2016: Innovating in the Digital Economy.* Geneva: World Economic Forum.

Bank of England (2015) *NMG Consulting Survey 2015.*

Bankwest Curtin Economics Center (2015) *Beyond Our Means? Household Savings and Debt.* Perth: Curtin University.

Barr, C., and Malik, S. (2016) 'Revealed: the 30-year economic betrayal dragging down Generation Y's income' *Guardian,* 16 March, www.theguardian.com/world/2016/mar/07/revealed-30-year-economic-betrayal-dragging-down-generation-y-income.

Barr, N., and Crawford, I. (1998) *The Dearing Report and the Government's Response: A Critique.* London: LSE Research Online. http://eprints.lse.ac.uk/archive/00000283.

Barreda, L. (2015) 'El PP critica el apoyo de Pablo Iglesias al humorista Facu Díaz: «No todo vale»' [The PP Criticized the Support of the Comedian Facu Pable Iglesiuas Diaz: Not anything goes], *ABC,* 10 January 2015. www.abc.es/espana/20150110/abci-iglesias-facu-diaz-201501091656.html

Barry, B. (1977) 'Justice between generations', in P.M.S. Hacker and J. Raz (eds) *Law, morality and society.* Oxford: Clarendon, pp. 268–284.

Bartlett D., and Steeke, J. (2013) *The Betrayal of the American Dream.* New York: Public Affairs.

Bateman, T. (2015) *The State of Youth Justice 2015: An Overview of Trends and Developments.* National Association for Youth Justice. http://thenayj.org.uk/wp-content/uploads/2015/10/State-of-Youth-Justice-Oct15.pdf.

Battin, T. (1997) *Abandoning Keynes: Australia's Capital Mistake.* London: Macmillan.

Bauman, Z. (1999) *In Search of Politics.* Cambridge: Polity Press.

Bauman, Z. (2011) 'The London riots – on consumerism coming home to roost', *Social Europe*, www.socialeurope.eu/2011/08/the-london-riots-on-consumerism-coming-home-to-roost.

Beck, U. (1992) *Risk society: Towards a new modernity*. London: Sage.

Beck, U. (2007) 'Beyond class and nation: reframing social inequalities in a globalizing world', *British journal of sociology*, 58(4), pp. 679–705.

Becker, G., and Stigler, G. (1977) 'De gustibus non est disputandum [In matters of taste, there is no dispute]', *American Economic Review*, 67(2), pp. 76–90.

Becker, G. (1964) *Human Capital: A Theoretical and Empirical Analysis with Special Reference to Education*. Princeton: Princeton University Press.

Becker, G. (1975) *Human Capital: A Theoretical and Empirical Analysis, with Special Reference to Education*, 2nd edn. New York: NBER.

Becker, G. (1976) *The Economic Approach to Human Behavior*. Chicago: University of Chicago Press.

Becker, G. (1994) *Human Capital: A Theoretical and Empirical Analysis, with Special Reference to Education*, revised edn. Chicago: University of Chicago Press.

Beilharz, P., Considine, M., and Watts, R. (1992) *Arguing About the Welfare State*. Sydney: Allen and Unwin.

Belfield, C., Cribb, J., Hood, A., and Joyce, R. (2014) *Living Standards, Poverty and Inequality in the UK: 2014*. London: Institute of Fiscal Studies Report R96.

Benedicto, J. (2012) 'The political cultures of young people: an uncertain and unstable combinatorial logic', *Journal of Youth Studies*, 16(6), pp. 712–729.

Bennett, A. (2011) 'The post-subcultural turn: some reflections 10 years on', *Journal of Youth Studies*, 14(5), pp. 493–506.

Bennett, W., Dilulio, J., and Walters, J. (1996) *Moral Poverty: And How to Win America's War Against Crime and Drugs*. New York: Simon & Schuster.

Bentham, J. (1843) 'Principles of the Civil Code', in J. Bowring (ed.) *The Works of Jeremy Bentham*, Vol I. Edinburgh: William Tait.

Bentham, J. (1789) *An Introduction to the Principles of Morals and Legislation*. Edinburgh: Stevenson.

Berkowitz, E.D. (1991) *America's Welfare State: From Roosevelt to Reagan*. Baltimore, Maryland: The Johns Hopkins University Press.

Berlant, L. (2011) *Cruel Optimism*. Duke University, Durham.

Berlin, I. (2002) *Liberty*. Oxford: Oxford University Press.

Bessant, J. (2000) 'Civil conscription or reciprocal obligation: The ethics of work-for the dole schemes', *Australian Journal of Social Issues*, 35, pp. 125–127.

Bessant, J. (2004) 'Mixed messages: Youth participation and democratic practice', *Australian Journal of Political Science*, 39(2), pp. 387–404.

Bessant, J. (2008) 'Hard wired for risk: Neurological science, "the adolescent brain" and developmental theory', *Journal of Youth Studies*, 11(3), pp. 347–360.

Bessant, J. (2009) 'The wives of North-Shore doctors: Social equity and the Higher Education Contribution Scheme', *Public Administration Today*, pp. 64–74.

Bessant, J. (2014a) 'A dangerous idea? Freedom, children and the capability approach to education', *Critical Issues In Education*, 55(2), pp. 138–153.

Bessant, J. (2014b) *Democracy Bytes: New Media, New Politics and Generational Change*. London: Palgrave Macmillan.

Bessant, J. (2016) 'Democracy denied, youth participation and criminalizing digital dissent', *Journal of Youth Studies*, 19(7), pp. 921–937.

Best, W. (1940) 'Arrests without warrant or judicial review: Preventive police action in Nazi Germany, as of February 28, 1933', in *Der Deutsche Polizei*. Darmstadt: L.C. Wittich Verlag, pp. 31–33.

Beveridge, W.B. (1942) *Social Insurance and Allied Services*. London: HMSO.

Beveridge, W.B. (1944) *Full Employment in a Free Society*. London: Allen and Unwin.

Billari, F., and Liefbroer, A.C. (2010) 'Towards a new pattern of transition to adulthood?', *Advances in Life Course Research*, 15(2–3), pp. 59–75.

Blair, T. (2009) *Speech by Tony Blair at the 'New World, New Capitalism' Conference*, The Office of Tony Blair, www.tonyblairoffice.org/speeches/entry/speech-by-tony-blair-at-the-new-world-new-capitalism-conference.

Blanchflower, D. (1999) *What Can be Done to Reduce the High Levels of Youth Joblessness in the World?* Geneva: International Labour Office.

Blatterer, H. (2007) 'Contemporary adulthood: Reconceptualising and uncontested category', *Current Sociology*, 55, pp. 771–792.

Blundell, R., Green, D., and Jin, W. (2016) *The UK Wage Premium Puzzle: How Did a Large Increase in University Graduates Leave the Education premium unchanged?* IFS WP 16/01. London: Institute for Fiscal Studies.

Bohstedt, J. (2010) *The Politics of Provisions: Food Riots, Moral Economy, and Market Transition in England, c.1550–1850*. London: Ashgate.

Bonin, H. (2001) *Intergenerational Accounting: Theory and Application*, New York: Springer.

Bordo, M., and Eichengreen, B. (1993) (eds) *A Retrospective on the Bretton Woods System: Lessons for International Monetary Reform*. Chicago: National Bureau of Economic Research and University of Chicago Press.

Borensztein, E., and Panizza, U. (2010) *The Costs of Sovereign Default: Theory and Reality*, VOXLACEA, http://vox.lacea.org/fckeditor.html?q=node/25.

Boswell, J. (1994) *Same-sex Unions in Premodern Europe*. New York: Villard Books.

Bourdieu, P. (1977a [1972]) *Outline of the Theory of Practice*. Cambridge: University Press.

Bourdieu, P. (1977b) 'Questions de politique,' *Actes de la Recherche en Sciences Sociales*, 16, pp. 55–89.

Bourdieu, P. (1984) *Distinction. A Social Critique of the Judgement of Taste*, Translated by R. Nice. Cambridge: Harvard University Press.

Bourdieu, P. (1986) 'The Forms of Capital', in J. Richardson (ed.) *Handbook for Theory and Research for the Sociology of Education*. New York: Greenwood Press, pp. 241–258.

Bourdieu, P. (1987) 'What makes a social class? On the theoretical and practical existence of groups', *Berkeley Journal of Sociology*, 32, pp. 1–17.

Bourdieu, P. (1988a) *Homo academicus*. Cambridge: Polity Press.

Bourdieu, P. (1998b) *Practical Reason: On the Theory of Action*. Stanford: Stanford University Press.

Bourdieu, P. (1989) 'Social space and symbolic power', *Sociological Theory*, 7(1), pp. 14–25.

Bourdieu, P. (1990a) 'A lecture on the lecture', in *Other Words: Essays towards a Reflexive Sociology*. Stanford: Stanford University Press, pp. 177–198.

Bourdieu, P. (1990b [1980]) *The Logic of Practice*. Cambridge: Polity Press.

Bourdieu, P. (1991) *Language and Symbolic Power*, (J. Thompson ed. and trans). Cambridge: Polity Press.

Bourdieu, P. (1993) 'Youth is just a word': in *Sociology in Question*. (R. Nice trans). London: Sage, pp. 94–102.

Bourdieu, P. (1995) 'Public opinion does not exist', in *Sociology in Question*, London: Sage, pp. 149–157.

Bourdieu, P. (1998) *Acts of Resistance: Against the New Myths of Our Time* Cambridge: Polity Press.

Bourdieu, P. (2000) *Pascalian Meditations*. Cambridge: Polity Press.

Bourdieu P., and Wacquant L. (1992) *An Invitation to Reflexive Sociology*. Cambridge: Polity Press.

Bouyon, S. (2015) 'Recent trends in EU home ownership', *ECRI Commentary No 15*. www.ceps.eu/system/files/ECRI%20Commentary%20No%2015%20SB%20 Recent%20Trends%20in%20Home%20Ownership%20in%20the%20EU-28%20 final_0.pdf.

Boyer, R. (1983) *The Influence of Keynes on French Economic Thought, Past and Present*. Paris: CEPREMAP. www.cepremap.fr/depot/couv_orange/co8404.pdf.

Brannen, J., and Nilsen, A. (2005) 'Individualization, choice and structure: a discussion of current trends in sociological analysis', *The Sociological Review*, 53(3), pp. 412–428.

Bridges, L. (2012) 'Four days in August: the UK riots', *Race & Class*, 54(1), pp. 1–12.

Brown, D. (2012) 'Criminal law reform and the persistence of strict liability', *Duke Law Journal*, 62, pp. 285–339. http://scholarship.law.duke.edu/cgi/viewcontent.cgi?article= 3358&context=dlj.

Brown, D. (2013) 'Criminalization and normative theory', *Current Issues in Criminal Justice*, 25(2), pp. 606–625.

Brown, D., Farrier, D., Egger, S., McNamara, L., Steel, A., Grewcock, M., and Spears, D. (2011) *Criminal Laws: Materials and Commentary on Criminal Law*. Sydney: Federation Press.

Brown, N., Sokal, A., and Friedman, H. (2013) 'The Complex Dynamics of Wishful Thinking: The Critical Positivity Ratio', *American Psychologist*, 68, pp. 801–813.

Brown, P., Lauder, H., and Ashton, D. (2011) *The Global Auction: The Broken Promises of Education Jobs and Incomes*. Oxford: Oxford University Press.

Brown, W. (2015) *Undoing the Demos: Neoliberalism's Stealth Revolution*. Cambridge: Zone.

Browne, J., and Elming, W. (2015) *The Effect of the Coalition's Tax and Benefit Changes on Household Incomes and Work Incentives*, IFS Briefing Note 159 IFS, London.

Burke, C. (2014) '"Fleeting pockets of anarchy": Streetwork. The exploding school', *Pedagogica Historica*, 50(4), pp. 433–442.

Burke, C., and Jones, K. (eds) (2014) *Education, Childhood and Anarchism: Talking Colin Ward*. London: Routledge.

Burke, E. (1812) *Reflections on the French Revolution* Vol. 5 London: F and C Rivington.

Burke, L. (2014) 'Reauthorizing the Higher Education Act – toward policies that increase access and lower costs', *Backgrounder #2941*, Heritage Foundation www.heritage.org/ research/reports/2014/08/reauthorizing-the-higher-education-acttoward-policies-that-increase-access-and-lower-costs.

Burkitt, I. (1997) 'The situated social scientist: Reflexivity and perspective in the sociology of knowledge', *Social Epistemology: A Journal of Knowledge, Culture and Policy*, 11(2), pp. 193–202.

Cameron, D. (2011) 'David Cameron on the riots: This is Criminality Pure and Simple', *Guardian*, 9 August 2011. www.guardian.co.uk/politics/video/2011/aug/09/david-cameron-riots-criminality-video

Canada, G., Druckenmiller, S., and Warsh, K. (2013) 'Generational theft needs to be arrested', *The Wall Street Journal*, 14 February, www.wsj.com/news/articles/SB10001 424127887323485704578257753243530078.

Cardarelli, R., Sefton, J., and Kotlikoff, L. (2000) 'Generational accounting in the UK'. *The Economic Journal*, 110(467), pp. 547–574.

Carlen, P. (2008) 'Imaginary penalities and risk-crazed governance' in P. Carlen (ed.) *Imagined Penalities*. Cullompton: Willan, pp. 1–25.

Carlisle, J.E., and Patton, R.C. (2013) 'Is social media changing how we understand political engagement? An Analysis of Facebook and the 2008 Presidential Election. *Political Research Quarterly.* doi:10.1177/1065912913482758.

Carney, T. (2006) 'Welfare to work: or work discipline revisited?', *Australian Journal of Social Issues*, 41(1), pp. 27–48.

Castaignde, J., and Pignoux, N. (2010) 'France', in F. Dunkel, J. Gryza, P. Horsfield, and L. Pruin (eds) *Juvenile Justice Systems in Europe: Current Situation and Reform.* Monchengladbach: Forum Verlag Godesberg.

Castles, F. (1983) *The Impact of Parties*. Beverly Hills: Sage.

Castles, F. (1985) *The Working Class and Welfare: Reflections on the Political Development of the Welfare State in Australia and New Zealand 1890–1980.* Sydney: Allen & Unwin.

Cavadino, M., and Dignan J. (2006a) 'Penal policy and political economy', *Criminology & Criminal justice*, 6(4), pp. 435–456.

Cavadino, M., and Dignan J. (2006b) *Penal system: A Comparative Approach*, London: Sage.

CEDA (Committee for Economic Development of Australia) (2015) *Australia's Future workforce?* Melbourne: CEDA. https://cica.org.au/wp-content/uploads/Australias-future-workforce.pdf.

Cerny, P. (1990) *The changing architecture of politics: Structure, agency, and the future of the state.* London: Sage.

Chang, O. (2016) 'People are outraged by the federal budget's internship program which pays $4 an hour (on top of existing payments)', *Business Insider Australia*, 4 May 2016. www.businessinsider.com.au/people-are-outraged-by-the-federal-budgets-internship-program-which-pays-4-an-hour-on-top-of-their-existing-payments-2016-5.

Children's Commissioner (2015) *Own Initiative Investigation Report Services provided by the Department of Correctional Services at the Don Dale Youth Detention Centre.* Darwin: Office of the Children's Commissioner.

Chote, R., Crawford, R., Emmerson, C., and Tetlow, G. (2010) 'Public Spending Under Labour', *IFS Election Briefing Note*. London: Institute of Fiscal studies.

Chrisafis, A. (2016) 'Nuit Debout Protests occupy French cities in Revolutionary Call for change', *Guardian*, 9 April 2016, www.theguardian.com/world/2016/apr/08/nuit-debout-protesters-occupy-french-cities-in-a-revolutionary-call-for-change.

Clarke, S., Corlett, A., and Judge, L. (2016) *The Housing Headwind: The impact of Rising Housing Costs on UK Living Standards.* London: Resolution Foundation.

Cockett, R. (1994) *Thinking the Unthinkable: Think-Tanks and the economic counter-revolution.* New York: Harper-Collins.

Cohen, S. (1972) *Folk Devils and Moral Panics*. London: MacGibbon and Kee.

Cole, A. (1998) *French Politics and Society*. Hemel Hempstead: Prentice Hall.

Coleman, G. (2104) *Hacker, Hoaxer, Whistleblower, Spy: The many faces of Anonymous.* London: Verso.

Coleman-Jensen, A., Rabbitt, M., Christian Gregory, C., and Singh, A. (2015) *Household Food Security in the United States in 2014.* ERR-194. U.S. Department of Agriculture, Economic Research Service, September. www.ers.usda.gov/media/1896841/err194.pdf.

Collin, P. (2007) 'Policies for youth participation and the development of new political identities', *National Youth Affairs Conference*, Melbourne. www.yacvic.org.au/includes/pdfs_wordfiles/YACVic_ConfProceedings_Papers.pdf.

Collin, P. (2008) *Young People Imagining a New Democracy: Literature Review.* Sydney: Whitlam Institute. www.whitlam.org/__data/assets/pdf_file/0005/82994/youngpeople_imaginingdemocracy_literature_review.pdf.

Commission of the European Communities (2009) *An EU Strategy for Youth – Investing and Empowering. A renewed open method of coordination to address youth challenges and opportunities.* Brussels: Commission of the European Communities. http://eur-lex.europa.eu/LexUriServ/LexUriServ.do?uri=COM:2009:0200:FIN:EN:PDF.

Committee for Economic Development Australia (CEDA) (2015) *Australia's Future Workforce?* Melbourne: CEDA. http://adminpanel.ceda.com.au/FOLDERS/Service/Files/Documents/26792~Futureworkforce_June2015.pdf.

Commonwealth of Australia (2016) *Higher Education Loan Programme: Impact on the budget. Report no. 02/2016.* Canberra: Parliamentary Budget Office.

Commonwealth of Australia, The Senate (2015) *Education and Employment References Committee, Getting our money's worth: the operation, regulation and funding of private vocational education and training (VET) providers in Australia, Commonwealth of Australia*,Canberra,www.aph.gov.au/Parliamentary_Business/Committees/Senate/Education_and_Employment/vocationaled/Final_Report).

Consejo de la Juventud de España (2013) *Observatorio de Emancipación nº1, Primer trimestre 2013* www.cje.org/es/publicaciones/novedades/observatorio-de-emancipacion/.

Consejo de la Juventud de España (2015) *Observatoria de Emancipacion no 10.* www.cje.org/es/publicaciones/novedades/observatorio-de-emancipacion-n-10-primer-semestre-2015/.

Conservative Party (1979) *Conservative General Election Manifesto.* www.margaret thatcher.org/document/110858.

Conservative Party (2015) *The Conservative Party Manifesto 2015* (online) www.bond.org.uk/data/files/Blog/ConservativeManifesto2015.pdf.

Cooke, R. (2016) 'The Boomer Supremacy: The dominance of baby boomers is becoming total', *The Monthly* (online) www.themonthly.com.au/issue/2016/march/1456750800/richard-cooke/boomer-supremacy.

Coombs, G., and Dollery, B. (2002) 'An analysis of the debate on intergenerational equity and fiscal sustainability in Australia', *The Australian Journal of Social Issues*, 37(4), pp. 363–381.

Coombs, G., and Dollery, B. (2004) 'The ageing of Australia: Fiscal sustainability, inter-generational equity and inter-temporal fiscal balance', *Australian Journal of Social Issues*, 39(4), pp. 459–470.

Cooper, D., and Wang, J.C. (2014) 'Student Loan Debt and Economic Outcomes.' *Federal Reserve Bank of Boston Current Policy Perspectives*, No. 2014.

Cooper, E. (2016) 'Housing affordability for young people worsening', *Pro Bono,* 26 April 2016.https://probonoaustralia.com.au/news/2016/04/housing-affordability-young-people-worsening/.

Corlett, A., Finch, D., and Whittaker, M. (2016) *Living Standards 2016: The experiences of low to middle income house-holds in downturn and recovery*, London: Resolution Foundation.

Côté, J. (2014) 'Towards a new political economy of youth', *Journal of Youth Studies*, 17(4), pp. 527–543.

Côté, J. (2016) 'A new political economy of youth reprised: rejoinder to France and Threadgold', *Journal of Youth Studies*, 19(6), pp. 852–868.

Côté, J., and Allahar, A. (1996) *Generation on Hold: Coming of Age in the Late Twentieth Century*. New York: New York University Press.

Côté, J., and Allahar, A. (2006) *Critical Youth Studies: A Canadian Focus*. Toronto: Pearson Education.

Cotrell, B. (2016) 'The rise of nationalism across the globe', 27 August 2016 www.facebook.com/unitedpatriotsfront/videos/332497977084661.

Coughlan, S. (2010) 'Student tuition fee protests ends with 153 arrests', *BBC*, www.bbc.co.uk/news/education-11877034.

Council of European Union (2006) *Modernising Education and Training: A Vital Contribution to Prosperity and Social Cohesion in Europe*, Joint interim report of the Council and of the Commission on progress under the 'Education & Training 2010 Work Programme (79/01) http://Eur-Lex.Europa.Eu/Lexuriserv/Site/En/Oj/2006/C_079/C_0792 0060401en00010019.Pdf.

Crawford, J.G. (1959) 'The Role of Government and the Place of Planning', in *The Industrial Development of Australia Symposium*. Sydney: UNSW.

Crawford, K. (2006) *Adult Themes: Rewriting the Themes of Adulthood*. Sydney: McMillan.

Cribb, S., Hood, A., and Joyce, R. (2016) *The Economic Circumstances of Different Generations: The Latest Picture*. London: Institute of Fiscal Studies. www.ifs.org.uk/publications/8583

Critchley, S. (2004) 'The Problem of Hegemony', *Political Theory Daily Review*, www.politicaltheory.info/essays/critchley.htmwww.politicaltheory.info/essays/critchley.htm.

Critchley, S. (2007) *Infinitely Demanding: Ethics of Commitment, Political of Resistance*. New York: Verso.

Critchley, S. (2012) *The Faith of the Faithless*. London: Verso.

Crouch, C. (2011) *The Strange Non-Death of Neoliberalism*. Cambridge: Polity.

Cruz-Castro, L., and Sanz-Menéndez, L. (2015) 'Policy Change and Differentiated Integration: Implementing Spanish Higher Education Reforms', *Journal of Contemporary European Research*, 11(1), pp. 103–123.

Daguerre, A., and Taylor-Gooby, P. (2002) 'Welfare Reform in the UK: 1985–2002', *Welfare Reform and Management of Societal Change Working Papers*, University of Kent. www.kent.ac.uk/wramsoc/workingpapers/index.html.

Das, U., Papaioannou, M., and Trebesch, C. (2012) *Sovereign Debt Restructurings 1950–2010: Literature Survey, Data, and Stylized Facts* 30, International Monetary Fund, Working Paper No. WP/12/203. www.imf.org/external/pubs/ft/wp/2012/wp 12203.pdf.

Davidson, K. (2015) 'These seven household names make a killing off of the prison-industrial complex', *US Uncut*, 30 August 2015. http://usuncut.com/class-war/these-7-household-names-make-a-killing-off-of-the-prison-industrial-complex/.

Davis, E. (2003) 'Comparing Bear Markets – 1973 and 2000', *National Institute Economic Review*, 183(1), pp. 78–89.

Davis, G. (2010) 'The republic of learning: higher education transforms Australia', *The Boyer Lectures*. Sydney: ABC.

Dawar, A. (2008) 'Teenager faces prosecution for calling Scientology "cult"', *Guardian*, 20 May 2008. www.theguardian.com/uk/2008/may/20/1.

Dawkins, J. (1988) *Higher Education; A Policy Statement*. Minister for Employment, Education and Training, Commonwealth of Australia: AGPS.

De Giorgi, A. (2016) 'Five theses on mass incarceration'. *The Free Library Crime and Social Justice Associates*, 13 August 2016. www.thefreelibrary.com/Five+theses+on+mass+incarceration.-a0444400587.

Dean, M. (2006) 'Governing the unemployed self in an active society', *Economy and Society*, 24(4), pp. 559–583.

DeNavas-Walt, C., and Proctor, B. (2015) *Income and Poverty in the United States: 2015*. Report Number: P60–252 Washington: US Census. www.census.gov/library/publications/2015/demo/p60-252.html.

Department of Employment (2015) *Evaluation of Work for the Dole 2014–15*, Canberra: Social Research Center ANU for the Department of Employment.

Department of Social Services (2014a) *A New System for Better Employment and Social Outcomes – Interim Report of the Reference Group on Welfare Reform to the Minister for Social Services*. www.dss.gov.au/sites/default/files/documents/06_2014/dss001_14_full_report_27_june_tagged.pdf.

Department of Social Services (2014b) *Pensions Review Background Paper*. www.dss.gov.au/our-responsibilities/seniors/publications-articles/pension-review-background-paper?HTML.

Derian, J. (1992) *Antidiplomacy: Spies, Terror, Speed, and War*. Oxford: Blackwell.

Dewey, J. (1916) *Democracy and Education*. New York: Free Press.

Díaz, F. (2014) '"The Comedian" in Tuerka', *Niaz*, 1 November 2014. www.naiz.eus/actualidad/noticia/20141104/decir-que-me-mofo-de-las-victimas-es-una-sandez-para-utilizarla-politicamentewww.naiz.eus/actualidad/noticia/20141104/decir-que-me-mofo-de-las-victimas-es-una-sandez-para-utilizarla-politicamente.

Dilmot, A. (2012) *Beauty and the Beast: Numbers and Public Policy*, Lecture delivered at Said Business School, Oxford University, 26 January 2012.

Dilthey, W. (2002 [1910]) *The Formation of the Historical World in the Human Sciences*, Vol. 3. New Jersey: Princeton University Press.

Downs, A. (1957) *An Economic Theory of Democracy*. New York: Harper and Row.

du Bois-Reymond, M. (1998) 'I don't want to commit myself yet: Young people's life concepts', *Journal of youth studies*, 1(1), pp. 63–79.

Dunleavy, J. (1991) *Democracy, Bureaucracy and Public Choice*. Hemel Hempstead: Harvester-Wheatsheaf.

Durrant-Whyte, H., McCalman, L., O'Callaghan, S., Reid, A., and Steinberg, D. (2015) *The Impact of Computerisation and Automation on Future Employment*. Canberra: CEDA.

Dworkin, R. (2012) *Justice for Hedgehogs*. Cambridge: Harvard University Press.

DyslexicCBeanie (2016) *Reclaim Australia Interview @ Parliament House Rally* www.youtube.com/watch?v=fABJVC6g0BUwww.youtube.com/watch?v=fABJVC6g0BU.

Eardley, T., Abello, D., and Macdonald, H. (2001) *Is the Job Network Benefitting Disadvantaged Job Seekers?: Preliminary Evidence from a Study of Non-Profit Employment Services*. Sydney: Social Policy Research Centre.

Edwards, K. (2007) 'From deficit to disenfranchisement: Reframing youth electoral participation', *Journal of Youth Studies*, 10(5), pp. 539–555.

EHRC (2014) *Briefing Paper 5: Race disproportionality in stops and searches under Section 60 of the Criminal Justice and Public Order Act 1994*, London: EHRC. www.equalityhumanrights.com/en/publication-download/briefing-paper-5-race-disproportionality-stops-and-searches-under-section-60.

Eisman, S. (2010) *Subprime Goes to College*, Testimony Hearings before the US Senate, Health, Education, Pensions and Labor Committee 24 June.

Eitzen, D.S., and Zinn, M. (2000) 'The Missing Safety Net and Families: A Progressive Critique of the New Welfare Legislation', *Journal of Sociology and Social Welfare*, March 2000, pp. 53–71.

Elias, N. (1970) *What is Sociology?* London: UCL.

Elliot, L. (2016) 'Each generation should be better off than their parents? Think again'. *Guardian*, 15 February 2016. www.theguardian.com/business/2016/feb/14/economics-viewpoint-baby-boomers-generation-x-generation-rent-gig-economy.

Emirbayer, M. (1997) 'Manifesto for a relational sociology', *American Journal of Sociology*, 103(2), pp. 281–317.

Toohey, P. (2016) 'Mind wars: The extremists taking Australia to dark place', *Daily Telegraph*, www.dailytelegraph.com.au/news/special-features/in-depth/white-extremism-in-australia/news-story/f45b4ed749f14a632e318fc9a93e82b1.

Esping-Andersen, G. (1990) *The Three Worlds of Welfare Capitalism*. Princeton: Princeton University Press.

Esping-Andersen, G. (2000) 'Three Worlds of Welfare capitalism', in C. Pierson, and F. Castles (eds) *The Welfare State Reader*. Cambridge: Polity Press, pp. 154–169.

EU EMPL Committee (2015) *Wage and Income Inequality in the European Union* www.europarl.europa.eu/RegData/etudes/STUD/2015/536294/IPOL_STU(2015)536294_EN.pdf.

EU MYPLACE (2015) *Project Final Report*, https://myplaceresearch.files.wordpress.com/2016/06/ga266831-myplace-final-summary-report.pdf.

Europa Press (2015) *Gomez Bermudez Archiva la Causa Contra Facu Diaz el Entender que no humillo a la Victimas del Terrorismo 15 January*. www.europapress.es/nacional/noticia-gomez-bermudez-archiva-causa-contra-facu-diaz-entender-no-humillo-victimas-terrorismo-20150115134210.html.

European Centre for the Development of Vocational Training nd, www.cedefop.europa.eu.

European Centre for the Development of Vocational Training (2016a) *ECVET in Europe Monitoring report 2015*. Luxembourg: Publications Office of the European Union.

European Centre for the Development of Vocational Training (2016b) *EU Skills Agenda*. Luxembourg: Publications Office of the European Union.

European Commission (2004) *The Future of Pension Systems*. Brussels: European Commission http://ec.europa.eu/public_opinion/archives/ebs/ebs_161_pensions.pdf.

European Commission (2015a) *Country Report Spain 2015*. Brussels: European Commission. http://ec.europa.eu/europe2020/pdf/csr2015/cr2015_spain_en.pdf.

European Commission (2015b) *Country Report France 2015*. Brussels: European Commission. http://ec.europa.eu/europe2020/pdf/csr2015/cr2015_france_en.pdf.

European Commission (2015c) *Country Report United Kingdom 2015*. Brussels: European Commission. http://ec.europa.eu/europe2020/pdf/csr2015/cr2015_uk_en.pdf.

European Commission (2015d) *Education and Training Monitor 2015*. Luxembourg: Publications Office of the European Union. http://ec.europa.eu/education/tools/docs/2015/monitor2015-spain_en.pdf.

European Commission (2015e) *Europe 2020 Strategy*. https://ec.europa.eu/info/strategy/european-semester/framework/europe-2020-strategy_en.

European Commission (2016) *Ten Actions to Help Equip People in Europe with Better Skills*. http://europa.eu/rapid/press-release_IP-16-2039_en.htm.

European Council (2000) *Presidency Conclusions, Lisbon European Council, 23 and 24 March 2000*, pa.eu/uedocs/cms_data/docs/pressdata/en/ec/00100-r1.en0.htm.

European Court of Auditors (2015) *EU Youth Guarantee: First Steps Taken But Implementation Risks Ahead.* www.eca.europa.eu/Lists/ECADocuments/SR15_03/SR15_03_EN.pdf.

European Group for Integrated Social Research (2001) 'Misleading trajectories: transition dilemmas of young adults in Europe', *Journal of Youth Studies*, 4(1), pp. 101–118.

European Parliament (2006) *The European Framework for Fiscal policies.* Brussels: European Parliament. www.europarl.europa.eu/atyourservice/en/displayFtu.html?ftuId=FTU_4.2.1.html.

European Union (2014) *New Modes of Learning and Teaching in Higher Education.* Luxembourg: EU.

European Youth Portal (2013) *The Residential Independence of Young People in Spain.* http://europa.eu/youth/es/article/50/6893_en.

Eurostat (2012) *EU Statistics on Income and Living Conditions* (EU-SILC). Brussels: Eurostat.

Eurostat (2014) *Homicides Recorded by the Police, 2002–2012 YB14* http://ec.europa.eu/eurostat/statistics-explained/index.php/File:Homicides_recorded_by_the_police,_2002-12_YB14.png.

Eurostat (2015a) *Unemployment Statistics.* http://ec.europa.eu/eurostat/statistics-explained/index.php/Unemployment_statistics.

Eurostat (2015b) *Mean and Median Income by Age and Sex.* http://appsso.eurostat.ec.europa.eu/nui/show.do.

Eurostat (2016) *At Risk of Poverty Rate by Age.* http://ec.europa.eu/eurostat/tgm/refresh TableAction.do?tab=table&plugin=1&pcode=tessi120&language=en.

EurWORK (2016) *Statutory Minimum Wages in the EU.* www.eurofound.europa.eu/observatories/eurwork/articles/working-conditions-industrial-relations/statutory-minimum-wages-in-the-eu-2016.

Evans, K. (2002) 'Taking control of their lives? Agency in young adult transitions in England and the new Germany', *Journal of Youth Studies*, 5(3), pp. 245–69.

Fairwork Ombusdman (2016) *Minimum Wage.* www.fairwork.gov.au/how-we-will-help/templates-and-guides/fact-sheets/minimum-workplace-entitlements/minimum-wages.

Farrugia, D. (2012) 'Reflexivity and the Structuring of Young People's Biographies', *TASA Conference*, www.tasa.org.au/wp-content/uploads/2012/11/Farrugia-David1.pdf

Farrugia, D. (2013a) 'Young people and structural inequality: beyond the middle ground', *Journal of Youth Studies*, 16(5), pp. 679–693.

Farrugia, D. (2013b) 'The reflexive subject: towards a theory of reflexivity as practical intelligibility', *Current Sociology*, 61(3), pp. 283–300.

Farrugia, D., Smyth, J., and Harrison, T. (2015) 'Moral distinctions and structural inequality: homeless youth salvaging the self', *The Sociological Review*, 64(2), pp. 238–255. doi:10.1111/1467-954X.12252.

Farthing, R. (2010) 'The politics of youthful anti-politics: representing the "issue" of youth participation in politics', *Journal of Youth Studies*, 13(2), pp. 181–195.

Farthing, R. (2014) 'Poverty, malnutrition and education in the UK', in L. Symaco (ed.) *Education, Poverty and Famine.* London: Bloomsbury.

Farthing, R. (2015) 'What's wrong with being poor? The problems of poverty, as young people describe them', *Children & Society*, 30(2), pp. 107–119.

Farthing, R. (2016) 'Writing in a role for structure: low-income young people's dual understanding of agency, choice *and* the welfare state', *Journal of Youth Studies* 19(6), pp. 760–775.

Fattah, E.A. (1997) *Criminology: Past, Present, and Future: A Critical Review*. London: Macmillan.

FBI (2014) *Uniform Crime Records 2012*. https://ucr.fbi.gov/crime-in-the-u.s/2012/crime-in-the-u.s.-2012/tables/1tabledatadecoverviewpdf/table_1_crime_in_the_united_states_by_volume_and_rate_per_100000_inhabitants_1993-2012.xls.

Fenna, A., and Tapper, A. (2012) 'The Australian Welfare state and the neo liberalism thesis', *Australian Journal of Political Science*, 47(2), pp. 155–172.

Fenna, A., and Tapper, A. (2015) 'Economic inequality in Australia: a reassessment'. *Australian Journal of Political Science*, 50(3), pp. 393–411.

Ferrer, F., Ferrer-Fons, M., and Soler-i-Martí, R. (2013) *Country-based reports on interview findings Spain*. MYPLACE (Memory, Youth, Political Legacy And Civic Engagement) www.fp7-myplace.eu.

Filandri, M., and Bertolini, S. (2016) 'Young people and home ownership in Europe', *International Journal of Housing Policy*, 16(2), pp. 144–164.

Fisher, T., and Reece, E. (2011) 'The punitive turn in social policies: Critical race feminist reflections on the USA, Great Britain and beyond', *Critical Sociology* 37(2), pp. 225–236.

Fishman, A. (2015) *Marketing to the Millennial Woman*. New York: Generational Targeted Marketing.

Flora, P., and Heindeheimer, A. (1981) 'The Historical Core and Changing Boundaries of the Welfare State', in P. Flora and A. Heidenheimer (eds) *The Development of Welfare States In Europe and America*. New Brunswick: Transaction, pp. 17–34.

Fondation Abbé Pierre (2015) *An Overview of Housing Exclusion in Europe 2015*, Paris: Fondation Abbé Pierre. www.fondation-abbe-pierre.fr/sites/default/files/content-files/files/an_overview_of_housing_exclusion_in_europe_2015_-_complete_report.pdf.

Foot, D., and Venne, R. (2005) 'Awakening to the intergenerational equity debate in Canada', *Journal of Canadian Studies*, 39, pp. 5–120.

Forsyth, H. (2014) *A History of the Modern Australian University*. Kensington: Newsouth.

Forsyth, J. (2010) 'The Big Mo is with the Tories', *The Spectator Magazine*. http://blogs.spectator.co.uk/2010/04/the-big-mo-is-with-the-tories/.

Fourcade-Gourinchas, M., and Babb, S. (2002) 'The Rebirth of the Liberal Creed: Paths to Neoliberalism in Four Countries', *American Journal of Sociology*, 108(3), pp. 533–579.

France, A., and Haddon, E. (2014) 'Exploring the epistemological fallacy: Subjectivity and class in the lives of young people', *Young*, 22(4), pp. 305–321.

France, A., and Threadgold, S. (2016) 'Youth and political economy: towards a Bourdieusian approach', *Journal of Youth Studies*, 19(5), pp. 612–628.

Fraser, N. (1995) 'Politics, culture and the public sphere: toward a postmodern conception', in L. Nicholson and S. Seidman (eds) *Social Postmodernism: Beyond Identity Politics*. New York: Cambridge University Press, pp. 287–314.

Freedman, M. (1999) *Prime Time: How Baby Boomers Will Revolutionize Retirement and Transform America*. New York: Public Affairs.

Freeman, R. (1976) *The Overeducated American*. New York: Academic Press.

Frey, C.B., and Osborne, M. (2013) *The Future of Employment*. Oxford: The Oxford Martin Programme on Technology and Employment.

Friedman, M. (1953) 'The methodology of positive economics', in *Essays in Positive Economics*. Chicago, IL: Chicago University Press, pp. 3–43.

Friedman, M., and Kuznets, S. (1945) *Income from Independent Professional Practice*, New York, NBER.

Fry, R. (2016) 'For first time in modern era, living with parents edges out other living arrangements for 18–34 year olds', *Pew Research Center*, 24 May 2016, www.pew socialtrends.org/2016/05/24/for-first-time-in-modern-era-living-with-parents-edges-out-other-living-arrangements-for-18-to-34 year olds/

Fryer, D., and Fagan, R. (1994) 'The role of social psychological aspects of income on the mental health costs of unemployment', *Community Psychologist*, 27(2), pp. 16–17.

Fuchs, C. (2013) 'The Anonymous movement in the context of liberalism and socialism', *Interface*, 5(2), pp. 345–376.

Fuchs, C. (2014) *Digital Labour and Karl Marx*. New York: Routledge.

Furchtgott-Roth D., and Meyer, J. (2015) *Disinherited: How Washington Is Betraying America's Young*. New York: Encounter Books.

Furedi, F. (2005) *The Politics of Fear. Beyond Left and Right*. New York: Continuum.

Furlong, A., and Cartmel, F. (2006) *Young People and Social Change: Individualisation and Risk in Late Modernity*. Milton Keynes: Open University Press.

Furlong, A., and Cartmel, F. (2007) *Young People and Social Change*. London: McGraw-Hill.

Furlong, A. and Cartmel, F. (2012) 'Social change and political engagement among young people: generation and the 2009/2010, British Election Survey', *Parliamentary Affairs*, 65(1), pp. 13–28.

Galbraith, J. (1958) *The Affluent Society*. New York: Houghton Mifflin.

Galbraith J., Wray, R., and Mosler, W. (2009) *The Case against Intergenerational Accounting: The Accounting Campaign against Social Security and Medicare*, Public Policy Brief, New York: The Levy Economics Institute, Bard College.

Galik, L., and Gilroy L. (2015) *Annual Privatization Report 2015: Criminal Justice and Corrections*. Reason Foundation. http://reason.org/files/apr-2015-criminal-justice.pdf.

Gallagher, P. (2006) *Australian Government Research on Ageing: Potential Impacts and Policy Responses*. Canberra: ANU.

Galston, W.A. (2004) 'Civic education and political participation', *PS: Political Science and Politics*, 37(2), pp. 263–266.

Gardiner, L. (2016) *Stagnation Generation: The Case for Renewing the Intergenerational Contract*. London: The Intergenerational Commission/Resolution Foundation.

Garland, D. (1996) 'The Limits of the Sovereign State', *The British Journal of Criminology*, 36(4), pp. 445–471.

Garland, D. (2001) *The Culture of Control: Crime and Social Order*. Oxford: Oxford University Press.

Germains, G. (2014) 'The lost generation', *Intern*, 2, pp. 17–21.

Giddens, A. (1990) *The Consequences of Modernity*. Cambridge: Polity Press.

Giedd, J. (2016) 'The Amazing Teen Brain', *Scientific American*, 1 May 2016.

Gillies, D. (2011) 'State education as high-yield investment: Human capital theory in European policy discourse' *Pedagogicky Casopis*, 2, pp. 224–245.

Ginsborg, P. (2009) *Democracy: Crisis and Renewal*. London: Profile Books.

Giroux, H. (2015) 'Schools as punishing factories: the handcuffing of public education, *Rise Up Times*, 21 August 2015. https://riseuptimes.org/2015/08/21/giroux-schools-as-punishing-factories-the-handcuffing-of-public-education/.

Gleick, J. (2014) 'Today's dead end kids', *The New York Review of Books*, 18 December 2014, pp. 36–38.

Glyn, A., and Wood, S. (2001) 'Economic policy under New Labour: How social democratic is the Blair Government?, *Political Quarterly*, 72(1), pp. 5–66.

Gokhale, J. (2009) *Measuring the Unfunded Obligations of European Countries*. Washington: National Center for Policy Analysis.

Goldrick-Rab, S. (2016) *Paying the Price: College Costs, Financial Aid and The Betrayal of the American Dream*. Chicago: University of Chicago.

Goldthorpe, J. (1987) *Mobility and the Class Structure in Modern Britain*. London, Clarendon Press.

Gordon, H., and Taft, J. (2011) 'Rethinking youth political socialization: teenage activists talk back', *Youth & Society*, 43(4), pp. 1499–1527.

Gough, I. (1979) *The Political Economy of the Welfare State*. London: Macmillan.

Gov.uk (2015) *Help to Buy*. www.gov.uk/government/news/help-to-buy-helping-130000-own-their-own-home.

Gov.uk (2016a) *National Minimum Wage Rates*. www.gov.uk/national-minimum-wage-rates.

Gov.uk (2016b) *National Living Wage*. www.gov.uk/government/publications/national-living-wage-nlw/national-living-wage-nlw.

Graeber, D. (2013) *Debt: The First Five Thousand Years*. London: Melville House.

Gray, J. (2007) *Straw Dogs*. New York: Farrar, Straus and Giroux.

Green, D., and Shapiro, I., (1994) *Pathologies of Rational Choice Theory*. New Haven: Yale University Press.

Green, S. (2002) *Rational choice theory: An overview*. Waco: Baylor University. http://business.baylor.edu/steve_green/green1.doc.

Greenville, J., Pobke, C., and Rogers, N. (2013) *Trends in the Distribution of Income in Australia*. Melbourne: Productivity Commission.

Grogger, J., and Karoly, L. (2005) *Welfare reform: Effects of a decade of change*. Cambridge: Harvard University Press.

Gross, M., and McGoey, L. (2015) *Routledge International Handbook of Ignorance Studies*. London: Routledge.

Guardian and London School of Economics (2011) *Reading the Riots: Investigating England's Summer of Disorder*. London: London School of Economics.

Gunter, A., and Watt, P. (2009) 'Goin' college, goin' work and goin' road: Youth cultures and transitions in east London', *Journal of Youth Studies*, 12(5), pp. 515–529.

Haas, J., and Vogt, K. (2014) 'Ignorance and Investigation', in M. Gross and L. McGoey (eds) *Routledge International Handbook of Ignorance Studies*. Abingdon: Routlege, pp. 17–32.

Habermas, J. (1989) *The Structural Transformation of the Public Sphere: An Inquiry into a Category of Bourgeois Society*. (trans T. Burger with F. Lawrence). Cambridge: MIT Press.

Habermas, J. (1996) *Between Facts and Norms: Contributions to a Discourse Theory of Law and Democracy*, (trans W. Rehg). Cambridge: MIT Press.

Habermas, J. (2004) 'Public space and political public sphere – the biographical roots of two motifs in my thought', *Commemorative Lecture*, 11 November 2004, Kyoto. http://ikesharpless.pbworks.com/f/Kyoto_lecture_Nov_2004,+Jurgen+Habermas.pdf.

Hall, G.S. (1904) *Adolescence: Its Psychology and its Relations to Physiology, Anthropology, Sociology, Sex, Crime, Religion and Education*. London: Chapman and Hall.

Hall, P. (1986) *Governing the Economy: The Politics of State Intervention in Britain and France*. New York: Oxford University Press.

Hall, P. (1989) *The Political Power of Economic Ideas: Keynesianism across Nations*. Princeton: Princeton University Press.

Hall, P. (1990) *Policy Paradigms, Experts and the State: The Case of Macro Economic Policy Making in Britain*. New York: Macmillan.

Hall, P. (1993) 'Policy Paradigms, Social Learning and the State: The Case of Economic Policy-making in Britain', *Comparative Politics*, 25, pp. 275–296.

Hall, P. (2001) 'The Evolution of Economic Policy-making in the European Union', in A. Menon and V. Wright (eds) *From the Nation State to Europe?* Oxford: Oxford University Press.

Hall, P., and Soskice, D. (eds) (2001) *Varieties of Capitalism: The Institutional Foundations of Comparative Advantage*. New York: Oxford University Press.

Hallpike, C. (1979) *The Foundations of Primitive Thought*. Oxford: Oxford University Press.

Hamblett, C., and Deverson, J. (1964) *Generation X*. London: Tandem Books.

Hamilton Project (2014) *Ten Economic Facts about Crime and Incarceration in the United States*. Washington: Brookings Institute. www.hamiltonproject.org/papers/ten_economic_facts_about_crime_and_incarceration_in_the_united_states.

Hammond, J.L., and Hammond, B. (1912) *The Village Labourer 1760–1832*. London: Longman Green.

Harrington, M. (1962) *The Other America: Poverty in the United States*. New York: Touchstone.

Harris, A., Wyn, J., and Younes, S. (2010a) 'Beyond apathetic or activist youth. "Ordinary" young people and contemporary forms of participation', *Young*, 18(1), pp. 9–32.

Harris, R., Simons, M., and Maher, K. (2010b) *New directions in European vocational education and training policy and practice Lessons for Australia*, Canberra: NCVER.

Harvey, D. (2005) *A Brief History of Neoliberalism*. Oxford: Oxford University Press.

Harvey, D. (2012) *Rebel Cities: From the Right to the City to the Urban Revolution*. London: Verso.

Hay, C. (2001) 'The "Crisis" of Keynesianism and the Rise of Neoliberalism in Britain: An Ideational Institutionalist Approach', in J.L. Campbell and O.K. Pedersen (eds) *The Rise of Neoliberalism and Institutional Analysis*. Princeton: Princeton University Press, pp. 193–218.

Hay, C. (2007) *Why We Hate Politics*. Cambridge: Polity Press.

Hay, C., and Stoker, G. (2009) 'Revitalising Politics: Have We Lost the Plot?', *Representation*, 45(3), pp. 225–236.

Hays, S. (1994) 'Structure and agency and the sticky problem of culture', *Sociological Theory*, 12(1), pp. 57–72.

Heffernan, M. (2011) *Wilful Blindness: Why We Ignore the Obvious at our Peril*. New York: Walker & Co.

Heller, P., Hemming, R., and Kohnert, P. (1986) *Aging and Social expenditures in the Major Industrialized Countries 1980–2025*, IMF, Occasional Paper no. 47 Washington: IMF.

Hendry, D., and Ericsson, N. (2006) (eds) *Understanding Economic Forecasts*. New York: McGraw Hill.

Henman, P., and Perry, J. (2002) 'Welfare dependency? A critical analysis of changes in welfare recipient numbers', *Australian Journal of Social Issues*, 37(3), pp. 315–335. http://search.informit.com.au.ezproxy.lib.rmit.edu.au/documentSummary;dn=200210424.

Henn, M., and Weinstein, M. (2006) 'Young people and political (in)activism: why don't young people vote?', *Policy & politics*, 34(3), pp. 517–534.

Henn, M., Weinstein, M., and Forrest, S. (2005) 'Uninterested youth? Young people's attitudes towards party politics in Britain', *Political Studies*, 53(3), pp. 556–578.

Henrichson, C., and Delaney, R. (2012) *The Price of Prisons: What Incarceration Costs Taxpayers*. New York: Vera Institute. http://archive.vera.org/sites/default/files/resources/downloads/price-of-prisons-updated-version-021914.pdf.

Henry, S., and Milovanovic, D. (1994) 'The constitution of Constitutive Criminology: A Postmodern approach to Criminological Theory', in D. Nelken (ed.) *The Futures of Criminology*. London: Sage.

Heywood, A. (2013) *Politics* (4th edn.) London: Palgrave Macmillan.

Hill, M. (1993) *The Welfare State in Britain: A Political History since 1945*. Brookfield, VA: Edward Elgar.

Hing, J. (2012) 'The Shocking Details of a Mississippi School-to-Prison Pipeline', *Truthout*, 3 December 2012. http://truth-out.org/news/item/13121-the-shocking-details-of-a-mississippi-school-to-prison-pipeline.

HM Government (2014) *Child poverty strategy 2014–2017*. www.gov.uk/government/uploads/system/uploads/attachment_data/file/324103/Child_poverty_strategy.pdf (accessed 11 July 2014).

Hoare, J., and Robb, P. (2006) 'Crime in England and Wales update to June 2006', *Home Office Statistical Bulletin 16/06*. www.homeoffice.gov.uk/ids.

Horspool, D. (2009) *The English Rebel: One Thousand Years of Troublemaking, from the Normans to the Nineties*. London: Penguin.

Howarth, R. (2005) 'Against High Discount Rates', in W. Sinnot-Armstrong, and R. Howarth (eds) *Perspectives on Climate Change: Science, Economics, Politics, Ethics*. Oxford: JAI Press.

Howker, E., and Malik, A. (2009) *The Jilted Generation*. London: Atlantic.

Husak, D. (2008) *Overcriminalization: the limits of the criminal law*. New York: Oxford University Press.

ICPR (2016) 'United Kingdom: England and Wales', *World Prison Brief*, Institute for Criminal Policy Research. www.prisonstudies.org/country/united-kingdom-england-wales.

IMF (2012) *Australia: Financial System Stability Assessment*. IMF Country Report No. 12/308. Washington: IMF. www.apra.gov.au/AboutAPRA/Publications/Documents/cr12308%5B1%5D.pdf.

IMF (2013) *France: Financial Sector Assessment Program— Technical Note on Housing Prices and Financial Stability*. IMF Country Report No 3/184. Washington: IMF. www.imf.org/external/pubs/ft/scr/2013/cr13184.pdf.

IMF (2016) *World Economic Outlook April*, IMF. www.imf.org/external/pubs/ft/weo/2016/01/weodata/index.aspx.

Infosys (2016) *Amplifying Human Potential: Education and Skills for the Fourth Industrial Revolution*. www.infosys.com.

International Labour Organization, ILO (2016) *World Employment and Social Outlook: Trends 2016*. Geneva: ILO.

Interviews (2012) Interviews conducted 12 April 2012.

Jaeger, H. (1985) 'Generations in history: reflections on a controversial topic', *History and Theory*, 24(3), pp. 273–294.

Jansson, B. (1997) *The Reluctant Welfare State — American Social Welfare Policies: Past,Present, and Future,* (Third Edition). New York: Haworth Press.

Jansson, K. (2007) *British Crime Survey – Measuring crime for 25 years*. London: BCS. nationalarchives.gov.uk/20110218135832/rds.homeoffice.gov.uk/rds/pdfs07/bcs25.pdf.

Jauregui, A. (2013) 'Anonymous DDoS petition: Group calls on White House to recognize distributed denial of service as protest', *Huffington Post*, 13 January 2013. www.huffingtonpost.com.au/entry/anonymous-ddos-petition-white-house_n_2463009.

Jencks, C. (1992) *Rethinking social policy: Race, poverty, and the underclass*. Cambridge: Harvard University Press.

Jennings, M.K., Stoker, L., and Bowers, J. (2009) 'Politics across Generations: Family Transmission Re-examined', *The Journal of Politics*, 71(3), pp. 782–799.

Joas, H., and Knobl, W. (2009) *Social Theory: Twenty Introductory Lectures*. Cambridge: Cambridge University Press.

Kalecki, M. (1943) 'Political aspects of full employment', *Political Quarterly*, 1943.

Kamenatz, A. (2006) *Generation Debt: Why Now is a Terrible Time to be Young*. New York: Riverhead Books.

Kauppi, N. (2002) 'Elements for a Structural Constructivist Theory of Politics', *Center for European Studies Working Paper Series #104*. Cambridge: Harvard University Press.

Keane, J. (1995) 'Structural transformations of the public sphere' *Communications Review*, 1(1), pp. 1–22.

Kensey, A. (2005) 'La Population des condamnes a de longues peines'. Unpublished PhD Thesis, Paris: University of Paris I Panthe on Sorbonne.

Kenworthy, L. (1999) 'Do social welfare policies reduce poverty? A cross-national assessment', *Social Forces*, 77, pp. 119–139.

Kenyon, E., and Heath, S. (2001) 'Choosing this life: narratives of choice amongst house sharers', *Housing Studies*, 16(5), pp. 619–635.

Kertzer, D. (1983) 'Generation as a Sociological Problem', *Annual Review of Sociology*, 9, pp. 125–149.

Keynes, J. (1971–1989) *The Collected Writings*: XXVI, *Activities 1940–1946. Shaping the Post-War World: Bretton Woods and reparations*, D. Moggridge (ed.). London: Macmillan.

Kimberlee, R.H. (2002) 'Why Don't British Young People Vote at General Elections?' *Journal of Youth Studies*, 5(1), pp. 85–98.

King, M.L. (1968) 'The Other America', Speech at Grosse pointe High School, 14 March 1968, Grosse Pointe Historical Society, www.gphistorical.org/mlk/mlkspeech/mlk-gp-speech.pdf.

Kingson, E.R. (2007) 'Generations at war: The sequel', *Together*, 14(2), pp. 5–6.

Kogan, M., and Hanney, S. (2000) *Reforming Higher Education*. London: Jessica Kingsley.

Kogler, H. (1997a) 'Alienation as epistemological source: Reflexivity and social background after Mannheim and Bourdieu,' *Social Epistemology: A Journal of Knowledge, Culture and Policy*, 11(2), pp. 141–164.

Kogler, H. (1997b) 'Reconceptualisng reflexive sociology: A reply', *Social Epistemology: A Journal of Knowledge, Culture and Policy*, 11(2), pp. 223–250.

Kohlberg, L. (1981) *Essays on Moral Development, Vol.I: The Philosophy of Moral Development*. San Francisco: Harper & Row.

Konrath, S., Bushman, B.J., and Campbell, W.K. (2006) 'Attenuating the link between threatened egotism and aggression', *Psychological Science*, 17, pp. 995–1001.

Korpi, W., and Palme, J. (2003) 'New politics and class politics in the context of austerity and globalization: welfare state regress in 18 countries, 1975–1995', *The American Political Science Review*, 97(3), pp. 425–446.

Kotlikoff, L., and Burns, S. (2004) *The Coming Generational Storm*. Cambridge: MIT Press.

Kotlikoff, L., and Raffelhüschen, B. (1999) 'Generational accounting around the world', *AEA Papers and Proceedings*, 89(2), pp. 161–166.

Kroll, A. (2010) 'Steve Eisman's next big short: For-profit colleges', *Mother Jones*, 27 May 2010. www.motherjones.com/mojo/2010/05/steve-eisman-big-short-michael-lewis.

Kus, B. (2006) 'Neoliberalism, Institutional Change and the Welfare State: The Case of Britain and France', *International Journal of Comparative Sociology*, 47(6), pp. 488–525.

Lacey N. (2009) 'Historicising Criminalization: Conceptual and Empirical Issues', *Modern Law Review*, 72(6), pp. 936–960.

Lacey N. (2012) 'Principles, Policies, and Politics of Criminal Law', in L. Zedner and J. Roberts (eds) *Principles and Values in Criminal Law and Criminal Justice*. Oxford: Oxford University Press.

Lakoff, G. (2004) *Don't Think of an Elephant*. London: Chelsea Green Publishing.

Lambert, M. (2014) *Privatization and the Public Good: Universities in the Balance*. Cambridge: Harvard Education Press.

Lamm, R.D. (1989) 'Columbus and Copernicus: New wine in old wineskins', *Mount Sinai Journal of Medicine*, 56(1), pp. 1–10.

Larson, R., and Lampman-Petraitis, C. (1989) 'Daily emotional states as reported by children and adolescents', *Child Development*, 60, pp. 1250–1260.

Laslett, P., and Fishkin, J. (eds) (1992) *Philosophy, Politics & Society: Justice Between Age Groups and Generations*, Vol 6. New Haven: Yale University Press.

Latournauld, W. (2014) 'Youth Unemployment: What Future for Generation Y?' *Cafebabel*, 18 December 2014. www.cafebabel.co.uk/society/article/youth-unemployment-what-future-for-generation-y.html.

Lazear, M. (2000) 'Economic imperialism', *The Quarterly Journal of Economics*, 115(1), pp. 99–146.

Leach, J., Broeks, M., Østensvik, K., and Kingman, D. (2016) *European Intergenerational Fairness Index: A crisis for the young*. London: Intergenerational Foundation.

Leadbetter, C. (1999) *Living on Thin Air: The New Economy*. London: Penguin Viking.

Leftwich, A. (2004) *What is Politics? The Activity and its Study*. Cambridge: Polity.

Lehmann, W. (2004) ' "For some reason I get a little scared": Structure, agency and risk in school-work transitions', *Journal of Youth Studies*, 7(4), pp. 379–396.

Leigh, A. (2013) *Battlers and Billionaires: The Story of Inequality in Australia*. Collingwood: Black Inc.

Levy, J. (1999) *Tocqueville's Revenge: State, Society, and Economy in Contemporary France*. Cambridge: Harvard University Press.

Levy, J. (2010) 'The Return of the State? French Economic Policy under Nicolas Sarkozy'. Paper presented at the annual meeting of the American Political Science Association, Washington.

Lewis, A. (1954) 'Economic development with unlimited supplies of labour', *The Manchester School*, 22(2), pp. 139–191.

Lewis, D. (2006) 'Online Communities of interest for Young People', International Conference on Engaging Communities, Brisbane.

Liddington, A. (2015) United Patriots Front: Leadership 360, www.youtube.com/watch?v=diTHFBKX8Wgwww.youtube.com/watch?v=diTHFBKX8Wg.

LiHumanite.fr (2015) 'En Île-de-France, un jeune sur deux contraint de rester vivre chez ses parents'. www.humanite.fr/en-ile-de-france-un-jeune-sur-deux-contraint-de-rester-vivre-chez-ses-parents-585370.

Lipset, S. (1996) *American Exceptionalism: A Two-Edged Sword*, New York: W.W. Norton.

Livingstone, S. (2012) 'Critical reflections on the benefits of ICT in education', *Oxford Review of Education*, 38(1), pp. 9–24.

Livingstone, S., Pitre, S., and Watling, J. (2005) 'Active Participation or just more information? Young people's take up of opportunities to act and interact on the Internet', *Information Communication and Society*, 8(3), pp. 287–314.

Longman, P. (1987) *Born to Pay: The New Politics of Aging in America*. Boston: Houghton Mifflin.

Lunt, I. (2008) 'Beyond tuition fees? The legacy of Blair's government to higher education', *Oxford Review of Education*, 34(6), pp. 741–752.

MacDonald, R. (2011) 'Youth transitions, unemployment and under employment. Plus ca change, plus c'est le meme chose?' *Journal of sociology*, 47(4), pp. 427–444.

Macdonald, R., and Marsh, J. (2004) 'Missing school', *Youth & society*, 36(2), pp. 143–162.

MacGregor, S. (1985) 'Making Sense of Social Security: Initiatives and Implementation 1979–1983', in P. Jackson (ed.) *Implementing Government Policy Initiatives: The Thatcher Administration (1979–1983)*. London: Royal Institute of Public Administration, pp. 229–251.

Maguire, M. (1997) 'Crime Statistics, Patterns and Trends', in M. Maguire, R. Morgan, and R. Reiner (eds) *The Oxford Handbook of Criminology* (2nd edn). Oxford: Oxford University Press, pp. 135–188.

Maguire, M. (2007) 'Crime data and statistics', in M. Maguire, R. Morgan, and R. Reiner (eds) *The Oxford Handbook of Criminology* (4th edn) Oxford: Oxford University Press.

Mannheim, K. (1952 [1928]) 'The problem of generations', in K. Mannheim, *Essays on the Sociology of Knowledge: Collected Works Vol 5*. London: Routledge, pp. 276–322.

Manning, N. (2009) *Young people and politics: apathetic and disengaged? A qualitative inquiry*. Koln: Lambert Academic.

Marsh, D., and Stoker, G. (eds) (2002) *Theory and Methods in Political Science*. London: Palgrave Macmillan.

Marshall, A. (1930) *Principles of Economics*, 8th edn. London: Macmillan.

Martin, A. (2012) 'Political Participation among the Young in Australia: Testing Dalton's Good Citizen Thesis', *Australian Journal of Political Science*, 42, pp. 211–226.

Mayo, E. (1949) *Hawthone and the Western Electric Company: The Problems of an Industrial Civilization*. London: Routledge.

McCarthy, D., Sefton, J., and Weale, M. (2011) *Generational accounts for the United Kingdom*. London: National Institute of Economic and Social Research.

McCormack, A. (2016) 'Generation Less: Why we're worse off than our parents' *Triple J Hack*. www.abc.net.au/triplej/programs/hack/generation-less-why-young-people-are-worse-off-than-their-parent/7320370.

McCracken, M. (2009) 'How Accurate are forecasts in a recession?', *Economic Synopses*, 9, pp. 2–5.

McDonald, K. (1999) *Struggles for Subjectivity: Identity, Action and Youth Experience*. Cambridge: Cambridge University Press.

McGuinness, F. (2016) *Income inequality in the UK*, House of Commons Briefing Paper No 7484. July. London: House of Commons Library.

McMullin J, Duerden, T., Comeau, and Jovic, E. (2007) 'Generational affinities and discourses of difference: A case study of highly skilled information technology workers', *The British Journal of Sociology*, 58(2), pp. 299–300.

Melbourne Institute of Applied Economic and Social Research (2016) *The Household, Income and Labour Dynamics in Australia Survey: Selected Findings from Waves 1 to 14*. Melbourne: MIAESR.

Merton, R.K. (1948) 'The Self-fulfilling prophecy', *Antioch Review,* 8(2), pp. 193–210.

Mestan, K. (2014) 'Paternalism in Australian welfare policy', Australian Journal of Social Sciences, 49(1), pp. 3–22.

Michael, J., and Adler, M. (1933) *Crime, Law and Social Science*. Montclair: Patterson Smith.

Michler, J. (2013) 'Austerity and the metaphors that bind', *Lady Economist,* https://lady economist.com/2013/04/08/household-as-metaphor-and-national-austerity-economics/.

Micklethwait, J., and Wooldridge, A. (2014) *The Fourth Revolution: The Global Race to Reinvent the State*. London: Penguin Random House.

Middaugh, E. (2012) *Service and Activism in the Digital Age: Supporting Youth Engagement in Public life*, DML Central Working Papers, UC Irvine.

Mill, J.S. (1972) *Utilitarianism, On Liberty and Considerations on Representative Government* (ed. H.B. Acton). London: Dent.

Mincer, J. (1958) 'Investment in Human Capital and Personal Income Distribution', *Journal of Political Economy*, 66(4), pp. 281–302.

Minguez, A. (2016) Economic crisis and the new housing transitions of young people in Spain, *International Journal of Housing Policy*, 16(2), pp. 165–183.

Ministry of Education Culture and Sport (2015) *Datos básicos del sistema universitario español*. www.mecd.gob.es/dms/mecd/educacion-mecd/areaseducacion/universidades/estadisticas.

Mirowski, P, and Plehwe, D. (eds) (2009) *The Road from Mont Pelerin: The Making of the Neoliberal Thought Collective*. Cambridge: Harvard University Press.

Mishra, R. (1999) *Globalisation and the Welfare State*. Cheltenham: Edward Elgar.

Mission Australia (2016) *Pre-budget Submission 2016–17*. Sydney: Mission Australia. www.treasury.gov.au/~/media/Treasury/Consultations%20and%20Reviews/Consultations/2015/2016%20Pre%20Budget%20submissions/Submissions/PDF/Mission%20Australia.ashx.

Moffitt, R. (2007) *Welfare Reform: The US Experience*, prepared for the Economic Council of Sweden Conference 'From Welfare to Work', Stockholm, 7 May 2007.

Moffitt, R. (2015) 'The deserving poor, the family, and the US welfare system', *Demography,* 52, pp. 729–749.

Morabito, A. (2016) 'Report: Millennials won't meet the average standard of living until 2034'. *Red Alert*, August. http://redalertpolitics.com/2016/08/17/report-millennials-wont-meet-average-standard-living-2034/#fD4uSFjcvEb5e6TZ.99.

Morris, N. (2006) 'Blair's "frenzied law making": a new offence for every day spent in office', *Independent*, 16 August 2006. www.independent.co.uk/news/uk/politics/blairs-frenzied-law-making-a-new-offence-for-every-day-spent-in-office-412072.html.

Mouffe, C. (2005a) *The Return of the Political*. London: Verso.

Mouffe, C. (2005b) *On the Political*. London: Routledge.

Mueller, J. (2011) 'The IMF, Neoliberalism and Hegemony', *Journal of Global Society*, 25(3), pp. 377–402.

Muncie, J. (2006) 'Governing young people: Coherence and contradiction in contemporary youth justice', *Critical Social Policy*, 26, pp. 770–793.

Muncie, J. (2008) 'The "punitive turn" in juvenile justice: Cultures of control and rights compliance in Western Europe and the USA', *Youth Justice*. 8(2), pp. 107–121.

Murphy, J. (2016) *A Decent Provision: Australian Welfare Policy, 1870 to 1949*. Abingdon: Routledge.

Murphy, J., Murray, S., Chalmers, J., Martin, S., and Marston, G. (2011) *Half a citizen: Life on Welfare in Australia*. Sydney: Allen & Unwin.

Murray, C. (1984) *Losing Ground: American Social Policy 1950–1980*. Basic Books.

Musselin, C. (2001) *The Long March of French Universities*. New York: Routledge.

Myles, J. (1984) *Old Age in the Welfare State*. Boston: Little Brown.

Nagel, T. (1975) 'Libertarianism without Foundations', *Yale Law Journal*, 85, pp. 136–151.

Nakata, S. (2008) 'Elizabeth Eckford's appearance at Little Rock: The possibility of children's political agency', *Politics*, 28(1), pp. 19–25.

Nakosteen, M. (1965) *The History and Philosophy of Education*. New York: Wiley.

Nash, L. (1978) 'Concepts of Existence: Greek Origins of Generational Thought' *Daedalus*, 107(4), pp. 1–21.

Nazario, J. (2009) 'Politically Motivated Denial of Service Attacks,' *Arbor Networks*, https://ccdcoe.org/publications/virtualbattlefield/12_NAZARIO%20Politically%20Motivated%20DDoS.pdf.

Neocleous, M. (2000a) 'Against Security', *Radical Philosophy*, 100, pp. 7–15.

Neocleous, M. (2000b) *The Fabrication of Social Order: A Critical Theory of Police Power*. London: Pluto Press.

Neocleous, M. (2008) *Critique of Security*. Edinburgh: Edinburgh University Press.

Newburn, T. (2015) 'The 2011 England Riots in Recent Historical Perspective', *British Journal of Criminology*, 55, pp. 39–64.

Newburn, T., Cooper, K., Deacon, R., and Diski, R. (2015) 'Shopping for Free? Looting, Consumerism and the 2011 Riots', *British Journal of Criminology*, 55(5), pp. 987–1004.

Newburn, T., Lewis, P., and Metcalf, J. (2011) 'A new kind of riot? From Brixton 1981 to Tottenham 2011', *Guardian*, 9 December 2011.

Nicholas, S., and Appleyard, D. (2008) 'Meet the families where no one's worked for THREE generations – and they don't care', *Daily Mail*. 21 March 2008. www.dailymail.co.uk/news/article-541598/Meet-families-ones-worked-THREE-generations-dont-care.html#ixzz4LnOBR2uh.

Nozick, R. (1974) *Anarchy, State, Utopia*. New York: Basic Books.

NullCrew (2013) @NullCrew_FTS. https://twitter.com/NullCrew_FTS/status/3091726 1020431.

Nussbaum, M. (1988) 'Nature, Function, and Capability: Aristotle on Political Distribution', in *Oxford Studies in Ancient Philosophy*. Oxford: Oxford University Press.

Nussbaum, M. (1995) 'Human Capabilities, Female Human beings', in M. Nussbaum, and J. Glover (eds) *Women, Culture and Development*. Oxford, Oxford University Press.

Nussbaum, M. (1997) 'Human rights theory: capabilities and human rights', *Fordham Law Review*, 66, pp. 273–300.

Nussbaum, M. (2000) *Women and Human Development*. Cambridge: Cambridge University Press.

Nussbaum, M. (2003) *The Fragility of Goodness*. Cambridge, Cambridge University Press.

Nussbaum, M. (2011) *Creating capabilities: The Human Development Approach*. Cambridge: Harvard University Press.

Nussbaum, M. (2015) *Political Emotions: Why Love Matters for Justice*. Cambridge: Harvard University Press.

O'Connor, J. (1973) *The Fiscal Crisis of the State*. New York: St. Martin's.

O'Malley, P. (2009) 'Responsibilization', in A. Wakefield and J. Fleming (eds) *The Sage Dictionary of Policing*. London: Sage, pp. 277–279. doi: http://dx.doi.org/10.4135/9781446269053.

OECD (1988) 'The Path to Full Employment: Structural adjustment for an active society', (Editorial), *OECD Employment Outlook*, OECD, Paris 7–12.

OECD (1997) *Ageing in OECD Countries – A Critical Policy challenge*, Social policy studies No. 20, Paris: OECD.

OECD (2008) *Growing unequal? Income distribution and poverty in OECD* countries. Paris: Organisation for Economic Co-operation and Development. (OECD).

OECD (2011) *Divided we fall: why inequality keeps rising*, Paris: OECD www.oecd.org/els/soc/49499779.pdf.

OECD (2014a) *Rising inequality: Youth and poor fall further behind*. Paris: Organisation for Economic Co-operation and Development.

OECD (2014b) *Education at a Glance*. OECD Indicators. www.oecd.org/edu/Education-at-a-Glance-2014.pdf.

OECD (2015a) 'Labour Force Statistics by Age and Sex' http://stats.oecd.org/.

OECD (2015b) *In It Together: why less inequality benefits all*, Paris: OECD www.keepeek.com/Digital-Asset-Management/oecd/employment/in-it-together-why-less-inequality-benefits-all_9789264235120-en.

OECD (2016a) Historical population data and projections https://stats.oecd.org/Index.aspx?DataSetCode=POP_PROJ.

OECD (2016b) *Social expenditure: aggregate data* https://stats.oecd.org/Index.aspx?DataSetCode=SOCX_AGG.

OECD (2016c) *OECD Outlook* (June), www.oecd.org/eco/outlook/economic-outlook-june-2016-catherine-l-mann-editorial-policy-makers-act-now.htm.

Offe, C. (1984) *Contradictions of the Welfare State*. Cambridge, Mass: MIT Press.

Offer, D. (1984) 'Normal Adolescents', *American Educator*, 9, pp. 34–39.

Offer, D. (1987) 'In defence of adolescents', *Journal of the American Medical Association*, 257(24), pp. 3407–3408.

Offer, D., and Offer, J. (1975) *From teenage to Young manhood: A psychological study*. New York: Basic Books.

Offer, D., and Schonert-Reichl, K.A. (1993) '"Myths or truths of adolescence?" Reply', *Journal of the American Academy of Child and Adolescent Psychiatry*, 32, pp. 1077–1078.

Offer, D., & Schonert-Reichl, K.A. (1992) 'Debunking the myths of adolescence: Findings from recent research', *Journal of the American Academy of Child and Adolescent Psychiatry*, 31(6), pp. 1003–1014.

Office of Budget and Management (2013) *Fiscal Year 2013: Historical Tables. Budget of the US Government*. Washington: OBM.

Oller, L., and Barot, B. (2000) 'The accuracy of European Growth and inflation Forecasts', *International Journal of Forecasting*, 16(2), pp. 293–315.

Olmedo, A., and Santa Cruz Grau, E. (2013) 'Neoliberalism, policy advocacy networks and think tanks in the Spanish educational arena, the case of FAES', *Education Inquiry*, vol. 4, www.education-inquiry.net/index.php/edui/article/view/22618.

Olsen, H.B. (2015) 'Let's talk about millennial poverty'. https://medium.com/@mshanna brooks/but-seriously-lets-talk-about-millennial-poverty-526066ad9adb#.6435tgdpw.

ONS (2015a) *English Housing Survey 2013–2014* www.gov.uk/government/statistics/english-housing-survey-2013-to-2014-headline-report.

ONS (2015b) Housing Summary Measures Analysis www.ons.gov.uk/ons/dcp171776_412657.pdf.

ONS (2016) *UK Labour Market 2016* www.ons.gov.uk/employmentandlabourmarket/peopleinwork/employmentandemployeetypes/bulletins/uklabourmarket/september 2016#young-people-in-the-labour-market.

Oord, T. (2007) *The Altruism Reader*. Philadelphia: Templeton Foundation Press.

O'Reilly, J., Eichorst, W., Gabos, A., Hadjivassilou, K., Lain, D., Leshcke, J., McGuinness, S., Kurekova, L., Nazio, T., Ortlieb, R., Russell, H, and Villa, P. (2015) 'Five characteristics of youth unemployment in Europe: Flexibility, education, migration, family legacies and EU policy', *Sage Open,* January–March, pp. 1–19.

Organisation for Economic Co-operation and Development (OECD) (1988) *Employment Outlook*. Paris: OECD.

Organization for Economic Co-operation and Development *(2011) OECD Employment Outlook*. Paris: OECD.

Organization for Economic Co-operation and Development (1985) *Social Expenditure, 1960–1990: Problems of Growth and Control*. Paris: OECD.

Parkinson, M. (2015) *Graduation Address: University of Adelaide*. www.adelaide.edu.au/news-image/Parkinson.pdf.

Pascual, A. (2007) 'Reshaping Welfare States', in A. Pascual and L. Magnusson (eds) *Reshaping Welfare States and Activation Regimes in Europe*. Brussels: PIE Peter Lang.

Patterson, J. (1988) *Grand Expectations: The United States, 1945–1974*. New York: Oxford University Press.

Pearce, F., and Snider, I. (1995) 'Regulating Capitalism', in F. Pearce, F., and I. Snider (eds) *Corporate Crime Contemporary Debates*. Toronto: University of Toronto Press, pp. 19–47.

Pearson, G. (1983) *Hooligan: A History of Respectable Fears*. Basingstoke: Macmillan.

Peck, J. (1998) 'Workfare: A geopolitical etymology', *Environment and Planning D: Society and Space*, 16(2), pp. 133–161.

Peel, M. (2003) *The Lowest Rung: Voices of Australian Poverty*. Melbourne: Cambridge University Press.

Pelaez, V. (2014) The Prison Industry in the United States: Big Business or a New Form of Slavery? *Global Research,* March 31 2014. www.globalresearch.ca/the-prison-industry-in-the-united-states-big-business-or-a-new-form-of-slavery/8289.

Pellandini-Simanyi, L. (2014) 'Bourdieu, ethics and symbolic power', *The Sociological Review,* 62(4), pp. 651–674.

Perez-Lanzac, C. (2014) 'Out of the job market at 23', *El Pais*. http://elpais.com/elpais/2014/11/07/inenglish/1415352012_379056.html.

Peterson, S. (2014) Juvenile Justice and Youth Justice in Spain. *Global Youth Justice,* August. http://blog.globalyouthjustice.org/?p=2735.

Pettit, P. (2007) 'A Republican Right to Basic income?', *Basic Income Studies*, 2(2), pp. 1–8.

Pew Research Center (2014) *Political Polarization in the American Public*. www.people-press.org/2014/06/12/political-polarization-in-the-american-public/.

Pew Research Center (2015a) *Black Child Poverty Rate Holds Steady, Even As Other Groups See Declines*. www.pewresearch.org/fact-tank/2015/07/14/black-child-poverty-rate-holds-steady-even-as-other-groups-see-declines/.

Pew Research Center (2015b) *Millennials and Political News*. www.journalism.org/files/2015/06/Millennials-and-News-FINAL-7-27-15.pdf.

Pew Research Center (2015c) *The Whys and Hows of Generations Research*. www.people-press.org/files/2015/09/09-3-2015-Generations-explainer-release.pdf.

Pew Research Center (2015d) *Most Millennials Resist the Millennial Label*. www.people-press.org/files/2015/09/09-03-2015-Generations-release.pdf.

Pew Research Centre (2015e) *A Deep Dive in Party Affiliation*. www.people-press.org/2015/04/07/a-deep-dive-into-party-affiliation/.

Phelps, E. (2012) 'Understanding electoral turnout among British young people: a review of the literature', *Parliamentary Affairs,* 65(1), pp. 281–299.

Piaget, J. (1932) *The Moral Judgment of the Child.* London: Kegan Paul, Trench and Trubner.

Piketty, T. (2014) *Capital in the Twenty-first Century.* Cambridge: Harvard University Press.

Pierson, P. (1994) *Dismantling the Welfare State? Reagan, Thatcher, and the Politics of Retrenchment.* New York: Cambridge University Press.

Pigou, A. (1928) *A Study in Public Finance.* London: Macmillan.

Pilcher, J. (1994) 'Mannheim's Sociology of Generations: An Undervalued Legacy', *The British Journal of Sociology,* 45(3), pp. 481–495.

Pilkington, E. (2015) 'Kentucky sheriff "steadfastly" defends officer who handcuffed 8-year-old', *Guardian,* 4 August 2015. www.theguardian.com/us-news/2015/aug/04/kentucky-sheriff-defends-officer-handcuffed-child.

Pilkington, H. (2014) 'Are young people receptive to populist and radical right political agendas? Turning Evidence into Policy', *MYPLACE Policy Forum,* Brussels, 20 November 2014.

Pinaud, M., and Desplats, F. (2012) *Manager la Generation Y (Travailler avec les 20–30ans).* Paris: Les Presses de Snel.

Piven, F., and Cloward, R. (1982) *The New Class War.* New York: Pantheon.

Platt, L. (2011) *Understanding Inequalities: Stratification and Difference.* Cambridge: Polity Press.

Plehwe, D. (2009) 'Introduction', in P. Mirowski, and D. Plehwe (eds) *The Road from Mont Pelerin: The Making of the Neoliberal Thought Collective.* Cambridge: Harvard University Press, pp. 1–42.

Polanyi, K. (2001 [1944] *The Great Transformation: The Political and Economic Origins of Our Time.* Boston: Beacon Press.

Popov, A. (2012) *Deliverable 2.1: Country based reports on historical discourse production as manifested in sites of memory (United Kingdom).* MYPLACE (Memory, Youth, Political Legacy And Civic Engagement).

Popov, A. (2014) *Intergenerational transmission of political heritage and historical memory (United Kingdom),* MYPLACE (Memory, Youth, Political Legacy And Civic Engagement) www.fp7-myplace.eu/documents/d2/UK_D2.3%20Final.pdf.

Popov, A., and Deák, D. (2013) 'Transnational analysis of historical discourse production and young people's socialization into memories of the 'difficult past' across Europe', *Sociological Review,* 63(S2), pp. 36–52.

Popper, K. (1959) 'Prediction and Prophecy in the Social Science' in P. Gardiner (ed.) *Theories of History.* New York: Free Press.

Portney, P., and Weyant, R. (eds) (1999) *Discounting and Intergenerational Equity.* New York: Resources for the Future.

Posner, R. (2010) 'The Crisis of capitalist democracy', in D. Porter (ed.) *Internetculture.* London: Routledge.

Powell, C., and Dépelteau, F. (2013) *Conceptualizing Relational Sociology: Ontological and Theoretical Issues.* New York: Palgrave Macmillan.

Prasad, M. (2005) 'Why is France so French? Culture, institutions, and neoliberalism, 1974–1981', *The American Journal of Sociology,* 111(2), pp. 357–407.

Print, M., Saha, L., and Edwards, K. (2004) 'Youth political engagement and voting', *Youth Electoral Study Report 2.* Sydney: Australian Electoral Commission.

Prison Reform Trust (2015) *Race.* www.prisonreformtrust.org.uk/ProjectsResearch/Race.

Productivity Commission (2016) *Digital Disruption: What do governments need to do?* Canberra: Commission Research Paper.

Propertychat.com.au (2016) 'The Boomer Supremacy summary' *Property Chat Forums: General discussions* (online) www.propertychat.com.au/community/threads/the-boomer-supremacy-summary.8795/page-3.

Quadagno, J. (1984) 'From poor laws to pensions: The evolution of economic support for the aged in England and America', *Milbank Memorial Fund Quarterly,* 62, pp. 417–446.

Quadagno, J. (1987) 'Theories of the Welfare State', *Annual Review of Sociology,* 13, pp. 109–128.

Quiggin, J. (1999) 'Human capital theory and education policy in Australia', *Australian Economic Review*, 32(2), pp. 130–144.

Raffelhüschen, B. (2002) 'Generational Accounting: Quo Vadis?', *Nordic Journal of Political Economy*, 28, pp. 75–89.

Ranciere, J. (2010) *Dissensus: On Politics and Aesthetics.* New York: Continuum.

Rawls, J. (1971 [1999]) *A Theory of Justice.* (Rev ed.) Cambridge: Harvard University Press.

Rawls, J. (2001) *Justice as Fairness: A restatement.* J. Kelly (ed.). Cambridge: Harvard University Press.

Rayner, J. (2016) *Generation Less: How Australia is Cheating the Young.* Melbourne: Redback.

Reagan, R. (1981) *Inaugural Address*, The American Presidency project. www.presidency.ucsb.edu/ws/?pid=43130www.presidency.ucsb.edu/ws/?pid=43130.

Redmond, G. (2008) *Children's Perspectives on Economic Adversity.* Florence: Unicef Innocenti Research Centre.

Regan, S. (2014) *Australia's Welfare System: A Review of the Reviews 1941–2013.* Canberra: Crawford School of Public Policy, ANU.

Reicher, S., and Stott, C. (2011) *Mad Mobs and Englishmen? Myths and Realities of the 2011 Riots.* London: Constable & Robinson.

Reiner, R. (2007) *Law and order: An Honest Citizen's Guide to Crime and Control.* Cambridge: Polity Press.

Reinhart, C., and Rogoff, K. (2009) *This Time is Different: Eight Centuries of Financial Folly.* Princeton: Princeton University Press.

Reinhart, C., and Trebesch, C. (2014) 'Sovereign-debt relief and its aftermath: The 1930s, the 1990s, the future?' VOX: CEPR, http://voxeu.org/article/sovereign-debt-relief-and-its-aftermath-1930s-1990s-future.

Rhodes, M. (1996) 'Globalization and West European welfare states: A critical review of recent debates', *Journal of European Social Policy,* 6, pp. 305–27.

Richards, S. (1998) 'The New Statesman Interviews Jack Straw', *New Statesman,* 3 April 1998, pp. 27–29.

Richardson, S. (2013) 'Entitlement reform: From tangled web to safety net'. *Basic Income Studies*, 8(1), pp. 105–137.

Ridge, T. (2002) *Childhood Poverty and Social Exclusion: From a Child's Perspective.* Bristol: The Policy Press.

Rimlinger, G. (1971) *Welfare Policy and Industrialization in Europe, America and Russia.* New York: Wiley.

Riots Communities and Victims Panel (2012) *After the Riots: The Final Report of the Riot Communities and Victims Panel* (online) http://riotspanel.independent.gov.uk/wp-content/uploads/2012/03/Riots-Panel-Final-Report1.pdf (accessed April 20th, 2012).

Roberts, K. (2001) *Class in Britain*. Basingstoke: Palgrave Macmillan.

Roberts, K. (2003) 'Change and continuity in youth transitions in Eastern Europe: Lessons from western sociology', *The sociological review*, 51(4), pp. 484–502.

Roberts, K. (2007) 'Youth Transitions and Generations: A Response to Wyn and Woodman', *Journal of Youth Studies*, 10(2), pp. 263–69.

Roberts, S. (2010) 'Misrepresenting "choice biographies"? A reply to Woodman' *Journal of youth studies*, 13(1), pp. 137–149.

Roberts, S. (2012) 'One step forward, one step beck: a contribution to the on-going conceptual debate in youth studies', *Journal of Youth Studies*, 15(3), pp. 389–401.

Robeyns, I. (2009) 'Justice as fairness and the capability approach', in: K. Basu, and R. Kanbur (eds) *Arguments for a Better World. Essays for Amartya Sen's 75th Birthday*. Oxford: Oxford University Press, pp. 397–413.

Robinson, H. (2014) 'Substance', *The Stanford Encyclopedia of Philosophy* (ed. E. Zalta). http://plato.stanford.edu/archives/spr2014/entries/substance/.

Rothman, L. (2012) 'A cultural history of mansplaining' *The Atlantic*.

Roche, S. (2007) 'Criminal Justice Policy in France: Illusions of Severity', *Crime and Justice*, 36(1). pp. 471–550.

Rorty, R. (1991) *Objectivity, Realism and Truth: Philosophical papers I*. Cambridge: Cambridge University Press.

Roser, M. (2016) 'Income Inequality'. https://ourworldindata.org/income-inequality/.

Roubini, N. (2016) *The Third Industrial Revolution: Potential Impacts of Technology on Employment*, World Economic Forum, http://reports.weforum.org/global-strategic-foresight/nouriel-roubini-new-york-university-the-third-industrial-revolution.

Rowlands, R., and Gurney, C.M. (2000) 'Young people's perceptions of housing tenure: A case study in the socialization of tenure prejudice', *Housing, Theory and Society*, 17(3), pp. 121–130.

Rudd, P., and Evans, K. (1998) 'Structure and agency in youth transitions: student experiences of vocational further education', *Journal of Youth Studies*, 1(1), pp. 39–62.

Rude, G., and Hobsbawm, E. (1973) *Captain Swing: A Social History of the great English Agricultural Uprising of 1830*. New York: W.W. Norton.

Rugg, J.J., and Quilgars, D.J. (2015) 'Young people and housing: A review of the present policy and practice landscape', *Youth and Policy*, 114, pp. 5–16.

Ryan, M. (2014) 'Sovereign bankruptcy: Why now and why not in the IMF?', *Fordham Law Review*, 82(5).

Ryan, W. (1976) *Blaming the Victim*. New York: Random House.

Sabbagh, C., and Vanhuysse, P. (2010) 'Intergenerational justice perceptions and the role of welfare regimes', *Administration & Society*, 42(6), pp. 638–667.

Saito, M. (2003) 'Amartya Sen's capability approach to education: A critical exploration', *Journal of Philosophy of Education*, 37(1), pp. 17–34.

Sauter, M. (2014) *The Coming Swarm: DDOS Actions, Hacktivism, and Civil Disobedience on the Internet*. London: Bloomsbury.

Sayer, A. (2005) *The Moral Significance of Class*. Cambridge: Cambridge University Press.

Schultz, T. (1961) 'Investment in Human Capital', *The American Economic Review*, 51(1), pp. 1–17.

Schwab, K. (2016) *The Fourth Industrial Revolution*. World Economic Forum.

Schwartz, H. (2001) 'Round Up the Usual Suspects! Globalization, Domestic Politics, and Welfare State Change', in P. Pierson (ed.) *New Politics of the Welfare State*. New York: Oxford University Press, pp. 17–44.

Sen, A. (1983) 'Poor, relatively speaking', *Oxford Economic Papers*, 35(2), pp. 153–169.

Sen, A. (1985) *Commodities and Capabilities*. Oxford.: Oxford University Press.

Sen, A. (1992) *Inequality Re-examined*. Oxford: Oxford University Press.

Sen, A. (1999a) *Development as Freedom*. Oxford: Oxford University Press.

Sen, A. (1999b) *On Human Development*. Oxford: Oxford University Press.

Sen, A. (2002) *Freedom and Rationality*. Cambridge: Harvard University Press.

Sen, A. (2004) 'Capability and well-being', in M. Nussbaum, and A. Sen, *The Quality of Life*. New York: Routledge, pp. 30–53.

Sen, A. (2009) *The Idea of Justice*. Cambridge: Harvard University Press.

Senate Economic References Committee (2015) *Out of reach? The Australian housing affordability challenge*. Canberra: Parliament of Australia.

Sennett, R. (2003) *Respect in a World of Inequality*. New York: Penguin.

Serres, M. (2015) *Times of Crisis*. London: Bloomsbury.

Settersten, R., Ottusch, T., Schneider, B., (2015) 'Becoming Adult: Meanings of Markers to Adulthood', in R. Scott, and S. Kosslyn (eds) *Emerging Trends in the Social and Behavioral Sciences*. New York: John Wiley & Sons, pp. 1–16.

Sewell, T. (2015) *Overt and convert Islam in Australia*. National Democratic Party of Australia. https://antifascistactionsydney.wordpress.com/2015/05/31/thomas-sewell.

Sewell, T. (nd) Rally tomorrow in Melton, Vic Hannah Watts Park @11am www.facebook.com/unitedpatriotsfront/videos/223861884614938.

Shattock, M. (2008) 'The Change from Private to Public Governance of British Higher Education: Its Consequences for Higher Education Policy Making 1980–2006', *Higher Education Quarterly*, 62(3), pp. 181–203.

Shattock, M. (2012) *Making Policy in British Higher Education 1945–2011*. London: Institute of Education.

Sherrif, N. (2015) 'UN expert slams US as only nation to imprison kids for life without parole', *Al Jazeera*, 9 March 2015.

Shildrick, T., Blackman, S., and MacDonald, R. (2009) 'Young People, Class and Place', *Journal of Youth Studies*, 12(5), pp. 457–465.

Shockley, W., and Pearson, R. (1992) *Shockley on Eugenics and Race: The Application of Science to the Solution of Human Problems*. Washington, DC: Scott-Townsend.

Shortis, C., (nd) Fly a National flag in public and you're a far-right extremist. Work it out. www.facebook.com/unitedpatriotsfront/videos/223861884614938).

Sickmund, M., Sladky, T., Kang, W., and Puzzanchera, C. (2015) 'Easy Access to the Census of Juveniles in Residential Placement'. www.ojjdp.gov/ojstatbb/ezacjrp/.

Simmons, J., and Dodd, T. (eds) (2003) *Crime in England and Wales 2002–2003*. London: National Statistics.

Skidelsky R. (2000) *John Maynard Keynes: Fighting for Britain, 1937–1946*. London: Macmillan.

Slaughter, S. (1998) 'Federal policy and supply side institutional resource allocation at public research universities,' *Review of Higher Education*, 21, pp. 209–244.

Slaughter, S., and Rhoades, G. (2004) *Academic capitalism and the new economy: Markets, state and higher education*. Baltimore: Johns Hopkins University Press.

Sloan, J. (2014) '"The outraged young": young Europeans, civic engagement and the new media in a time of crisis', *Information, Communication & Society*, 17(2), pp. 217–231.

Smith, A. (1979) *Inquiry into the Nature and Causes of the Wealth of Nations* (1776). R.H. Campbell, A.S. Skinner, and W.B. Todd (eds). Indianapolis: Liberty Fund.

Smith, A. (1776–1904) *An Inquiry into the Nature and Causes of Wealth of the Nations*. E. Cannan (ed.), 5th edn. Methuen, London.

Smith, V. (2008) *Rationality in Economics: Constructivism and Ecological Forms*. Cambridge: Cambridge University Press.

Smyth, P. (1994). *Australian Social Policy: The Keynesian Chapter*. Sydney: UNSW Press.

Smyth P. (1998) 'Remaking the Australian Way', in P. Smyth, and B. Cass (eds) *Contesting the Australian Way: States, Markets and Civil Society*. Cambridge: Cambridge University Press.

Smyth, P., and Cass, B. (eds) (1998) *Contesting the Australian Way: States, Markets and Civil Society*. Cambridge: Cambridge University Press.

Softpedia (2012) *NullCrew Hacks South African ISP Directory, 450 Account Details Leaked*. http://news.softpedia.com/news/NullCrew-Hacks-South-African-ISP-Directory-450-Account-Details-Leaked-281630.shtml.

Softpedia (2013) *DHS's Study in the States Website Hacked by NullCrew*. ews.softpedia. com/news/DHS-s-Study-in-the-States-Website-Hacked-by-NullCrew-318719.shtml.

Soler-i-Marti, R. (2012). 'Youth political involvement update: Measuring the role of cause-oriented political interest', *Journal of Youth Studies*, 18(3), pp. 396–416.

Solum, L.B. (2001) 'To our children's children's children: The problem of intergenerational ethics', *Loyola of Los Angeles Law Review*, 35(1), pp. 163–234.

Soros, G. (2008). *The New Paradigm for Financial Markets*. New York: Public Affairs.

Sparrow, A. (2011) 'David Cameron announces recall of parliament over riots', *Guardian*, 9 August 2011. www.theguardian.com/uk/2011/aug/09/david-cameron-announces-recall-parliament.

Standing, G. (2011) *The Precariat*. London: Bloomsbury.

Standing, G. (2014) *A Precariat Manifesto*. London: Bloomsbury.

Stanley-Hall, G. (1904) *Adolescence*. New York: D. Appleton and Company.

Steinmo, S., Thelen, K., and Longstreth, F. (eds) (1992) *Structuring Politics: Historical Institutionalism in Comparative Analysis*. New York: Cambridge University Press.

Stiglitz, J. (2015) *The Great Divide*. London: Allen Lane.

Stiglitz, J. (2001) *Information and the Change in the Paradigm of Economics*. Nobel Prize Lecture, Nobel Academy, Stockholm.

Stiglitz, J., Sen, A., and Fitoussi, J-F. (2009) *Report by the Commission on the Measurement of Economic Performance and Social Progress*. www.stiglitz-sen-fitouussi.fr.

Stoerger, J. (2009) 'The digital melting pot: bridging the digital native–digital immigrant divide', *First Mind*, 14(7). http://firstmonday.org/ojs/index.php/fm/article/view/2474/2243.

Stokes, B. (2015) *Who are Europe's Millennials?* Pew Research Center. www.pew research.org/fact-tank/2015/02/09/who-are-europes-millennials/.

Stolzenberg, L., and D'Alessio, S. (1997) 'Three strikes and you're out: the impact of California's new Mandatory Sentencing law on Serious Crime rates', *Crime and Delinquency*, 43(4), pp. 457–469. doi:10.1177/0011128797043004004.

Strange, S. (1997) *Casino Capitalism*. Manchester: Manchester University Press.

Strauss, W., and Howe, N. (1997) *The Fourth Turning*. New York: Broadway Books.

Sukarieh, M., and Tannock, S. (2015) *Youth Rising? The Politics of Youth in the Global Economy*. Abingdon: Routledge.

Sunstein, C. (2007) *Worst Case Scenarios*. Cambridge: Harvard University Press.

Swortz, D. (2002) 'The sociology of habit: The perspective of Pierre Bourdieu', *The Occupational Therapy Journal of Research*, 22, pp. 615–636.

Tannock, S. (2001) *Youth at Work: The Unionized Fast-Food and Grocery Workplace*. Philadelphia: Temple University Press.

Tapper, A. (2002) *The intergenerational report is not about intergenerational equity, but about fiscal sustainability*, www.onlineopinion.com.au/view.asp?article=1875.

Taylor, C. (1989) *Sources of the Self.* Cambridge: Cambridge University Press.

Thatcher, M. (1987) Interview for *Woman's Own*, 23 September 1987, Margaret Thatcher Foundation. www.margaretthatcher.org/document/106689.

Thompson, E.P. (1971) 'The moral economy of the English crowd in the 18th century', *Past & Present*, 50, pp. 76–136.

Thompson, J. (2003) 'Intergenerational equity: issues of principle in the allocation of social resources between this generation and the next', *Parliamentary Library Research Paper no 7*. Canberra: Parliament of Australia, Canberra.

Thompson, J. (2009) *Intergenerational Justice: Rights and Responsibilities in an Intergenerational Polity*. Abingdon: Routledge.

Threadgold, S. (2011) 'Should I pitch my tent in the middle ground? On "middling tendency", Beck and inequality in youth sociology', *Journal of Youth Studies* 14(4), pp. 381–393.

Threadgold, S., and Nilan, P. (2009), 'Reflexivity of contemporary youth, risk and cultural capital', *Current Sociology*, 57(1), pp. 47–68.

Tiefensee, A., and Westermeier, C. (2016) *Intergenerational Transfers And Wealth In The Euro-Area: The Relevance Of Inheritances And Gifts In Absolute And Relative Terms*. Berlin: Frei Universitat.

Titmuss, R. (1958) *Essays on the Welfare State*. London: Macmillan.

Tonry, M. (2011) *Punishing Race: A Continuing American Dilemma*. Oxford: Oxford University Press.

Trading Economics (2015) 'France home ownership rate', *Trading Economics*, www.tradingeconomics.com/france/home-ownership-rate.

Treadwell, J., Briggs, D., Winlow, S., and Hall, S. (2013) 'Shopocalypse now: consumer culture and the 2011 Riots', *British Journal of Criminology*, 53, pp. 1–17.

Tremmel, J.C. (2009) *A theory of intergenerational justice*. London: Earthscan.

Triple J. (2016) 'Boomer Supremacy: Does the older generation dominate Gen Y', *Triple J Breakfast Blog* www.abc.net.au/triplej/breakfast/blog/s4417154.htm.

Troll, L. (1970). 'Issues in the study of Generations', *Ageing in Human Development*, 1(3), pp. 199–218.

Trow, M. (1974) 'Problems in the Transition from Elite to Mass Higher Education', in *Policies for Higher Education, from the General Report on the Conference on Future Structures of Post-Secondary Education*. Paris: OECD, pp. 55–101.

Tulloch, J., and Lupton, D. (2003) *Risk and Everyday Life*. London: Sage.

Twenge, J. (2014) *Generation Me: Why Today's Young Americans Are More Confident, Assertive, Entitled – and More Miserable Than Ever Before*. New York: Atria.

Tymoigne, E., and Wray, L. (2013) *Modern Money Theory 101: A Reply to Critics*. Levy Economics Institute of Bard College, www.levyinstitute.org/pubs/wp_778.pdf.

UK Children's Commissioners (2015) *Report of the UK Children's Commissioners UN Committee on the Rights of the Child: Examination of the fifth Periodic Report of the United Kingdom of Great Britain and Northern Ireland*.

Unger, R. (2014) *A Religion of the Future*. Cambridge: Harvard University Press.

UNICEF France (2015) *Every Child Counts. Everywhere, Anytime*. Paris: UNICEF France.

United Patriots Front (2016) *The Unholy Quran: The Religion of Peace?* www.facebook.com/unitedpatriotsfront/videos/223861884614938.

Uprichard, E. (2008) 'Children as "being and becomings": Children, childhood and temporality', *Children and Society*, 22(4), pp. 303–313.

US Census Bureau (2015a) Age of Householder: All Races by Median and Mean Income: 1967 to 2014 www.census.gov/hhes/www/income/data/historical/household/index.html.

US Census Bureau (2015b) Age of Householder: White Not Hispanic by Median and Mean Income: 1999 to 2014 www.census.gov/hhes/www/income/data/historical/household/index.html.

US Department of Education (2017) *What is Vocational education?* Washington: National Center for Education Statistics. https://nces.ed.gov/pubs/web/95024-2.asp.

US Department of Labor (nd) *Wages* www.dol.gov/general/topic/youthlabor/wages.

US Senate Committee on Health Education Labor and Pensions (2010) *Emerging Risk? An Overview of the Federal Investment in For-Profit Education*, www.help.senate.gov/hearings/emerging-riskd-an-overview-of-the-federal-investment-in-for-profit-education.

Vail, M. (2014) 'Varieties of liberalism: Keynesian responses to the great recession in France and Germany', *Governance: An International Journal of Policy, Administration, and Institutions*, 27(1), pp. 63–85.

Van Horn, R., and Mirowski, P. (2009) 'The rise of the Chicago School of Economics and the birth of neoliberalism', in P. Mirowski and D. Plehwe (eds) *The Road from Mont Pelerin: The Making of the Neoliberal Thought Collective*. Cambridge: Harvard University Press, pp. 139–180.

Van Parijs, P. (1999) 'The disenfranchisement of the elderly and other attempts to secure intergenerational justice', *Philosophy and Public Affairs*, 27(4), pp. 292–333.

Vesnic-Alujevic, L. (2012) 'Political participation and web 2.0 in Europe: A case study of Facebook', *Public Relations Review*, 38, pp. 466–470.

Vollebergh, W., Iedema, J., and Raaijmakers, Q. (2001) 'Intergenerational transmission and the formation of cultural orientations in adolescence and young adulthood', *Journal of Marriage and Family*, 63, pp. 1185–1198.

Vromen, A., and Collin, P. (2010) 'Everyday youth participation? Contrasting views from Australian policy-makers and young people', *Young*, 18(1), pp. 97–112.

Vromen, A., Xenos, M., and Loader, B. (2014) 'Young people, social media and connective action: from organisational maintenance to everyday political talk', *Journal of Youth Studies*, 18(1), pp. 80–100. doi:10.1080/13676261.2014.93319.

Wacquant, L. (1992) 'Toward a social praxeology: The structure and logic of Bourdieu's sociology', in P. Bourdieu, and L. Wacquant (eds) *An Invitation to Reflexive Sociology*. Cambridge: Polity Press.

Wacquant, L. (2009) *Punishing the Poor: The Neoliberal Government of Social Insecurity*. Durham: Duke University Press.

Wacquant, L. (2013) 'Symbolic Power and Group-Making: On Pierre Bourdieu's Reframing of Class', *Journal of Classical Sociology*, 13 (2), pp. 274–291.

Wacquant, L. (2009) *Punishing the Poor: The Neoliberal Government of Insecurity*. Durham: Duke University Press.

Wagner, P., and Rabuy, B. (2016) 'Mass Incarceration: The Whole Pie 2016', *Prison Policy Initiative*. www.prisonpolicy.org/reports/pie2016.html?gclid=CKC565LQ7c0CFc1uGwodZWYLHg Once.

Walker, A., Kershaw, C., and Nicholas (2006) *Crime in England and Wales 2005/06*, www.homeoffice.gov.uk/rds/index.htm.

Walker, P. (2015) 'Pension uprating costs seven times original estimate', *Financial Times: advisor*. www.ftadviser.com/2015/06/12/pensions/personal-pensions/pension-uprating-costs-seven-times-original-estimate-kM9iPNyOLNQmvcUikSElgL/article.html.

Walther, A. (2006) 'Regimes of youth transitions: Choice, flexibility and security in young people's experiences across different European contexts', *Young* 14(2), pp. 119–139.

Wang, W., and Parker, K. (2014) 'Record Share of Americans Have Never Been Married', *Pew Research Center*.

Watt, N. (2011) 'David Cameron Flies Back to UK for Emergency Meeting on Riots', *Guardian*, 9 August 2011. www.guardian.co.uk/politics/2011/aug/09/david-cameron-london-riots-cobra.

Watts, R. (1987) *The Foundations of the National Welfare State*. St Leonards: Allen and Unwin.

Weick, K. (1995) *Sensemaking in Organisations*. London: Sage.

Weick, K., Sutcliffe, K., and Obstfeld, D. (2005) 'Organizing and the process of sense-making', *Organization Science*, 16(4), pp. 409–421.

Weiss, L. (2003) *States in the Global Economy: Bringing Domestic Institutions Back In*. Cambridge: Cambridge University Press.

Weiss, E.B. (1991) 'Intergenerational Equity: A Legal Framework for Global Environmental Change', in *Environmental Change and International Law*. Tokyo: United Nations University Press.

Weiss, L. (1998) *The Myth of the Powerless State*. Ithaca: Cornell University Press.

Wenar, L. (2012) 'John Rawls', in E.N. Zalta (ed.) *Stanford Encyclopedia of Philosophy*. https://plato.stanford.edu/entries/rawls/.

Western, B., and Wildeman, C. (2009). 'The black family and mass incarceration.' *The Annals of the American Academy of Political and Social Science*, 621, pp. 212–242.

Whitlam, G. (1985) *The Whitlam Government 1972–1975*. Melbourne: Penguin.

Wildeman, C. (2009) 'Parental imprisonment, the prison boom, and the concentration of childhood disadvantage', *Demography*, 46(2), pp. 265–280.

Wilkins, L. (1965) *Social Deviance*. London: Tavistock.

Wilkinson, R., and Pickett, S. (2009) *The Spirit Level*. London: Allen Lane.

Willetts, D. (2010) *The Pinch: How the Baby Boomers Took Their Children's Future – And Why They Should Give It Back*. London: Atlantic.

Williams, A., Coupland, J., Folwell, A., and Sparks, L. (1997) 'Talking about Generation X: Defining them as they define themselves', *Journal of Language and Social Psychology*, 16(3), pp. 251–277.

Williams, B. (2006) *Ethics and the Limits of Philosophy*. Abingdon: Routledge.

Williams, Z. (2011) 'The UK riots: the psychology of looting', *Guardian*, 10 August 2011. www.theguardian.com/commentisfree/2011/aug/09/uk-riots-psychology-of-looting.

Wilson, G., and Grant, E. (2012) *Consequences of the Global Financial Crisis*. Oxford: Oxford University Press.

Wilson, J., and Herrnstein, R. (1985) *Crime and Human Nature*. New York: Basic Books.

Wilson, W. (2014) *Housing Benefit: Shared Accommodation Rate SN/SP/5889* London: House of Commons Library.

Wincott, D. (2013) 'The (golden) age of the welfare state: Interrogating a conventional wisdom', *Public Administration*, 91(4), pp. 806–822.

Wittgenstein, L. (1953) *Philosophical Investigations*. New York: Blackwell Publishing.

Woodman, D. (2009) 'The mysterious case of the pervasive choice biography: Ulrich Beck, structure/agency, and the middling state of theory in the sociology of youth', *Journal of Youth Studies*, 12(3), pp. 243–256.

Woodman, D. (2010). 'Class, individualisation and tracing processes of inequality in a changing world: a reply to Steven Roberts', *Journal of Youth Studies*, 13(6), pp. 737–746.

Woodman, D. (2011) 'A generations approach to youth research', in S. Beadle, R. Holds-worth, and J. Wyn (eds) *For We are Young And ...? Young People in a Time of Uncertainty: Possibilities and Challenges.* Melbourne: Melbourne University Press, pp. 29–48.

Woodman, D. (2013) 'Researching "Ordinary" Young People in a Changing World: The Sociology of Generations and the "Missing Middle" in Youth Research', *Sociological Research Online*, 18(1). 7, www.socresonline.org.uk/18/1/7.html 10.5153/sro.2868.

Woodman, D., and Threadgold, S.R. (2014) 'Critical youth studies in an individualized and globalized world: making the most of Bourdieu and Beck', in P. Kelly and A. Kamp (eds) *A Critical Youth Studies for the 21st Century.* Leiden: Brill.

Woodman, D., and Wyn, J. (2014) *Youth and Generation: Rethinking change and inequality in the lives of young people.* London: Sage.

World Bank (2014) *GINI Index.* http://data.worldbank.org/indicator/SI.POV.GINI.

World Bank (2016) *World Bank Data.* http://data.worldbank.org/country/australia?view=chart.

World Bank (nd) *Unemployment, youth total labor force ages 15–24*, http://data.world-bank.org/indicator/SL.UEM.1524.ZS.

World Economic Forum (2016) *The Future of Jobs, Global Challenge Insight Report.* www3.weforum.org/docs/WEF_Future_of_Jobs.pdf.

Wright, E. (1978) *Class, Crisis and the State.* London: New Left Books.

Wyn, J., and Dwyer, P. (1999) 'New directions in research on youth transitions', *Journal of Youth Studies*, 2(1), pp. 5–21.

Wyn, J., and White, R. (2000) 'Negotiating social change: The paradox of youth', *Youth & Society*, 32(2), pp. 165–183.

Wyn, J., and Woodman, D. (2006) 'Generation, youth and social change in Australia', *Journal of Youth Studies*, 9(5), pp. 495–514.

Wyn, J., and White, R. (1997) *Rethinking Youth.* St Leonards: Allen and Unwin.

Young-Bruehl, E. (2012) *Childism: Confronting Prejudice Against Children.* New Haven: Yale University Press.

Younge, G. (2011) *Reading the Riots: Investigating England's Summer of Disorder.* London: *Guardian*/LSE.

Zedner, L. (2007) 'Pre-Crime and Post-Criminology', *Theoretical Criminology*, 11(2).

Zedner, L. (2009) 'Fixing the future? The pre-emptive turn in criminal justice', in B. McSherry, A. Norrie, and S. Bronnit (eds) *Regulating Deviance: The Redirection of Criminalisation and the Futures of Criminal Law.* Hart Publishing.

Zimring, F. (2005) 'The unexamined death penalty: capital punishment and reform of the model penal code', *Columbia Law Review*, 105(4), pp. 1396–1416.

Zizek, S. (2011) 'Shoplifters of the World Unite!' *London Review of Books*, 19 August.

Zizek, S. (2014) *Trouble in Paradise.* London: Allen Lane.

Zuckerman, E., Roberts, H., McGrady, R., York, J., and Palfrey, J. (2010) *Distributed Denial of Service Attacks Against Independent Media and Human Rights Sites.* Cambridge: The Berkman Center for Internet & Society at Harvard University.

Zuniga, G., Jung, N., and Valenzuela, H. (2012) 'Social media use for news and individuals' social capital, civic engagement and political participation', *Journal of Computer Mediated Communication*, 17(2), pp. 319–336.

Index

Page numbers in *italics* denote tables, those in **bold** denote figures.

3